MW00412110

TRENCH Buddies

OVERCOMING LIFE'S
BATTLES TOGETHER

SANDI MICHON

Printed by CreateSpace
an Amazon.com company

LIBRARY OF CONGRESS CATALOGING-IN-PUBLICATION DATA
has been applied for.

ISBN: 978-0-692-33573-4

Dedication

This book was a battle. Writing a book on spiritual warfare invites spiritual warfare, and God has walked me through each concept as I faced them in my own life – to write from experience rather than theory. God has been my Faithful Teacher. Hopefully, these words are His, and will bring Him much glory.

Trench Buddies is lovingly dedicated to Jesus Christ – the Ultimate Trench Buddy and Source of all lasting victory. I offer this book to Him as an act of simple, yet arduous obedience.

Just as spiritual warfare is a corporate battle, so it has been with this book. So many people have contributed to the finished product. I am indebted to the faithful prayer team that tirelessly bombarded God's throne for me and Trench Buddies ministry. So many people granted me time and expertise through interviews and explanations. An editing team poured over the text catching typos and enhancing the content. Women (Jan, Carla, Elaine, Jess, and Deb) with administrative gifts broke through my frequent paralysis with order and encouragement. Pari Hoxha graciously provided the cover design.

My family, and particularly my husband, Ron, have been my most ardent supporters. They have walked through many of my training battles with me. They have endured my incessant conversations and musings as I wrestled through the book content – always providing encouragement and wise input. I love them dearly.

Finally, I am thankful for my trench buddies – the women who love me deeply and battle for my soul. Patti Brigham and Lianne Azevedo top the list, reinforced by the women in our Bible study, and other godly women whose counsel I treasure.

My prayer from the start is that every person involved with Trench Buddies would somehow be blessed by participating. I pray the reader will be as well.

Forward

Victory in Jesus... my Savior forever....

These are familiar song lyrics, but not necessarily a familiar experience for many believers in Jesus Christ. Why not?

This book attempts to answer that question.

Victory assumes a battle, and war assumes an opponent. We are in an invisible war that rages against our soul, but most of us are not very well trained.

Trench Buddies offers a frank look at this war and provides incredibly practical battle strategies using interesting, thought-provoking military parallels. The content has revolutionized the power of the Bible in my life and equipped me to "war well." It has trained me to battle better for my own soul, and to help others find more frequent victories.

I pray it does the same for you.

Introduction

We love.

Or, at least we want to.

People are in pain all around us. They are losing life's battles. Our culture is rocked by the explosions of divorce, death, disease, depression and despair.

In our globally-connected world, people feel more alone than ever before.

For decades, I have listened to, talked with, cried with, cooked for, and struggled alongside people in deep pain. I am haunted by their pain, and haunted by my own lingering questions: How do I love well? How do I love at the deepest level? How do I battle for the very soul of another?

The people that have helped me the most through my own pain have looked beyond the superficial. They looked beyond the rhetorical "I'm fine" to see that I wasn't. When the real pain bled to the surface, they didn't pat me on the back and hand me a super-hero band-aid. They hunkered down for the costly, messy ministry to my soul. They listened, learned, challenged, and loved. They became my trench buddy.

A trench buddy doesn't care if your hair is a mess, your make-up is streaming down your cheeks, your clothes aren't the latest style, or if you struggle with your weight. It's no longer about how you look, what you earn, or where you live. It doesn't even matter that you're sitting there caked with mud from the battlefield.

They see beyond all that. They see your soul. Trench buddies see with clarity the difference between spiritual life and death – so they battle core issues.

They know that sin is at the core of every explosion – and that every battle is spiritual at the core.

Jesus

Jesus Christ is the ultimate trench buddy template. He saw the mess we were in. He could have tried to fix society. He could have eradicated poverty. He could have set Himself up as an earthly king. Although He addressed all the other issues of life in His Word – He came to give His life – to battle for our souls. He is the Source of all victory.

During his earthly life, Jesus gave, sacrificed, and served – but He also got down to people's deepest needs. Look at how He dealt with the Samaritan woman at the well in Sychar. (John 4) What began as a casual conversation about thirst and water turned into a deeper conversation about living water that eternally quenches man's thirst.

Jesus is the Trench Buddy that modeled "messy ministry." He went to the outcasts, the lepers, and the demon-possessed. Even His ministry to the Samaritan woman was socially unacceptable for Jesus as a Jew.

Jesus modeled and mentored this type of ministry to His disciples – and told them to teach it to others. Just as a soldier trains to be proficient in battles, believers in Jesus Christ need to as well.

My passion is to be a better trench buddy – and for the church to be filled with believers trained to battle for each other's souls – and for us all to walk in the victory we have in Christ.

This book was birthed over ten years ago – first in a class – and secondly at a combat readiness center in Savannah, Georgia.

Class

When my daughter was a junior in high school, I wanted to prepare her for the rigors of secular college as a young woman of faith. We planned a comparative worldview class and invited seven of her girlfriends to join us. As we wrestled with Scripture and the culture, we discussed the temptations they faced, and how to overcome them. With my military background, I asked them if they had a trench buddy – someone who would battle for their souls – someone to be completely honest with, no matter what.

Five women in the group became trench buddies. They are still trench buddies today and they use the term often. They have been through highs and lows – and when they need someone at the soul level – they know who to call. It brings me great joy to see them relate to each other like that. The five women are also still strong believers.

Combat center

The nuts and bolts of this book came through my experience as a war exercise evaluator at the Combat Readiness Center in Savannah, Georgia. Our unit was participating in an Operation Readiness Exercise (ORE) that tests a unit's ability to go to war.

Units train diligently for months, and then practice their skills in realistic war exercises prior to formal inspections. Hundreds of Airmen "deploy" to these readiness centers and are subjected to every imaginable situation. War scenarios include chemical attacks, bombings, plane crashes, enemy combatants breaching the base, casualties, and communications breakdown. Military members are evaluated as they respond to each new war challenge. The goal is ATSO, the military acronym that stands for Ability to Train, Survive and Operate.

When the heat is on and the unexpected happens, the military wants to know if personnel can stay alive and successfully support the overall mission.

As an exercise evaluator, I knew what was coming. It was my job to evaluate how my section performed their tasks under the pressure of "war." Even though it was an exercise, it was very intense. During a full-on chemical attack, hundreds of

Airmen performed their jobs in bulky chemical warfare gear replete with gas masks. In the Georgia heat, the extra layers of protection were like wearing parkas in the Bahamas. Canteens were equipped with gas mask tubes to ward off debilitating dehydration. Carefully-guarded "entry control points" between base sectors kept chemical contamination contained. An unauthorized intruder was wrestled to the ground when he tried to gain access to a secure building. Chaplains had to deal with those who cracked under the pressure. Players that ignored attack warnings lay littered on the field, tagged "dead," encumbering other personnel with the task of casualty collection. Leaders huddled in the command and control section, surveying the damage, and recalculating plans to survive and thrive. Regardless of the obstacles, the mission governed every strategy.

It was here that I first noticed the stunning disconnect between how we train for war versus how we train for life. The experience deeply impacted me on several levels, but one aspect particularly stood out to me.

Every person in the exercise was expected to know the Airman's Manual from cover to cover. This 5"x7" spiral-bound manual contains information critical to survival. It has sections on war, attack levels, types of chemical attacks, their antidotes, weapon usage, security practices, explosives recognition, and combat medical treatment for your buddies and yourself (Self-Aid-and-Buddy-Care /SABC). Knowledge contained in the manual could make the difference between life and death for yourself and others – and it could make or break mission success. It could determine victory or defeat.

During the exercise, the Airman's Manual was to be carried at all times (It fit perfectly into the side trouser pocket on the battle dress uniform). An inspector could stop participants and ask them any question pertaining to information in the manual. You were expected to know it – because in a real war – there's no time to look it up.

Parallels

I was astounded by the spiritual parallels.

The notion of sending an untrained soldier into war is unthinkable. What are the chances of survival? How would it affect those around him or her? How would it affect the integrity of the unit?

Countries spend millions, if not billions on defense training. We even form alliances and train together for even greater effectiveness. Why? Because evil is always with us. There will always be dictators and tyrants with dreams of global domination through cruel or simply deceptive strategies. We live in a fallen world where the lust for power must be placed in check. The 20th century proved to be the bloodiest in history and the 21st century was ushered in by terrorism on a global scale – with still no real solutions in sight.

We understand defense training, but remain dangerously ignorant of the urgent training needed for the unseen spiritual war that rages all around us. There are very few who unequivocally deny the reality of a spirit world and the distinction between two sides – good and evil. For the Christian, God has called us to wage war on a spiritual level that has an eternal outcome. A war for the soul.

God has provided a Manual (the Bible) to equip us for victory in this battle we call life. It should be read from cover to cover. Maybe, like in the exercise, it should be on us, or more importantly, in us at all times. It is not information simply for head knowledge, but to survive and thrive in the mission we've been called to accomplish – and to know God Himself.

Spiritual training should be practiced exhaustively in realistic scenarios so that the right response becomes automatic. Our lives should be inspected regularly in order that weak areas can be corrected before the "real deal" happens. Our training should be a high priority, worthy of our time and money. We should also care that our buddies are trained, because our lives might depend on their skills if we get hit.

Training

In my 28 military years, training was a constant priority with readiness as the objective. The military didn't assume you remembered last year's training; you were trained again and again to make sure you did. It wasn't just training to grow in your job, or in your leadership skills – but in how to stay alive to do those things. It was training to fight, and fighting to win – always for a greater purpose beyond you.

I've done hundreds of interviews in my public affairs military career, spanning Desert Storm and into Operation Enduring Freedom and the Global War on Terrorism. I've covered heroes from Normandy and prison camp survivors from Vietnam, welcomed home Desert Storm veterans, participated in regional war exercises, and covered troop deployments in Iraq and Afghanistan. All these experiences have deepened my burden to write this book, but a few have burned images into my heart.

In the military, there is an unspoken protocol followed when a fallen soldier is transported home. When an aircraft is tagged for an HR flight (human remains), any available flightline personnel gather at the aircraft as the caskets are loaded. Personnel form two, silent, parallel columns, and snap to attention and salute as the caskets pass through their lines for a final flight home. It is heart-wrenching to see the cost of war up-close and personal. The casualty is someone's father, mother, son, daughter, brother, sister, or friend. These highly-trained military members sacrificed their lives for the mission, but how much more tragic would it be if the death was due to ignorance or neglect of duty? We are talking real lives. There is a human toll.

We understand casualty counts as the cost of physical war, but often miss the tragedy of the broken lives all around us as a result of spiritual warfare.

This book introduces simple but profound parallels between military training and the direct correlation to spiritual situations. It is broken down into six sections: war, weapons, explosives, security, self-aid-and-buddy-care, and victory/ peace. Actual information from the Airman's manual is included to illustrate the teaching. To enhance the parallel, a fictional personal profile is woven through each section to help apply the training concepts.

As you can imagine, to cover such expansive topics is like trying to fit an ocean into a thimble, so my aim is introductory at best. It is to spark a thought. Virtually every person exposed to these analogies has immediately expanded them with their own examples and applications. My passionate hope is that you, the reader, will do the same.

Once you get it – you'll see it everywhere.

Battle better

Our hearts break for the broken.

The apostle Paul's did too. He said to the Corinthians, "Who is led into sin without my intense concern?" (II Corinthians 11:29)

Many of my battles involved being led into sin. More than once, I have been the bloodied soldier fallen on the battlefield of life and have been enormously grateful for those trained troops that risked the shelter of the foxhole to drag me to safety and tend to my wounds.

They mentored me in the Manual.

It is through the training of Scripture that I can "Aim High" for "Semper Fi" (Always Faithful) and "Be all that I Can Be." In the fight of faith, there are no conscientious objectors – we are all in this together.

May this book hold up a mirror, clarify our mission, motivate us to follow the Manual – and deepen our devotion and service to Jesus Christ – our Savior and Commander-in-Chief.

May we love – and battle – as Jesus did. In the end, may we, like Paul, say, "I will most gladly spend and be extended for your souls."

Enlisted in His service,
Sandi Michon

Table of Contents

End notes

Section

1

WAR

AMBUSH: A Personal Profile

She never saw it coming.

Jane sat with her head in her hands in the dark, quiet apartment. Her two daughters slept in the bedroom down the hall, but Jane had never felt so alone.

Her chestnut hair fell over her hunched shoulders. An athletic, shapely, size 4, she had a dazzling smile, smoky green eyes, high cheekbones and a creamy complexion, but tonight Jane felt ugly to the core. She had a quick mind and had always excelled in school, but she had never felt so stupid.

Did stupid start when she had felt the smartest? She knew what she had wanted in life, and was very good at getting it. Somehow though, once she got it, it never seemed to satisfy. Maybe that's what opened the door to drinking, clubbing, and ultimately the affair that ruined her marriage, and the deceptions that destroyed her friendships. Driven by independence, she had become like a blind boxer, flailing at anyone within arm's reach.

Jane shuddered as vignettes played through her mind like a series of rocket attacks. Shell-shocked from sin, she was blind to the emotional blood oozing from the shrapnel in everyone that loved her. She felt invincible, never realizing that prolonged shock kept her unaware of her own injuries. She kept fighting, but in each successive attack, she struggled to recognize who she was fighting, and especially what she was fighting for.

Her life had become a cacophony of explosions. It rattled her nerves and shattered her confidence. She was no longer brave and strong, and it was exhausting to pretend she was. Even though Jane went through the motions of work and taking care of the kids, inside she was a defeated soldier huddled in the corner of her heart, afraid to open the door, not knowing who to trust – out of ammo, out of ideas, out of options.

She thought she had been trained for spiritual warfare. Jane was brought up in a Christian home and went to Christian school. She had a handsome, faithful husband, two beautiful kids, and they had already upgraded to the second home while still in their 20s. Yet, it all unraveled over the span of two years.

When did work replace worship? When did deception replace delight? Did fun replace fight? How had the fight for freedom made her a prisoner-of-war?

With one final explosion, her bravado shattered. It was time to surrender – not to the enemy that had tormented her for years – but to the God Who had died to ensure her victory.

Her tears dripped through her fingers, silently falling to the floor. Within minutes, weeping gave way to heart-wrenching sobs as she lowered herself to the carpet, facedown, prostrate in prayer.

"God, help me..."

"...contend earnestly for the faith which was once for all
handed down to the saints."
Jude 1:3[1]

1
WAR 101

War was not on Jane's life agenda. It never made her to-do list.

Jane is like most of us. Who in their right mind wants war?

Hardly anyone, but it's unavoidable.

War is a reality of life.

War simply defined is "a state or period of armed hostility or active military operations – most often between nations or parties within a nation."[2] One definition goes even deeper and terms war as "a struggle for men's minds."[3]

War is ugly, bloody, grueling, excruciating and costly. Wars have littered our landscapes with dead bodies and devastation throughout history.

In his statement, "War is hell," Union General William Tecumseh Sherman succinctly described the horror of war, and unwittingly set before us a surprisingly ironic truth that is the focus of this book.[4] Any seasoned soldier will agree that war is hell, but the profound twist is that the denial of war can invite a certain, vastly-worse hell. As long as good and evil co-exist, the hell of battle is infinitely more desirable than the inevitable hell of unrestrained evil.

War is an inescapable reality of life – sometimes nationally – always personally. If I am not purposing to fight for the good, I am surrendering to the evil. If I am not actively pursuing the right, and willing to battle all that oppose it, then I naturally default to the wrong.

Personal neutrality is a fatal fallacy. To opt out is to concede defeat.

"All that is necessary for evil to triumph is for good men to do nothing" said Sir Edmund Burke and it serves as a reminder that apathy already chooses a side.[5]

English writer and philosopher G. K. Chesterton presented a slightly different angle. "War is not the best way of settling differences; it is the only way of preventing their being settled for you."[6]

As society has softened into selfishness, fighting for truth, good and freedom has become anathema to us. We enjoy privileges earned by others, but eschew the sacrifice required to keep them. We bend to accommodate and tolerate, seeking a false peace that inexorably leads to the brink of hell – unopposed evil.

John Stuart Mill cited another aspect possibly uglier than war:

"War is an ugly thing, but not the ugliest of things. The decayed and degraded state of moral and patriotic feeling which thinks that nothing is worth war is much worse. The person who has nothing for which he is willing to fight, nothing which is more important than his own personal safety, is a miserable creature, and has no chance of being free unless made or kept by the exertions of better men than himself."[7]

These applications have profound implications when applied to the Christian today – and the appeal to be the better men and women recognized by Mill.

The Bible and war

The Bible is replete with war references for our instruction – from Cain and Abel in Genesis, to the cataclysmic climax in Revelation. From beginning to end, the Bible chronicles the heavenly conflict between God and Satan played out on earth as the battle between good and evil. The sides are clearly defined and mankind's history plays out dramatic clashes as God and Satan vie for the hearts and souls of men.

This war is unseen, but it is real, and the stakes are very high. In our typical notion of war, there is a danger of physical death that terminates an earthly life. Death in spiritual warfare has an eternal impact. Maybe that's why Jesus implores His disciples not to fear those who can kill the body, but not the soul – but rather fear him which is able to destroy both soul and body in hell. (Matthew 10:28)

Victory is possible

As the ultimate Commander-in-Chief, God sets up clear parameters for perpetual victory. When His people follow His authority, He abundantly provides protection. Conversely, Biblical history shows how God's people suffered horribly when they forgot what side they were on, were seduced into enemy alliances, and lulled into complacency. In a state of compromise and prosperity, they were no longer able to distinguish danger – to discern truth from lies. When they neglected God's commands intended to keep them sharp, defeat and captivity were the inevitable consequences that stood in sharp contrast to the victory God desired for them.

The Bible provides a vivid portrayal of physical warfare and spiritual warfare. The second book of the Bible says that "the Lord is a warrior, the Lord is His name." (Exodus 15:3) Our God is a God of war, but not like the hawkish, malevolent Being many imagine. God is the all-powerful Lord of hosts whose supreme love is shown by the great price He exacted to personally pay for our victory. In human terms, He is the five-star general who dies for His troops, but then conquers even death to come back and lead them to victory. He goes before them, works through them, comes behind them, and wages "air war" to cover them.

The Old Testament contains bloody battles from both sides. The book of Psalms records the heart cries to God from those caught in the throes of personal and national wars. Military jargon is common as the psalmists cry out for protection, refuge, victory and restoration. God is David's fortress, shield, buckler, high tower and deliverer. In Psalm 144:1-2, David says, "Blessed be the Lord, my rock, who trains my hands for war, and my fingers for battle." David knew the sting of battle, from other nations and from his own family. He also knew the reality of battle in his own heart as he struggled with sin.

The New Testament shifts predominantly to spiritual warfare. In Ephesians 6, the enemy is "principalities and powers of the air" and the armor outlined there is for internal use – to protect the mind and soul where the fiercest battles rage. There are references to war and soldiers, but the battles are cosmic, and faith is the prize for which to contend. Military references alert us to spiritual battles that intensify at the end of the age when God ultimately wages the physical war of all wars.

In light of the reality of spiritual war, the Bible becomes more than a "life manual" – it is vital to the very survival of our soul. But, it is noteworthy that the Bible is a "life" manual, because the Christian war is much more about pursuing life than death – it is a fight for life and wholeness. This is most easily understood in medical situations like fighting cancer or fighting to save a nearly-severed limb. This fight attaches value to all people but valiantly battles that which brings death. Medical battles may inflict pain and suffering, but always with the objective of healing and life.

Love is the motive

Jesus presents a startling paradox in the fifth chapter of Matthew. (Matthew 5:44) He tells us to love our enemies, but never to compromise with truth to do so. Like no other battle scenario, the Christian must fight spiritual battles with a motive of love.

To explore war as a topic is daunting, but looking at key concepts of physical warfare can stimulate a startling awareness of spiritual war – and what can happen if you're unprepared for both. We easily understand the risks associated with sending an untrained soldier into battle, but we just as easily dismiss the need for disciplined training for spiritual soldiers – believers in Jesus Christ. Churches are filled with shattered souls wondering why they feel so weak and defeated, blaming each other instead of recognizing the real enemy, and training for strength and victory that is already ours in Christ.

To a Soldier/Airman/Marine/Seaman, war is a given. It's what you train for, and if need be, it's what you die for.

If you are a Christian, the war is on. It may be to the death...

Are you fit or flabby? Are you trained for battle? Are you part of a trained unit? Are you under a chain of command? Can you handle your weapon? Can you identify the enemy? Can you recognize explosives so you don't step on them? If a fellow soldier gets wounded, do you know how to help him/her? Have you even been to basic training?

Preparation prompts courage. So, does a lack of preparation then prompt fear?

George Washington said, "There is nothing so likely to produce peace as to be well-prepared to meet the enemy."[8] How does that apply to us spiritually? Have we ever examined ourselves that way?

Military inspections are a way of life. Whether you're standing in formation for a physical inspection or in a full-on training exercise to test unit readiness to go to war – you have to assess your weaknesses to move toward strength.

Who wants war? Probably not you – me neither. But we're in one. I didn't really get this concept for years, so I lived in defeat. Once I faced the unpleasant truth of war, both as a military member and a believer in Jesus Christ, I began to train for, and gain more victories.

Theologian/Pastor John MacArthur reviews our position in his book, *The Truth War*. "War is one of the most calamitous consequences of evil. It is catastrophic. It is always ugly. It should never be glamorized, and no sane person should ever desire the conflict or savor the strife of war," he writes. "There are times, however, when evil makes warfare absolutely necessary."[9]

MacArthur further defines the distinctiveness of spiritual warfare: "The truth war is not a carnal war. It is not about territory and nations. It is not a battle for lands and cities. It is not a clan war or a personality conflict between individuals. It is not a fight for clout between religious denominations. It is not a skirmish over material possessions. It is a battle for the truth."[10]

Like us, the church wants to avoid war. According to MacArthur, the church "has grown lazy, worldly, and self-satisfied. Church leaders are obsessed with style and methodology, losing interest in the glory of God and becoming grossly apathetic about truth and sound doctrine."[11] A spiritual clash of ideas is always present, but we eschew controversy. We no longer know how to engage the culture with a bold confidence coupled with love and respect.

We are called to be ambassadors – to bring the good news of the gospel to people. We are also called to be soldiers – to pull down false ideas and lies spawned by Satan.

What is your personal readiness for war – and ultimately – your potential for victory and peace?

CHAPTER 1: WAR 101

Most important "take-away" thought(s):

Churches are filled with shattered souls, wondering why they feel so weak and defeated. Blaming each other instead of recognizing the real enemy, and training for strength and victory that is already ours in christ.

There is nothing so likely to produce peace as to be well prepared to meet the enemy.

1. On a scale of 1-10 (1 as lowest), how would you rate your awareness of war in your spiritual life? What are the implications of your rating? In other words, how does that impact your approach to life?

10   I feel caught up in hypervigilism rather than training.

2. In what areas are you fighting for the good? How are you actively pursuing the right?

Fighting for victory in the lives of my children + grand children. Break the generational curses!

At work, fighting for families + children to receive a good start with a high quality education.

3. Are there any areas of life in which you have opted out? If so, which ones, and why?   Ministry — not clear what I can commit to — my calling.

Physical Health — need to plan for exercise and nutrition

Spiritually — I need to go deeper, reflect

Emotionally — I need to stop giving to feel valued.

I would like to journal consistently to my grand childre—

4. For what, if anything, are you willing to risk you personal comfort or safety?

my children + grand children

5. If you acknowledge war as a reality in your daily life, on a scale of 1-10, how would you rate your level of training for this ongoing conflict? Explain.

6   I can do hard, I know how to recognize the enemy.
     I know how to set boundaries
I am not yet disciplined enough

"Your right hand, O LORD, is majestic in power, Your right hand, O LORD,
shatters the enemy."
Exodus 15:6

2
THE REALITY OF AN ENEMY

Almost everyone above the age of 15 can remember exactly where they were on September 11, 2001. What initially appeared to be a freak accident quickly turned into a horrible realization of war when the second plane hit the east World Trade Center tower. News anchors were stunned speechless. One after the other began reporting the unfolding events as a "concerted, deliberate attack." The Pentagon was subsequently hit, followed by the forced crash in Pennsylvania.

"What we have feared has come to pass," reported one newscaster, voicing the sentiments of millions of horrified Americans that sat glued to television coverage. In less than 12 hours, an entire nation went through a dramatic paradigm shift that changed life as we had previously known it.

We were at war.

The stark reality of war initiated a series of actions necessary to survival – contingencies planned long in advance, and tested repeatedly – even though the exact details could never be fully predicted.

But, the first response to an act of war is not so much an action as it is an acute awareness – there is an enemy. When an unseen enemy turned civilian airliners into giant guided missiles on suicide missions to destroy thousands of innocent people, they became a visible threat. It was a shocking, uncomfortable awareness.

As details unfolded after the tragic attacks that fateful September day, many admitted to overlooking multiple warning signs in the complacency of everyday life. The absence of "combat caution" was precisely what the terrorists used to great advantage to accomplish their deadly mission. In a nation not fully convinced they were at war with an unseen enemy, the enemy operated freely – with devastating results.

Ignorance gives an enemy a powerful strategic advantage.

Spiritual ignorance

Imagine our vulnerability in spiritual warfare when we fail to acknowledge the reality of the enemy. As believers in Christ, we see that the Bible identifies our enemies as the world (man's systems that operate contrary to God), the flesh (the influence of our fallen nature) and the Devil (also called Satan/Lucifer, leader of a demonic host of fallen angels). Unfortunately, the culture increasingly presents these three elements as posing no real threat. The culture increasingly says society can save us, man is perfectible without God, and Satan is an imaginary cartoon character wearing a red suit with horns. (Just today, I saw a man sporting a tattoo depicting a cartoon Satan with a saxophone – apparently for parties in hell.)

It was interesting to watch a Nightline segment aired in March 2009 that debated the reality of Satan. This powerful spiritual enemy was reduced to a nebulous force whose agenda, if he existed at all, was up for grabs. In proudly presenting their viewpoint against Satan, Deepak Chopra and Carlton Pearson found it intellectually inferior to believe in such a nonsensical spirit being. One surprising presenter of this viewpoint was Bishop Pearson, a former fundamentalist minister, who "had grown beyond" those elemental beliefs, but also offered no real explanation for evil.

In contrast, a Christian on the segment presented a biblical definition of the enemy of our souls, described experiential dealings with his forces, and defined specific victory strategies for the conquest.

From an emotional standpoint I might feel better listening to those that deny I have an enemy, but from a military viewpoint, I vastly prefer the uncomfortable knowledge of the enemy – that will fight me whether I believe in him or not.

Know your enemy

To deny the fact that we have an enemy is to develop a false sense of safety – to our own peril. Victory in war is far more likely when strategists learn as much as they can about the enemy, and plan accordingly.

A few years back, I interviewed an older Navy veteran who was part of the crew that captured the German U-boat 505 about 150 miles off the coast of Africa on June 4, 1944. In the days before global satellite monitoring, the American crew was able to disable the submarine, capture the crew, and tow the submarine back to Bermuda. The real booty was German codebook information which was pivotal in turning the tide of the war effort. The more the allies knew about enemy plans, the more successful they were at countering them.

Acclaimed Chinese General Sun Tzu offers war strategy unintentionally crucial to the Christian. "If ignorant both of your enemy and yourself, you are certain to be in peril," he said.[1]

Satan exposed

The apostle Paul understood this principle well. He admonished the Corinthian church to forgive others so that Satan would not get an advantage –"for we are not ignorant of his devices." (II Corinthians 2:11) Future chapters on explosives will define some of Satan's devices, but we must be aware that our enemy has devices planned against us. Paul taught the Ephesian believers extensively about spiritual warfare, and instructed them to put on the full armor of God that they "may be able to stand against the wiles of the devil." (Ephesians 6) It is disconcerting to acknowledge that Satan has specific strategies to knock us down, but this knowledge is also a key part of our victory.

To concede that we have an enemy should not prompt paranoia and cowardice. Rather, it should propel us to preparation through study and strategy, and thus build courage.

What does the Bible say about our enemy? Satan is a murderer from the beginning, he is the father of all lies, he is the author of confusion, he comes to steal, kill and destroy, and he can appear as an angel of light. With this basic information, we learn how to "fingerprint" the enemy in our surroundings. Further study shows he is subtle, crafty, and he plants doubt, rebellion and despair. What we don't know about him can hurt us.

Consistent with the nature of our enemy is the strategy of misinformation. We see this strategy, through his subtle approach, just three chapters into the Bible. In Genesis, the serpent twists God's words as he tempts Eve, who then adds to God's words in her own confusion. The serpent counters with a full-on lie, gets her to doubt God, and Adam and Eve lose a major battle. Today, we still suffer the consequences of their loss.

History is riddled with battles won through strategic confusion. In the days and weeks preceding the infamous D-Day invasion on the shores of Normandy, France, the allied forces flooded communication channels with conflicting information regarding their attack plans. It still cost the lives of many men to secure the Normandy beaches in June of 1944, but information confusion greatly hindered the German defense.

Confusion hinders the believer's defense as well. Jesus said, "You shall know the truth and the truth will set you free." (John 8:32) Truth cuts through confusion – like the sword of the Spirit presented as the Word of God in the book of Ephesians. The Bible is the source for reliable and vital intelligence about the enemy, and in the arena of spiritual warfare, Jesus is our Commander in Chief.

The apostle Paul once served as the poster boy for misinformation. Before he clashed with the Truth in Christ Jesus on the road to Damascus (Acts 9), Paul believed wrong information so fervently that he was killing Christians, and thought he was doing God a favor! God knocked Paul (then Saul) off his high horse (literally) and blinded the religious scholar physically so he could begin to see spiritually. In the years that followed, Paul intimately learned the danger of lies and the power of truth – and fought the "good fight of faith" until he was beheaded in Rome.

Because of his own experiences with lies, Paul repeatedly warned the churches he planted in Asia Minor about false teachers. He wanted victory for Christ-followers and exhorted them to recognize those that creep into churches undetected to promote false doctrine. (Jude 1:4) In the book of Jude, Paul describes wolves in sheep's clothing – what we might translate as double agents.

Abraham Lincoln could have been thinking about this reference during the Civil War when he wrote: "The shepherd drives the wolf from the sheep for which the sheep thanks the shepherd as his liberator, while the wolf denounces him for the same act as the destroyer of liberty. Plainly, the sheep and the wolf are not agreed upon a definition of liberty."[2]

A modern military example of a terrorist in U.S. Army clothing is illustrated by the Fort Hood murders involving Maj. Nidal Hisan. He trained with fellow Americans, wore the right uniform, yet believed ideas that were antithetical to the U.S. military's objectives. As a counselor to soldiers leaving for or returning from overseas deployments – against predominantly Islamic-led tyranny – Major Hisan undermined their sacrifice by questioning their mission. His dual role was sadly recognized when his conflicted ideas prompted the alleged murder of 13 of his fellow soldiers. He clearly had a different definition of liberty fueled by his ideology.

The enemy within

Paul was a spiritual war veteran. He knew the enemy and he knew firsthand the vulnerability created through wrong information. He begged believers to take the threat seriously. But, Paul's murderous past also gave him the distinct awareness of another ever-present enemy – ourselves.

Cartoonist Walt Kelly gave his character Pogo a deep nugget of truth: "We have found the enemy and he is us."[3] British theologian Charles Spurgeon adds emphasis with, "Beware of no man more than of yourself; we carry our worst enemies within us."[4] Scripture describes us as enemies before we encounter Jesus as Savior. In Romans 5:10, it says that while we were yet enemies, Christ died for us. Interestingly, even as His enemies, God waged war FOR us – not to vanquish us, but to gain us as sons and daughters – and even friends! (John 15:15)

Even after Paul walked with God for years, he never forgot the battle front of the war waging within his own soul. In the book of Romans, he vividly describes the continuous conflict between his flesh (his carnal, sinful, temporal instincts) and the Spirit (the Holy Spirit fueling our new, eternal nature). He teaches the same principles to the believers in Galatia saying that the flesh wars against the Spirit for dominance in our lives. We must yield to the Spirit which brings great fruit, and must beat down the flesh which brings debauchery and death. Even as a blood-bought, redeemed believer, I must fight an ever-present battle within me, and never underestimate its power.

The enemy around us

Each year, the Parade Magazine publishes a list of the top ten cruelest dictators in the world. Consistently jockeying for position in the top ten are: Robert Mugabe (Zimbabwe), Omar al-Bashir (Sudan), Kim Jong-Il (North Korea), Than Shwe (Burma), King Abdullah (Saudi Arabia), Hu Jintao (China), Seyed Ali Knamene'i (Iran), Isaias Afewerki (Eritrea), Gurbanguly Berdymuhannedov (Turkmenistan), and Muammar al-Qaddafi (Libya). Their ideologies decimated literally millions of lives – in some countries, up to 25 percent of their population. Across the board, each dictator was shrewd in gaining control and brutally violent to keep control.

A look back just one century highlights people like Hitler, Stalin, Mao Zedong and Pol Pot, at whose hands millions lost their lives. The war of ideas matters, and our young century is threatened with the top-ten list, their successors, and other murderous leaders like Osama bin Laden (now killed) that lead international terrorist cells rather than a specific country.

Ideas fuel cruelty. Virtually everyone on the cruel list represents ideologies contrary to the truth of Scripture and embodied in the very nature of God. (I readily acknowledge Christian cruelty in history but would list them as anomalies completely inconsistent with God's Word.) This is the world system we are at war with – a battle of ideas – that gain power shrewdly and maintain it through cruelty.

John MacArthur, Bible teacher and prolific author, highlights this battle of ideas in his book, *The Truth War*. He sounds very much like the drill instructor you hate in the beginning, but love when the training saves your life. He chides Christians for preferring play to the idea of actually fighting for doctrinal truth.

He says truth is the highest of prizes, and this serious warfare requires the utmost diligence. Truth is what we fight for and MacArthur defines it as, "recognition that ultimate truth is an objective reality. Truth exists outside of us and remains the same regardless of how we may perceive it. Truth by definition is as fixed and constant as God is immutable."[5]

As previously stated, the key to victory is to discern the enemy. When God's absolute truth is abandoned, the enemies to truth don't disappear, but morph into mere shadows of truth now difficult to define, and more difficult to combat. In our obsession with tolerance, we invite every idea to the table as an equal player and lose any transcendent truth worth fighting for. This inevitably invites a "might-makes-right" outcome. Chilling examples are found on American college campuses. As truth gives way to relative ethics, a high percentage of college students today can no longer call Hitler's actions wrong on the basis of any transcendent principles. And yet, Hitler's rise to power came through scary shadows of truth, and he is quoted as saying, "How fortunate for leaders that men do not think."[6]

Ideas based on truth?

All ideas are not equal, or truth becomes contradictory, and is therefore no longer truth.

The military demands adherence to clear objectives and to an unwavering military code of ethics and justice. Anything less promotes disunity and erodes strength. As previously mentioned, the military got a wake-up call to tolerance with Major Hasan on November 5, 2009. He was a U.S. Army psychiatrist and Muslim of Pakistani descent with alleged ties to radical Islamic Anwar al-Awlaki. Ultimately, Hasan's conflicting ideas may have pushed him to murder the very people he had sworn to serve. Sadly, history abounds with many other examples.

A world system opposed to God's truth gains more ground each decade – ushering in the "perilous times" long ago predicted in Scripture in Paul's epistle to Timothy. Instead of the church standing firm against the onslaught, MacArthur says many have grown lazy, worldly, and self-satisfied.

Our combat caution has waned – and our vulnerability is on the rise.

It is critical that we recognize our tri-dimensional enemy (the world, the flesh, and the devil) but equally important to know why we are fighting. MacArthur says it well, "...not for the thrill of vanquishing some foe or winning some argument, but out of a genuine love for Christ, Who is the living, breathing embodiment of all that we hold true and worth fighting for."[7]

CHAPTER 2: THE REALITY OF AN ENEMY

Most important "take-away" thought(s):

Truth cuts through Confusion

I vastly prefer Knowledge of the enemy- That will fight me whether I believe in him or not.

Satan
murderer
Father of all lies
Author of confusion - misinformation

steal
kill
Destroy
Angel of light
Plants, doubt, rebellion, despair

1. Describe your feeling on September 11, 2001. Can you think of a similar feeling when you first experienced the awareness that you had a spiritual enemy – and he had just delivered a massive strike in your life?

Sept. 11 - shock, stunned, at a loss, afraid for Brian, disoriented

Spiritually - when I read Dr. Bernard Nathanson's Book Aborting America and realized the intention deception that I had fallen for to my ruin.

2. What if you don't believe spiritual warfare is real? What are the ramifications of that belief? You will feel it's affects anyway.

You will likely die having no escape - Realize it too late

3. Why is it important to know the enemy we fight against? How does that play out practically in life?

We're not in the dark, we can develop a strategy and plan.
We can train so the impact is less devastating.

4. We face a three-prong enemy. Name them. List at least one way you struggle with each of them.

Satan
ourselves
Societal ideas

5. How does all of this practically apply to gaining greater victories in your spiritual walk?

Be aware
Be intentional

"Be on the alert, stand firm in the faith, act like men, be strong."
I Corinthians 16:13

3
THE ALERTNESS OF WAR

On September 12, 2001, our nation could no longer pretend we did not have an enemy. While we pursued a frantic search for intelligence information to better identify the enemy, we remained on full alert.

The military has several measurements of threat – and clearly defined actions that accompany each level. Military bases daily establish a Force Protection condition (FPCON) and there are also national and international levels posted each day, depending on events and intelligence information.

After 9/11, FPCONs were taken very seriously. Gates were heavily guarded with full ID checks and thorough vehicle inspections. Buildings were locked down and entry guards posted. Anything remotely suspicious or out-of-the-ordinary was immediately reported and investigated. Reserve forces were activated and thousands left their normal civilian routines and poured through military gates to report for duty. Those not in the military clamored for information, and our military public affairs office regularly received calls from average citizens asking questions, or reporting activities they thought might matter. They were no longer familiar with their surroundings. Terrorism was front-and-center on our national radar screen, and we were now alert and diligent.

High alert

In the face of such diligence, the enemy was severely hampered and would have to work twice as hard to strike again. The average citizen has no idea how many plans were actually detected. Only people with Top-Secret clearances to classified information were privy to how much potential terrorist activity was thwarted through diligence and reliable intelligence.

As stated earlier, complacency causes us to miss a lot of war's warnings. We relax, our guard is down. We get familiar with our surroundings. We get careless – and we pay for it.

To get a quick picture of what "high alert" looks like, imagine something most of us have experienced. You wake up suddenly in the dark of night. You're not really sure what woke you, but you think you hear an unfamiliar sound. Is it outside? Is it downstairs? The sense of fear is palpable and running up and down your spine. You hold yourself perfectly still – straining every sense to gain more information so you can evaluate the threat. You review every detail that happened before you went to bed. Did I lock the door? Did I leave the window open? Were all the kids home? Every thought and action is concentrated on assessing the situation, and deciding the next course of action.

If that is true at home, how much more does it happen during an active war when you know the enemy is armed, close by, and has a clear mission to destroy? A sense of imminent danger heightens the senses and encourages scrutiny. High alert brings critically-needed focus.

The apostle Peter addressed this focus when he told believers to "be sober, be vigilant; because your adversary the devil, as a roaring lion, walks about seeking whom he may devour." (I Peter 5:8) Nehemiah understood vigilance when he instructed the people to work on the wall (around Jerusalem) with a tool in one hand and a weapon in the other. (Neh. 4:17) Paul tells the Corinthians to "watch, stand fast in the faith, act like men, and be strong." (I Cor. 16:13)

It's hard to read any part of the Bible without finding references to the need to be on alert. Perhaps it's because we have to do it on purpose because our default setting is undisciplined complacency. We want to feel safe and at peace – even when the facts show we are not. It did not take long after September 11th to default back into familiarity and diminished threat. Even though terrorism is alive and thriving a decade later, we no longer call our military effort the "Global War on Terrorism." We are more concerned about making people comfortable than rightly identifying the true nature of our enemy. Dangerous stuff.

So much of the Old Testament is peppered with prophets sent by God to communicate multiple threats God's people had ceased to see. Sadly, they ignored most of the warnings – and suffered the consequences. The prophet Isaiah assesses them in chapter 56 as: "watchmen that are blind, they are all without knowledge; they are all dumb dogs, they cannot bark; dreaming, lying down, they love to slumber." (v.10) The prophet Jeremiah warns them to walk in the right paths and to hear the sound of the trumpet (calling them to war), but they would not walk in it, nor hear or obey (Jer. 6:16-17). The chilling consequences of their rebellion are in verse 19: "Hear, O earth: behold, I am bringing disaster on this people, the fruit of their plans, because they have not listened to My words, and as for My law, they have rejected it also."

In the New Testament, the apostle Paul speaks of this same attitude with the Thessalonians. He talks about people saying "peace and safety" but sudden destruction comes upon them and "they shall not escape" (I Thess. 5:3). He exhorts them not to sleep (take their ease and shut their eyes to the danger), but to watch and be sober.

Covert war

The believer's war is a covert war. In our current fight against terrorism, it's challenging to spot the enemy because the differences can be so subtle. They live among us, act like us, and appear to be good people. Gone are the days when the enemy marches into battle with bright red uniforms.

Former Marine and gifted Bible teacher, Chuck Swindoll emphasizes our need to see the reality of spiritual warfare, and how tricky it can be. He says, "A war is on – an invisible war – though many would deny it. It is the war to destroy human souls, and the opening salvo and earliest tactic of this war is deception."[1]

Vigilance is tiring, but vulnerability is our only other option. There's no such thing as "dumb and happy" in war. Ignorance isn't bliss – it's deadly.

Are you paying attention? Be assured the enemy is. Are you aware of your personal threat condition? How about your family and friends? What areas of your life require more scrutiny because of a greater potential for danger?

The right mental mindset puts warfare on a front burner where it belongs. It provides the right perspective for planning and victory.

CHAPTER 3: THE ALERTNESS OF WAR

Most important "take-away" thought(s):

1. Have you ever thought about the concept of monitoring your personal threat level at different times of your life? Why, or why not?

Yes HALT
Hungry
Angry
Lonely
Tired

2. In the event of a spiritual threat, what are you trying to protect? Where are you most vulnerable?

Trying to protect my self from sinning (listening to the lies) and my family

3. What factors in society distract us from staying alert to the threats around us?

Business, Work, drama

4. What are some things that would raise spiritual threat levels in your life? Certain situations, environments, or people? Explain. What are some precautions that might be put in place?

5. Can you think of Bible characters that let down their guard and ignored threat levels? What did their lack of diligence cost them?

"Or what king, when he sets out to meet another king in battle,
will not first sit down and consider whether he is strong enough with ten
thousand men to encounter the one coming against him with twenty thousand?
Luke 14:31

4
IMPORTANCE OF STRATEGY

December 7, 1941, is "a date which will live in infamy" because that was the day 353 Japanese aircraft executed a surprise attack on Pearl Harbor. Four battleships, three cruisers, three destroyers, and 188 aircraft were ruined, and 2,402 lives were lost by the time the smoke cleared.

The event crystallized the enemy and put the country on high alert. America was at war.

The enemy clearly had a strategy, and we needed a strategic plan to protect our nation and eventually take the war to two fronts. President Roosevelt mustered the sharpest military minds to craft plans best suited to outwit the enemy and bring about victory.

Strategy is essential to the execution of war. A familiar adage says that if you fail to plan, you plan to fail. Tanks, troops and torpedoes are all types of war tactics, but it is strategy that pulls them all together under a specific mission. Chinese General Sun Tzu says it well: "Strategy without tactics is the slowest route to victory. Tactics without strategy is the noise before defeat."[1]

Military strategy is a dynamic process. As battles are won and lost, it's necessary to assess, adjust and regroup, never losing sight of the goal. Strategy is the engine that drives the defense train and connects the cars.

Additionally, strategy is not a knee-jerk reaction, but usually a selection of deliberate responses planned way in advance. The Department of Defense maintains detailed defense plans based on the analysis of the global geopolitical landscape and the contingencies they represent. The "what-ifs" are considered, and the "what-thens" are developed. These plans are closely guarded and constantly practiced in realistic, simulated exercises to give command leaders experience and confidence – and also to assess what happens to the plans in a dynamic environment.

I participated in some of these Department of Defense, joint-forces exercises and was impressed by the extensive training scenarios. There was a sense of urgency, realism, and gravity as we watched the simulated air, land, and sea military maneuvers play out on huge screens in the command and control section. At times, the simulated scenario was hard to distinguish from real-world news headlines. It was a sobering experience. It was not an elaborate video game – it could become real in a heartbeat.

Clear defense objectives

I recently came across a National Defense Strategy for 2008. What stood out to me was that it was concise and orderly. The defense objectives were organized into five categories: defend the homeland, win the long war, promote security, deter conflicts, and win our nation's war. With objectives clearly defined, tactics were then developed to accomplish the strategy. This framework drove all subsequent details of readiness and implementation. Strategy drives priorities. With a clear plan, I can readily distinguish what adds to my plan and what detracts from my plan, and adjust accordingly.

Rational, coherent strategies are thought out long in advance. You can't wait until you're in the situation to figure out what to do, although the immediacy of the moment might alter some details. When the explosions rocked Pearl Harbor, within hours, military maps and copious defense plans surely lined the walls of Washington war rooms. The resulting, fine-tuned strategy became the framework for the military movement of men, machines and money.

Strategy is vitally important to victory and, sadly, few Christians seem to understand this principle. In apparently willful ignorance of enemy strategy – and lack of their own defense strategy – many Christians live in "ambush mode" thereby spending more time in sickbay than on the battlefield. This phenomenon has thinned the ranks and weakened God's forces – just as predictably as it would regular troop strength.

A sampling of Satan's strategies include: keep believers busy with non-essentials, tempt them to overspend and go into debt, make them work long hours to maintain empty lifestyles, over-stimulate minds with TV and computers so they can't hear God's voice, put glamorous models on TV and in magazines to keep them focused on outward appearance – dissatisfied with self and mate, etc. The enemy has specific plans to defeat us. We must have a counter-strategy.

Jesus addressed the practical importance of strategy when He spoke about how foolish it would be to try to build a house without a plan, and how that man would be mocked when he couldn't finish the job. Jesus takes the same concept and applies it to the military. "Or what king, going to make war against another king, does not first sit down and consult whether he is able with ten thousand to meet him who comes against him with twenty thousand?" (Luke 14:31)

The strategy of Jesus

Jesus remains the best example for... well... everything.

He had a clear strategy while He walked the earth. He came to do the will of His Father (John 8:28), to seek and to save the lost (Luke 19:10), to set the captives free (Luke 4:18), and to break the power of the enemy (Luke 10:19). The apostle Paul spells out Jesus' strategy to the Galatians: "Who gave Himself for our sins, that He might deliver us from this present evil world according to the will of God and our Father." (Galatians 1:4) His strategy actually sounds a little like the National Defense Strategy – especially the part about winning the long war. Jesus was in it to win the eternal war, and He did.

Jesus also faced wars on multiple fronts while on earth. People from His hometown rejected Him, the religious groups plotted against Him, the government officials condemned Him, and one of His own betrayed Him. Even Satan aimed a few temptation missiles His way in the fourth chapter of Matthew. Jesus had fasted for 40 days in the wilderness and was hungry. At His physically weakest point, the enemy, Satan, tempted Jesus to sell out to personal ambition in three tactical temptations. Jesus stuck to His strategy – which in His case – was keeping His Word. He simply referred back to His game plan each time with, "It is written." He remained unwavering and resolute to His mission.

Jesus sets the example and He also provides the details of our strategy through His Word. We, too, must integrate the Word into strategies specific to our battles.

A very godly friend recently shared how she discovered the importance of strategy during an extremely difficult series of life battles. "I was a Christian for 20 years, I went to church, and I loved the Lord," she said, "but I was ambushed by circumstances, and felt overwhelmed and helpless." She attended a seminar by Becky Tirabassi that showed her a way to develop strategies – practical ways to pursue victory in the Christian life. Each day, she listed personal issues like anger, sadness, relationships, etc. in a journal and searched specific Scriptures in that area to formulate immediate marching orders.

In the chaos of battle, we can forget our mission. Truth brings clarity back. She said it turned her life around to have a clear strategy to follow each morning. "We worship God in spirit and truth – our walk is spiritual, but it is also practical," she said.

As a nurse, this same friend observed how health care issues require strategies all the time. "We assess the symptoms, determine what systems are being attacked, and figure out a strategy to beat it," she observed. "Why is it so hard to translate that into our spiritual health?" That question is even more puzzling when we see how pivotal strategy is to success in sports, business, relationships, hobbies and investments.

Where the stakes are highest – in spiritual battle – our strategy is often weakest.

In the midst of communist intrigue in the 1920's, Leon Trotsky voiced a warning relevant to Christians: "You may not be interested in strategy, but strategy is interested in you."[2]

Elisabeth Elliot is well-acquainted with strategies – in both the physical and spiritual realms. The Belgian-born, American missionary was a young wife and mother when she and husband, Jim, served as missionaries to the Auca Indians in Equador in the 1950s. In 1956, Jim was murdered by the very people they served. Their daughter, Valerie, was only 10-months-old at the time.

Assaulted by grief, anger, and surely doubt – Elisabeth clung to her battle strategy for the souls of men and continued a work with the Quichua Indians for two more years. While there, she learned the Aucan (now known as Huaorani) language and in 1958, took up her husband's work to reach the Aucan people. Elisabeth Elliot was so strong in her commitment to her strategy that the Auca nicknamed her "Gikari," which means "woodpecker." She returned to the United States in 1963. Her strategy didn't change, but her tactics took her to different venues to share God's Word.

Despite her victories, now 80-something Elisabeth has lost two husbands, and experienced enemy strategies that made her want to quit. Looking back, she learned that when the long-term strategy dims in discouragement, a short-term strategy gets you back in the battle: "Just do the next thing."[3] Get up. Get dressed. Brush your teeth. Make coffee. Press on. Wise words from a wise woman.

Incidentally, death does not always signify a failed strategy. Even though Elisabeth Elliot's husband, Jim, died young, he died as a soldier in the battle he was called to fight. He lived a strategic, focused life, and fulfilled his own words: "When the time comes to die, make sure all you have to do is die."[4]

Strategic planning – it's not about you

Both the Elliots and my friend are great examples of another important aspect of strategy – it is not rooted in personal preference.

Military defense strategies have an overarching goal that extends far beyond the advantage of any individual or special interest group – or at least they should in a country that values freedom. When top military brass brainstorm strategy, they are in submission to other authorities, and plan for the greatest corporate good. Imagine the chaos if one general privately plans for his own gain. It happens in other countries – usually called a coup – and it generally brings great instability, fear and limited freedom.

The military mission always supersedes personal interest and this principle brings focus, unity, strength and victory. Army Chaplain (Col.) Phillip Wright has watched this principle in action during deployments in Southwest Asia. He noted that soldiers thrived in hardship when they kept the mission in focus. As a deployed chaplain in Afghanistan, Wright has helped military members develop strategies to thrive in war zones far from home. "If you only think about your own needs, it's very easy to slip into defeat mode," he said. "You have to remember why you are there."

Solomon brings biblical wisdom to the topic in Proverbs 16:9. "A man's heart plans his ways, but God directs his steps," is a perfect example of correct strategy. Make personal plans, but be willing to submit them to God. Jim Elliot developed a strategy based on his heart's passion, but allowed God to direct his steps with regard to timing, location, etc. His plans revolved around the One he sought to serve.

Oswald Chambers captures the same thought in *My Utmost for His Highest:* "Keep your life so constant in its contact with God that His surprising power may break out on the right hand and on the left. Always be in a state of expectancy, and see that you leave room for God to come in as He likes."[5]

The prophet Jeremiah warns about self-serving strategies in Jeremiah 7:24: "They did not listen, nor bow their ear, but walked in their own plans, in the stubbornness of their evil heart and went backward, not forward."

In the military, it's clear that the mission is not about you – but motives can get muddy with Christians – the mission gets motivated by "me." Even when it's not, Christian strategy can be reduced to slogans – pithy sayings that have lost meaning to many believers.

Here's one you've probably heard hundreds of times:

"Seek ye first the kingdom of God and His righteousness and all these things will be added unto you."(Matthew 6:23) Matthew's gospel articulates a clear mission but we've become almost deaf to it by repetition. In God's mission, self is not entirely lost, but subjugated to achieve a far greater victory. Bruce Wilkinson explores this overarching strategy in his book, *Experiencing Spiritual Breakthroughs.* He says that we should go after the King's agenda (kingdom) as our highest priority and seek to live in His righteousness and not our own. When a good soldier selflessly serves his country, the military takes care of the soldier's needs. The soldier doesn't seek food, clothing, shelter – these are provided for him as long as he serves the mission. This frees the soldier to focus on the higher calling.

The apostle Peter speaks of the supernatural resources we have in Christ, but emphasizes the need for strategy to use those resources. Peter says, "Therefore, brethren, be all the more diligent to make certain about His calling and choosing you; for as long as you practice these things, you will never stumble; for in this way the entrance into the eternal kingdom of our Lord and Savior Jesus Christ will be abundantly supplied to you." (I Peter 1:10)

The apostle Paul embraced the Christian's overall goal as stated in the West-minster Catechism: "Man's chief end is to glorify God and enjoy Him forever."[6] He also illustrates that God's mission is a life-long strategy. Despite a lengthy enlistment in God's army, Paul tells the Philippian believers that he hasn't yet "arrived," but "presses on to lay hold of that" for which he was laid hold of by Christ Jesus. His strategy is clear in chapter 3: "I press on toward the goal for the prize of the upward call of God in Christ Jesus." In his last letter to Timothy, Paul had executed his strategy and declared "mission complete." In II Timothy 4, just before Paul suffered a martyr's death, he stated: "I have fought the good fight of faith, I have finished the course, I have kept the faith." (II Tim. 4:7)

Peter and Paul shared God's mission and strategy – only the particulars changed depending on each person's gifting and role in the work of God. A read through the New Testament reveals one clear strategy after another, executed to win the fight of faith.

Survive or thrive?

Finally, it's also important to note that strategy is not just to survive – but to thrive – as Jim Elliot did during his short life. His death was not a failure. His victories became evident as the work he pioneered bore fruit in the years following his death.

There are critical times in life when survival is the only thing on the radar screen, but it is not meant to be a way of life. Imagine an army stuck in survival mode, hunkered down in foxholes with no other strategy than making it through the day – for months on end. The soldiers that stormed Omaha Beach on D-Day (June 1944) stayed in survival mode for 14 days while they were pinned on the beach under German fire, but they never intended to stay there. According to the D-Day veteran I interviewed, survival was important, but victory was still the overriding strategy. If those men had stayed in survival mode they never would have overrun the Germans and helped push them out of France.

Too many Christians are in survival mode today – hunkered down in the church and in the details of their own lives. Their prayer is to simply get through each week. There is no battle for higher ground. An arsenal of resources remains untapped, and we continue to lose societal ground.

The apostle Paul's survive and thrive strategies seemed to be one in the same. He spent time in prison, was stoned and left for dead in Lystra, shipwrecked three times, and spent a night and a day in the deep. He knew times of hunger and thirst, need and exposure. (II Corinthians 11:25) Rather than cower because life dealt him some hard blows, Paul refused to let anything disqualify him from the race set before him.

He repeatedly exhorted believers to abound, use their talents, and stay in the fight of faith. He tells the Colossians (1:10) to "walk in a manner worthy of the Lord, to please Him in all respects, bearing fruit in every good work and increasing in the knowledge of God." Jesus prompts us to live in a "thrive strategy" in John's gospel: "My Father is glorified by this, that you bear much fruit, and so prove to be My disciples." (John 15:8)

A military soldier goes through multiple tests to prove his mettle. Imagine a soldier enlisting and then sitting on the sidelines throughout the war. A soldier too tired, scared or apathetic to fight is a burden to the mission. While fear is a natural emotion when facing battles, a skilled soldier senses a "rightness" about the call to battle. "This is what we train for," is what I have heard in countless interviews with troops heading to Iraq and Afghanistan.

In numerous civilian and military interviews, I posed the survive-versus-thrive question and the word "focus" came up many times. In survival mode, the focus is narrow, the strategy limited. Focus and strategy expand in thrive mode – beyond self to a much broader sphere. A few people even noted that you can be in both modes at the same time – in different parts of your life.

We are meant to thrive, and our strategy should reflect a plan for victory. Massachusetts Pastor Jeff Chandler said too many get stuck at 2 Corinthians 4:7-8 which speaks of "being afflicted but not crushed, perplexed but not despairing, persecuted but not forsaken, and struck down but not destroyed." He said those conditions are reality for many, but a greater reality should be 2 Corinthians 2:14: "Thanks be to God who always leads us in triumph in Christ." Chandler compared surviving to being on the defensive while thriving pursues an active offense. "Those living with an offensive approach understand the ongoing battle and so are always alert, actively engaged, and constantly drawing upon all the resources God has made available to us."

The enemy of our souls has a strategy against us, and he fights to win. The most effective spiritual soldier is the one who strategizes for victory – uses all the resources in his chain-of-command --and executes the clear mission with courage. Like the Israelites facing off against the enemies resident in the Promised Land, it's time for the church to take what's rightfully theirs.

CHAPTER 4: IMPORTANCE OF STRATEGY

Most important "take-away" thought(s):

1. Have you ever thought about the concept of monitoring your personal threat level at different times of your life? Why, or why not?

2. In the event of a spiritual threat, what are you trying to protect? Where are you most vulnerable?

3. What factors in society distract us from staying alert to the threats around us?

4. What are some things that would raise spiritual threat levels in your life? Certain situations, environments, or people? Explain. What are some precautions that might be put in place?

5. Can you think of people in the Bible that let down their guard and ignored threat levels? What did their lack of diligence cost them?

And Jesus came up and spoke to them, saying,
"All authority has been given to Me in heaven and on earth."
Matthew 28:18

5
LEADERSHIP AND AUTHORITY

Authority is the glue that holds the military together, and the first clip from the "glue gun" is emptied on new recruits on Day Zero of boot camp.

"They were yelling at us before we even got off the bus," said Army specialist Michael Azevedo. The 17-year-old was not feeling well when he arrived, and things quickly got worse. "They ran us into a 200-foot enclosure and 'smoked' us. Drill sergeants screamed at everyone barking orders, demanding punishing calisthenics for random reasons. People were throwing up everywhere," Azevedo said, describing the military initiation dubbed "Shark Attack."

Basic training authority is loud, nose-to-nose, around-the-clock, and purposely humiliating to the proud or stubborn. One thing immediately becomes painfully clear – you don't get to make the rules – you follow them. Every aspect of training is designed to test your ability to submit to authority and ultimately to work as an orderly team.

"They screamed at us 24/7," said new Marine Joseph DeJesus. The self-described former rebel learned the value of authority when Marine basic training stripped him down mentally and physically, and rebuilt him and fellow recruits into a functional unit with a clear purpose. Every military branch executes the same basic training goal: strip, and then equip.

Talk with anyone who has been through basic training and they all have a story to tell, funny now, but not so much at the time. Personally, I was so paranoid that I found myself saluting everyone. I struggled to make sense of all the insignia at the joint-service Defense Information School I attended after Basic. If they wore a uniform and had stuff on their shoulder, I saluted, just to be safe, especially with foreign officers.

Why such a heavy emphasis on authority? It brings structure, order, responsibility, accountability – and hopefully, education, motivation and inspiration when entrusted to ethical and gifted leadership. Authority, according to

Merriam Webster Dictionary, is "a power to influence or command thought, opinion or behavior."[1] It is the skeleton that supports the muscle of any military.

Responsibility is clearly delineated for all ranks, and strength is directly related to a consistent application of proper authority. This priority is reflected in the Uniform Code of Military Justice (UCMJ) which details insubordination and specifies the penalties when authority is dishonored. This dishonor can occur by wrong use of authority, or by usurping proper authority in any way. True military authority should command respect because authority acts respectably.

Authority paradox

There is an interesting juxtaposition when it comes to military authority and power. Anyone who enlists (or is commissioned) in the military knows that once you sign – they "own you." When you submit to military authority, you cede your rights to them. They tell you what to do, when, where, how, and for how long. You submit your life individually, yet this submission and dedication is the stuff of strong forces. The individual relinquishes power, yet then participates in a greater aggregate power. To give up power to get more power seems illogical, but that is precisely what happens.

When individuals operate within a defined chain of command, they have minimal personal power, but also have access to even greater delegated power from every upper echelon. A mere private then functions with the potential power of the entire military above him or her.

Imagine then the consequences of personal autonomy in the military. Imagine the full fallout if, at any level of authority, the subordinate replies to an order with, "Nah, I just don't feel like doing that." Or, "That's not in my best interest right now." Such responses are dealt with harshly because military strength only occurs when the individual subjugates his or her rights to the greater good – through submission to authority.

Spiritual principles of authority

It's easy to see the authority principle as it applies in military venues. We get it. We appreciate it. But, on a personal level, we tenaciously cling to autonomy, and seldom see why we lack strength and power. This is especially true of Christians battling in the unseen realm of spiritual warfare. This issue of authority breaks or builds soldiers, but it also determines whether we are weaklings or warriors in the faith.

In a culture that exalts personal autonomy, words like authority and submission have become negative, emotionally-charged words. Bumper stickers blurt "Question Authority." It has become the cultural norm for young adults to challenge authority at every level. A wife is thought to be debased if she "lowers" herself to submit to her husband's delegated authority. Because true authority and submission are maligned and discarded, a growing cultural anarchy is moving into the vacuum.

A partial reason for this trend is due to distorted definitions and examples. History is littered with heinous examples of abusive authority, so it takes a truly great example to illustrate the right use of authority and power.

Here's the best One I know:

This Individual freely relinquished authority to have it. He received authority through submission and obedience. He used authority to serve others, never Himself. He showed the unifying power of authority, and used it for good, never evil. He delegated authority and trained people to use it properly. Wrong authority abused Him, but He remained faithful to His mission. He had all power, yet gave up His life and used His authority for redemption.

This exceptional example of true authority is Jesus Christ. Although He was God, He took on the form of a servant. He came to serve – not to be served – to give His life as an excruciating ransom. He willingly restricted His deity and submitted fully to His Father. During His role in earthly ministry, He said: "...I seek not my own will but the will of the Father who sent Me." (John 6:38)

Jesus displayed a servant authority and He brings great dignity to submission by setting the example Himself. Submission carries no negative connotation when presented as a godly pattern to follow. Jesus consistently displayed proper authority that builds up, encourages, strengthens, equips, instructs in righteousness, etc.

Entire books are written about the authority of God. He is the righteous, relational Ruler worthy of receiving full submission. He is referred to as the "Lord of hosts" or "God Almighty" nearly 500 times in Scripture, with both terms signifying authority as in a military context. God is the ultimate "large-and in-charge." The primary point in this chapter is that Jesus came to oppose a wrong authority – a satanic authority that is selfish, destructive, dishonest, opportunist, beguiling and deadly. This is the opposite of all that Jesus modeled.

Who gets to be in charge?

Spiritual warfare is ultimately a battle of authority. All authority is fueled by one of two kingdoms and it is imperative to discern which kingdom is behind which authority at any given time, regardless of the person or position.

This is vital for two reasons: control and influence.

We've already seen that military service means giving up autonomy. To come under authority is to give control to another – to cede your rights. This is true in many aspects of life. The Internal Revenue Service takes authority over my money. Traffic laws control my speed limit, which lane I drive on, and when I stop and go. Courts control behavior and the consequences of bad behavior. There are many authorities that control my physical life, but only two that vie for control in my spiritual life.

In Charles Kraft's book, *I Give You Authority*, he writes, "Human obedience... whether to God or Satan, gives whichever master specific rights in a person's life."[2]

It's not always easy to discern authority sources in the beginning. Hitler stands as a stark example of an authority that promised provision and protection but eventually used his control for mass genocide and imperial expansion. This is typically true of tyrants – and also for Satan – who lures us with promises and controls us through punishment. Satan first appears as an angel of light to gain control, and wields it recklessly once attained.

Given the track record of the two competing sources of authority (never posed as equals), it is imperative for the Christian to consistently submit to God's authority in order to yield to true, trustworthy power.

The second key aspect to authority is influence –having the capacity to be a compelling force. When Jesus spoke in the synagogues, people were astonished at his wisdom. Even in His humanity, Jesus embodied authority, and greatly influenced crowds wherever He went.

The fact that authority carries influence is illustrated by the impact generated through parents, teachers, pastors, husbands, coaches, bosses, etc. Positions of authority, particularly those delegated by God, carry great influence. Any of these positions can wield good or bad authority, and yield good or bad results. Discernment is essential.

Ask any adult who was traumatized as a child by abusive parents. Because children cannot readily discern wrong authority, there is often an unguarded influence that creates debilitating wounds that last a lifetime. How many women are shattered by ungodly spousal authority, and live for decades with a tattered self-image from unchecked negative influence?

To recognize wrong authority does not mean rebellion. When a person discerns wrong use of authority, particularly if it is only sporadic, he or she should set clear boundaries on how much influence that person or position is allowed to exert. Believers are not exempt from this abuse. In spiritual warfare, even Christians can exercise authority from the wrong kingdom if they knowingly or unknowingly submit to the enemy's control through sin, generational influence, or lack of complete submission to God.

Suppose a husband constantly belittles his wife due to his own insecurities. A Christian wife still loves and submits to her husband, but guards her heart against receiving wrong influences connected to his destructive use of authority. She rejects the lies, but not the person. This is very different from rebellion and is critical to winning spiritual battles by staying under the influence of only God's authority.

The apostle Paul alludes to this principle of discerning authority in his letter to the Corinthians: "For the weapons of our warfare are not fleshly, but mighty through

God to the pulling down of strongholds, pulling down imaginations and every high thing that exalts itself against the knowledge of God, and bringing every thought into the obedience of Christ."(II Cor. 10:4-5) Ungodly authority will reveal itself by content contrary to God's truth. The battle-savvy believer hones this skill of discerning wrong influence ushered in by wrong use of true authority.

Kraft said that Christians need to discern the kingdom behind authority, or they will end up following wrong leaders.

Good leaders learn by submission

It is also noteworthy that the best leaders are those who have learned how to follow. In the military, many say that the best officers come from the enlisted ranks. They have a sound foundation of following orders before they gain a position to give them, and their authority generally carries a greater degree of humility. Obedience is good preparation for skilled stewardship of authority. As Christians, we are always under God's authority – no matter how much authority we are entrusted with here on earth.

Joshua is a great biblical example of this principle. He served faithfully under Moses for 40 years and was elevated to full authority over the Israelites when Moses died. Joshua fully understood that power for victory came only through God – through personal and corporate submission and obedience – rather than military might. When faced with conquest for the Promised Land, he prepared the people by checking their hearts. He said, "Sanctify yourselves [be clean under God's authority] and tomorrow the Lord will do great things among us." (Joshua 3:5) Joshua obeyed God, the people obeyed Joshua (and God,) and they experienced great victories in occupying the lands that God promised. Submission is the only true posture for victory.

Just the opposite is illustrated in the book of Judges. After Joshua died, Judges recorded the chronic slide into chaos and oppression when God's people threw off God's authority. The theme is captured by the recurrent phrase: "They did what was right in their own eyes." This repeatedly led them to submit to ungodly nations and suffer under their control. They seesawed between prosperity and oppression – only experiencing deliverance when God sent judges to bring them back under God's authority – but then sadly wandering again and again. Despite repeated rescues, Judges ends on a dismal note, brilliantly illustrating the cause-and-effect of submitting to wrong authority.

In spiritual warfare, victory is completely dependent on submission to God – and on being rightly related to His delegated authorities. This is even more crucial when we are entering enemy territory (like Joshua), or when we are trying to take back territory from the enemy (like Judges). When we have ceded authority to Satan, we win back ground only when we refuse him any further control – and submit completely to God's control.

Divided submission = defeat

Consider a believer who follows after God – seemingly in submission – but harbors a secret sin such as pornography, drug use, or unforgiveness. As much as the Christian wants to walk in power, divided allegiance to sin drains power, and the believer begins to function in dull defeat – going through the motions, but lacking true fullness and victory that comes from full submission.

This authority path to victory is clearly delineated in James, chapter 4, which begins with wars and fighting. James gives instructions in verse 7: "Therefore submit yourselves to God. Resist the devil, and he will flee from you." James then echoes Joshua's call to purity and God's authority in the next verse: "Draw near to God, and He will draw near to you. Cleanse your hands, sinners; and purify your hearts, double-minded ones."

The power to resist the enemy is unmistakably linked to the choice to submit. Submit – resist – in that order. If we are not submitted to God, then Satan is still pulling strings. We then become more marionette than soldier, and resistance is impossible.

Submission to God also has to be genuine. In Acts 19, Paul performed many miracles with the power he possessed under God's authority. Some Jewish exorcists watched Paul and attempted to cast out demons in the same way, but without the same authority. The seven sons of Sceva had claimed authority over an evil spirit in a man, saying: "we adjure you by Jesus whom Paul preaches." In verse 15, the evil spirit answered: "Jesus I know, and I comprehend Paul, but who are you?" Without authority born from a personal, intimate relationship with Jesus Christ, the seven sons were exposed as frauds. They could not adjure by the Jesus in whom they believed. The man with the evil spirit then attacked and overpowered them, and the imposters fled the scene naked and wounded. Fighting the enemy without God's full authority can be very painful.

God's superior authority

In spiritual warfare, as powerful as Satan's army can be, authority sides are not evenly stacked. In I John 4, John tells believers to test every spirit to see if they are of God because false teachers masquerade as true teachers. He then encourages God's people by showing them which side is stronger. "You are of God, little children, and you have overcome them because **He who is in you is greater than he that is in the world.**" (I John 4:4)

All power to combat the enemy's authority in our lives is centered at the cross where God's greatness was displayed. Satan is referred to as the "prince and the power of the air – the spirit that is now working in the sons of disobedience" in Ephesians 2. He roams the earth seeking who he may devour, and has impressive authority to do so. Ironically, Satan's authority manifests itself in lawlessness – the chaotic result of disordered authority. Jesus came to destroy the works of the devil (I John 3:8) and He accomplished it through the cross.

It's also interesting that Paul refers to his struggle with sin as the "law of sin and death" working within him. Law implies authority. This classic battle of spiritual authority is experienced as the flesh (with its law of sin) battles against the Spirit (God's authority within). In Romans 6, the cross broke the power of sin. We can be slaves to sin, or slaves of righteousness – the issue is authority. There is no getting around it. Just like basic training teaches – we'd be a lot better off if we accepted the fact that we don't get to make the rules – we just need to follow the right ones.

The authority of sin is like a bully – only this bully fights on a battleground rather than a playground. Like all bullies, he needs to be confronted. It's much easier standing behind our heavenly Father – which is a picture of fighting under His authority.

God's authority is infinitely more powerful – and He wins in the end. For those taking up the battle after Jesus died and rose again, submitting to God's authority is the only path to victory. Like a general giving His troops a final briefing, Jesus speaks to His disciples in Matthew 28:

> "All authority has been given to Me in heaven and on earth. Go therefore and make disciples of all the nations, baptizing them in the name of the Father and the Son and the Holy Spirit, teaching them to observe all that I have commanded you; and lo, I am with you always, even to the end of the age."

We can submit and obey – or we can stubbornly resist. Luke records the penetrating words of Jesus that challenges us all: "But, why do you call me 'Lord, Lord,' and not do the things which I say?" (Luke 6:46)

"Jesus meant there would be those who confess Him as Lord, but do not follow Him as their Supreme Authority," said John Bevere in his book, *Enemy Access Denied*.[3]

He adds: "They live in a manner that does not support what they confess. They obey the will of God as long as it does not conflict with the desires of their own heart. If the will of God takes them in a different direction than the one they desire, they choose their own path yet still call Jesus, 'Lord.'"[4]

Being rightly related to God's authority is found only in submission – and obedience.

Victory is possible only to those who do both.

CHAPTER 5: LEADERSHIP AND AUTHORITY

Most important "take-away" thought(s):

1. What is the culture's general attitude towards authority? What is your personal attitude?

2. What are the advantages of authority? What happens when authority breaks down?

3. How does Jesus bring dignity to authority? What does He model?

4. Authority carries influence. Why can this be dangerous? In what ways can you guard your heart with authority figures in your life?

5. What are some considerations for using your own authority?

"I have been crucified with Christ; and it is no longer I who live, but Christ lives in me; and the life which I now live in the flesh I live by faith in the Son of God, who loved me and gave Himself up for me." Galatians 2:20

6
SIGNING UP FOR PAIN

Brandon Forshaw was a Marine in full "battle rattle" guarding a base in Africa when he set his sights on possibly the most grueling military special operations training – Air Force pararescue. He wanted to become a "PJ," slang for pararescue members.

Forshaw was one of 75 men selected from a demanding application process. The initial 10-week indoctrination course quickly whittled that number to 18. Every day started at 4 a.m. and demanded punishing physical challenges, purposely unrelenting stress, academic training and constant tests for mental endurance. Some training was underwater, and surfacing for air was only allowed after designated tasks had been accomplished. Instructors often harassed the tasks (like tying the air hose in a knot) to ramp up the pressure.

"It was like Ground Hog Day [the movie] on crack," said Forshaw of the tortuous monotony. "They try to make you quit – if you quit in training – you'll quit in a real mission," he said.

As a former Marine with deployments to Iraq and Africa under his belt, quitting was never an option for Forshaw. That determination gave him the mental victory for the hellish training requirements. The 18 "indoc" grads then crisscrossed the country attending courses relating to sea, land, air, and medical care. After months of parachute jumps, navigational swimming, escaping from an upside-down submerged helicopter (blindfolded) – every scuba challenge you can imagine – search-and-rescue training, weapons drills, and combat medicine, it all culminated with a two-week field training exercise.

"The training was intense, and attention to detail was huge," said Airman Forshaw. The grueling field exercise simulated multiple real-life situations including a helicopter crash with 20 casualties. His team of five trainees had to drag casualties from the burning hulk, while grenades detonated to provide just the right amount of chaos. Patients were dragged to safety, triaged and treated. Brawn and brain were strained to the max – to stay alive – and accomplish the mission.

When the smoke cleared, Forshaw emerged as one of 10 (from the original 75) to earn the prestigious title "pararescueman."

Why such intense training?

Their motto says it all: "This we do that others may live."

But, it should add, "This we continue to do..."

Training never stops

Easing up on training is not an option in the military. Forshaw is attached to the 920th Rescue Wing at Patrick Air Force Base in Florida, and his qualification as a pararescueman requires continuous training. He must stay current and add to his skills in order to be optimally ready for every possible scenario. Training is meticulously scheduled because the most successful attacks come how and when they are least expected.

Because of the dynamic nature of war, continuous training is a priority.

Army Ranger Ed Cope understands continuous, relentless training. Rangers are the Army's elite special operations unit called in for harrowing reconnaissance missions into enemy territory, and their grueling training weeds out the weak and undisciplined. "Attitude is everything," said Cope, regarding the rigorous Ranger training. "We want someone who will give 110 percent – someone who gives just 100 percent will hit a wall and stop," he said.

"We want people who will push themselves through the wall to find resources they never knew they had."

Special Forces are seasoned military members. They volunteer to pursue punishing training for special missions, but what about new recruits? Special ops guys may be considered the overachievers, but what about the "average Joe?" Do they need training too? Of course. Everyone does. Any unit is only as strong as the weakest member.

So, how does the military take shaggy new recruits and train them for battle? How does it take disparate groups of people from all walks of life and turn them into cohesive, disciplined units?

It doesn't happen by accident, but through *carefully constructed, sequential training to accomplish specific objectives*. Personal comfort is not part of the equation. Neither is personal preference. Frankly, they don't care what you think – they just care that you get trained – at all levels – so you add to the success of the mission.

Basic training

Joseph DeJesus is a great example of an average Joe. Through 13 weeks of Marine basic training, DeJesus was stripped of his "civilian" identity so they could instill a new identity. He learned marksmanship, land navigation, combat skills, and endurance – just to name a few. Ten-mile hikes carrying 75-pound packs were the norm. Classroom training included Marine Corps history and core values. Boot camp closed with an intense, week-long, around-the-clock test called "the crucible" to see if you have what it takes to be a Marine. It's when the highest percentage of new recruits is cut. DeJesus said the pressure was intense, and he averaged about an hour of sleep each night.

"You suck it up – and just do the next thing," he said. "I signed up for this."

DeJesus made it through basic training and then entered into combat training for the next five weeks. At the end of combat instruction, recruits were able to take over a simulated city and defend it from the instructors who were trying to regain it. They did. He successfully made it through his first phase of training.

This experience turned his life upside-down. "Me" became "we." He learned that his unit was only as fast as the slowest person. The boy was now a man. Prior to enlisting, this teenager picked the words "crazy, burnt-out, and immature" to describe himself. He now says, "I'm a member of the greatest fighting force in the world." He now takes pride in who he is and what he does. He carries himself differently.

Military training is pain with a purpose.

Cost of neglect

When the systematic, regimented and thorough approach to military training is compared to a Christian's approach to spiritual training, the bleak contrast is disturbing. Perhaps some of the parallels have already jumped out at you.

Sadly, most people carefully equip themselves for every other aspect of life EXCEPT the spiritual. If military training brings discipline, maturity, fitness, readiness, respect for authority, core values and increased odds of survival and victory, what is the predictable cause and effect when spiritual training is minimal or missing? If military training systematically equips soldiers to be competent, confident and courageous, does a lack of spiritual training produce incompetence, insecurity and cowardice? Such conclusions would certainly be logical.

Military training is for every rank in every branch—it is vital for officers and enlisted – no one is exempt.

In contrast, Christians often think it's only the pastor's job to pursue disciplined, on-going spiritual training. I remember my shock when introducing a group of women to the inductive Bible study method which teaches a systematic, careful study of God's Word. After a relatively simple lesson which required scrutinizing a Bible passage, one woman remarked, "I thought this was the pastor's job."

Pastors do play an essential role in teaching and equipping, and may even be considered the "special forces" in a spiritual sense, but that hardly negates the personal responsibility each believer must take to excel as a disciple of Jesus Christ. The idea that only pastors should constantly train and grow in their Christian position is akin to thinking that only military officers, and not the enlisted forces, should train. What good are trained leaders if no one else is trained to execute the mission?

The thought of sending an untrained soldier to war is unthinkable and cruel. The odds for victory would be slim and they would likely get themselves killed along with both the trained and untrained around them. How is it that we continue to neglect spiritual training even though we witness greater defeat, regular ambush, and frequent defections in God's army of believers?

Christian apologist Ravi Zacharias has travelled the globe for three decades and says the American church has become shallow. In our self-indulgence, many are lazy in training, preferring comfort to sacrifice, individuality over corporate good – not knowing who we are or what we believe. Many aren't even sure what the mission is.

Disciplined learners

As Christians, we are called to be "disciples," which means "disciplined learners." God has saved us, and called us with a holy calling, (II Timothy 1:9) and a heavenly calling. (Hebrews 3:1) We are to grow in the grace and knowledge of our Lord Jesus Christ. (II Peter 3:18) We are to grow up in all aspects of Him who is the head, even Christ. (Ephesians 4:15) We are called to a fight of faith (I Timothy 6:12) and told to endure hardness as a good soldier. (II Timothy 2:3) The apostle Paul, as we stated earlier, was a spiritual war veteran and he constantly stressed the need for continual training to remain strong in the faith. Though he had very impressive credentials and plenty of battle scars, he assessed that he had not attained; he had not "arrived." Paul's goal was always to press on, higher and stronger, to the high calling of Jesus Christ. What he modeled he expected – encouraging disciples to go beyond the elemental teaching of Christ – to press on to full maturity. (Hebrews 6:1)

Just how should we view our discipleship and what are we supposed to be learning? A military parallel is very useful here. When a person enlists in the military, he or she declares an allegiance to the country they serve. They make a commitment and accept all associated terms and conditions. They willingly submit to the required training and separate themselves from normal routines to concentrate on preparation. They give up control of their lives, submit to authority, learn to work together and become proficient in every area, especially in their talent/job role. They train constantly for war, but help anywhere when needed in between battles. They do so for a glory and purpose beyond themselves. Their individual behavior reflects on the whole, they move where they are needed, and the good of the team governs conduct and goals. They are all students of the same military doctrine – they live by the book – whether it's fixing people, aircraft, or dismantling bombs.

As professing believers in Christ, our allegiance is to Him, our citizenship is in heaven, we are no longer our own, we train for His service, and we're enlisted for life. War is not a contingency – it's a way of life. Our life is corporate, our individual role for a team mission. Ultimately, every action is for the glory of God. Our military doctrine is the Word of God – which fills our minds, renews our hearts, and empowers our conduct.

Where do we start?

So where do we start? One of the first things the military does is assess aptitudes. Every potential recruit takes the Armed Services Vocational Aptitude Battery (ASVAB) which determines individual strengths and weaknesses. The results determine which career fields the recruit is best suited (eligible) for. The test may reveal aptitudes unknown to the recruit. In the spiritual parallel, each believer possesses different talents, passions and spiritual gifts. For the mission of the church, and the effectiveness of the individual, it's strategic to help believers assess their strengths and where those strengths best benefit the church.

Once enlisted (or commissioned), military training is organized and strategic. Everyone gets the same basic foundation – no one is exempt. Early on, authority, structure, identity and teamwork are firmly established because the overall mission guides the process. After "basic training" each recruit has a developmental path to take them through their career – always building on the basics, and growing in their particular career field. There are training specialists at every level supervising the training progress. Supervisors assess training progress in every evaluation, and mandatory mentoring monitors personal and professional growth at least twice a year. With all the investment of time and money in each recruit, the military does all it can to ensure success.

Once a believer "enlists" in the "army of God" through saving faith, they are often left to fend for themselves with minimal training. They receive a manual (the Bible) and hopefully attend one to two hours of teaching each week – which may or may not be systematic. Ironically, most churches contain an assortment of capable, intelligent people who have completed orderly, challenging training for their careers – but are not similarly challenged when it comes to spiritual training.

Instead of robust spiritual training, doctrines are dumbed down, and few believers are challenged to tackle the tough and complex issues of our day through a biblical lens. Unfortunately, what we expect, we get.

The result is similar to what happened during Desert Storm during the early 1990's. Ordinary Iraqi citizens were forced to fight with little training and old weapons. When Americans bore down on their troops, hundreds of Iraqi "conscripts" dropped their weapons and raised their hands in surrender. Similarly, the culture constantly bombards believers in areas in which they should have deep doctrinal training, and these poorly-trained converts surrender at the lowest level of cultural attack. They are unable to stand their ground so they retreat instead of advancing as ordered. Just as allied forces easily took control of Iraq, the culture easily overwhelms the church and takes control of believers.

Attitudes about training

Writing a single chapter on training is challenging because it is the emphasis of the entire book. Every chapter is essentially on training, so what principles are important from a general standpoint?

A disclaimer is in order first. Not all churches neglect systematic training. More and more churches offer new believer classes to review basic doctrines. Many churches help their members discover their spiritual gifts and help them use and improve them in church ministry. More and more churches are challenging growth through courses and workshops and more in-depth Bible studies. This is good news and these churches should serve as models.

Perhaps the hardest challenge all churches face is the attitude towards spiritual training. Too many people think it's unnecessary. They prefer the passive, "just-teach-me-but-don't-require-anything-of-me" mentality – a mentality built largely through TV viewing and a plethora of passive entertainment. There's an "I'm tired from the rest of my life, so go easy on me with spiritual training" attitude – unaware that spiritual training is the foundation for all of life. Lack of spiritual training may also be precisely why every other area of life feels harder.

Some battles are the training

Too many Christians forget that many hard things in life ARE the training, and not simply the thing to train for.

Confused?

The military gives a crucial lesson here when it comes to training.

When the technical instructor (TI) is screaming in your face, humiliating you at every opportunity, and generally making your life miserable – you don't get mad at the instructor, complain and quit. Why? Because you realize the hard stuff is part of the training. It's what you signed up for. It's what you have to go through to live out your role in the mission.

How could Brandon Forshaw endure his tortuous weeks of training when so many dropped out? His mindset was fixed – his expectations were correct. He succeeded mentally to succeed physically and emotionally. When his instructors harassed his training, he knew it wasn't out of spite. They knew the challenges he could face – and the harder they made it, the better trained he would be to survive and thrive in the real situations. The mature trainees get that – and stay in the game as a result.

A popular song by Laura Story illustrates the proper attitude about hardships as spiritual training. In her song, "Blessings," she sings about "praying for peace, comfort for family, protection while we sleep, healing and prosperity." We want God to ease our suffering, but her lyrics say: "All the while, You hear each spoken need, yet love us way too much to give us lesser things." The chorus gives us a much-needed perspective that relates to God using hard things to train us:

> 'Cause what if Your blessings come through raindrops
> What if Your healing comes through tears
> What if a thousand sleepless nights
> Are what it takes to know You're near
> What if trials of this life are Your mercies in disguise

At the close of the last stanza, she adds:

> What if my greatest disappointments
> Or the aching of this life
> Is the revealing of a greater thirst this world can't satisfy
> And what if trials of this life
> The rain, the storms, the hardest nights
> Are Your mercies in disguise

Laura Story's lyrics reflect her life lessons on God's training through hard things. Story's story includes years of trials early in her marriage as her husband battled life-threatening medical problems. According to her testimony, all the wrong approaches to spiritual training – the "why me?" and "why this"— were slowly understood as God's mercy to train them for His call on their lives. Attitudes about the events God chooses to train us often determine the line between quitters and victors. The book of Exodus is full of wilderness experiences that God purposely led them into for the express purpose of testing and training.

A science class parallel is also helpful to illustrate this point. How many students have endured lengthy lessons on science principles? Isn't the lecture enough to get the points across? Apparently not. What follows most science lectures are lengthy labs to test the principles taught. The professor is not being cruel to assign the lab, but seeks to test the students' knowledge and provide hands-on instruction to prove the validity of the lesson.

God does much the same thing, but His labs are often perceived as punishment rather than training for a deeper grasp of the lessons. Again, the constant whining in Exodus illustrates incorrect responses to God's "labs."

Two types of training

Forshaw also illustrates two types of training we need to understand as Christians. The first type of training is the kind that is self-initiated. In Forshaw's case, he needed to work out rigorously to be in good physical shape. He needed to study to be intellectually sharp. He needed to swim intensely to be in shape for the grueling underwater training. This training was self-imposed – but it wasn't enough. Having done all he could, the rest of the training was inflicted upon him by authorities who knew exactly what he needed to learn, the "hows" and the "whys." He understood his personal responsibility but readily accepted the role others played in perfecting his skills – a role completely beyond his control.

As believers, we also have two types of training – what we personally pursue versus what is applied to us by God's all-knowing hand. Our personal spiritual disciplines (prayer, fasting, Bible study, service...) contribute to our spiritual readiness, but God adds whatever specialized training is needed to prepare us for His plan for our lives. Both are critical for our ability to endure and win the battle for our souls. One you get to choose, the other you don't – but you always get to choose your reaction. Forshaw cites his mother's sage advice when he explained his own attitude towards training. "Life is 90 percent reaction and 10 percent action," he said, meaning you only get to choose about 10 percent of life's events.

Mature believers understand this principle and it strengthens them spiritually. A gifted teacher and former missionary said she now responds to difficult circumstance with, "Lord, what are You trying to teach me through this?" More sage advice.

God and gunnery sergeants

Marine gunnery sergeants can give us a glimpse of God's heart. In Lt. Carey Cash's book, *A Table in The Presence*, Chaplain Cash calls them a "breed apart," and describes them: "Their faces are weathered, their hands are gnarled, their eyes are wrinkled at the corners. They are, without a doubt, the toughest men in the Corps, and the Marines know it."[1] Called "gunneys" for short, their toughness is grounded in love, although Cash says the term is seldom heard in an infantry battalion. Severity in training could save a Marine's life in combat.

"Gunneys know this. Most of them have been around long enough to see the grim consequences of less-than-instant obedience; the Marine who thinks twice about his squad leader's orders can easily get shot by the enemy. The Marine who doesn't pay attention to the exact grid coordinates can find himself wandering into a firefight. In the end, the tenacity and toughness of our gunnery sergeants was a form of good, fatherly authority, and yes, it was grounded in love," wrote Cash in his book describing the 5th Marine Regiment's march into Iraq.[2]

Survivors have a new appreciation of the fierce love that prompts "gunney" toughness. In military preparation and parenting – those who love us and care for our welfare train us – hard. How much more with God? Our Heavenly Father has modeled tough love through a battle-scarred, incarnate Christ, and teaches us through the Holy Spirit. He gives us His divine nature and a mission to accomplish during our lifetime. God then gives us teachers, a Manual, a channel of communication – and specific challenges that cause us to grow.

This is perhaps the most misunderstood principle in the church today. Prosperity teaching gains ground – and breeds weakness. The apostle Paul is our biblical gunney sergeant telling it like it is. He tells the Philippians that he counts everything as loss in his allegiance to Christ. His primary goal is to "to know Him and the power of His resurrection and the *fellowship of His suffering*, being conformed to His death..." (Philippians 3:10) Jesus assures His disciples that they will have tribulation in this world, but to have courage. (John 16:33)

Wrong teaching in this area leads to poor morale, and loss of perseverance and courage. Imagine the difference if we expected a loving God to bring tough training into our lives to equip us for our service to him – and to strengthen us for the fight. We would not shake our fist and walk away, but we would grit and submit – and emerge stronger for our endurance.

Transformation

The goal for each shaggy new military recruit is transformation – and the spiritual goal is the same. In Luke 6, Jesus details the hardships that should reflect the Christian mission and says: "A pupil is not above his teacher; but everyone, after he has been fully trained, will be like his teacher." (Luke 6:40) Paul confirms the transformational goal of Christian training to the Corinthians: "But we all, with unveiled face, beholding as in a mirror, the glory of the Lord, *are being transformed into the same image* from glory to glory, just as from the Lord, the Spirit." (II Cor. 3:18)

The military is constantly assessing their training approaches to be sure transformation is actually happening – that men and women are fully-equipped for the mission. As the geopolitical culture shifts, so do training goals and methods. Training is a mandate.

When transformation is lacking in the church, however, very little is done to examine why – or to aggressively pursue solutions. Typically, the bar is simply lowered to achieve a false sense of success, but recurring battles reveal the lack of real readiness for war. It has become "normal" to see the church as more of an infirmary than a training camp. The lack of training causes the church to be more occupied with tending to the wounded than successfully reaching out to a world at war spiritually. If more people are in "sick call" than out on the battlefield, it is easy to see why there are less victories and a loss of spiritual ground.

After the resurrection, Jesus gave His followers a training mandate that He fully intends to participate with: "... All authority has been given to Me in heaven and on earth. 'Go therefore and make disciples of all the nations, baptizing them in the name of the Father and the Son and the Holy Spirit, teaching them to observe all that I commanded you; and lo, I am with you always, even to the end of the age." (Matt. 28:18-20) A small band of spiritual brothers, transformed by Christ's training, obeyed His mandate and turned the world upside-down.

Spoils of war

Besides determining who gets to be in authority, the objective of most wars is also peace. It is interesting that Paul addresses this goal in Hebrews 12, right after the well-known chapter on the heroes of the faith. "All discipline for the moment seems not to be joyful, but sorrowful; yet to those who have been trained by it, afterwards it yields the peaceful fruit of righteousness." (Hebrews 12:11) The discipline of training is difficult, but overwhelmingly redemptive. Think of all that we miss by seeking to avoid it – both in our lives and in the lives of those around us.

Training will occur one way or the other and the outcome is crucial – for defeat or victory. We can be trained by default and let our natural inclinations lead us to corrupt desires, self-will, deception and sin – accursed children trained in greed (II Peter 2:10-14), or we can intentionally be trained in righteousness by the Book. (II Timothy 3:16) Paul gives the Galatians a clear contrast between the training the world offers by default and what we intentionally pursue through the Holy Spirit. In the ever-present war between the flesh and the spirit, we default to the flesh with immorality, impurity, sensuality, idolatry, sorcery, enmities, strife, jealousy, outbursts of anger, disputes, dissensions, factions, envying, drunkenness, and carousing. By contrast, fighting the fight of faith, through the Holy Spirit reaps love, joy, peace, patience, kindness, goodness, faithfulness, gentleness and self-control. (Galatians 5:22-23)

What would happen if the church was highly trained in spiritual warfare? What would happen if they walked victoriously in the Spirit instead of regularly losing to the flesh? The right training reaps the right results. Love, joy, peace, etc. would not only be the spoils of war – but would spoil war as we know it.

What if the "average Christian" pursued spiritual training with the same attitude as the "average Joe" recruit? The end result would turn our lives upside-down. Only instead of "me-to-we" outcome, it would turn the "me" into "He."

CHAPTER 6: SIGNING UP FOR PAIN

Most important "take-away" thought(s):

1. The PJ (Pararescue) motto is: "This we do that others may live..." If their difficult training is for rescuing others, how does our level of spiritual training affect our ability to help others in battles that challenge their faith? Give possible scenarios.

2. How would you describe how many believers view spiritual training? What is the expectation? How does that attitude affect the church's ability to accomplish their mission?

3. Describe how you separate yourself from the routine to concentrate on preparation.

4. How do the concepts of excellence and readiness apply to the Christian life? Your life? How do you achieve spiritual excellence in a practical way? How do you achieve spiritual readiness in a practical way?

5. How is training linked to transformation? Do you see many transformed lives in your circle of Christian acquaintances? If not, why?

The things which you have heard from me in the presence of many witnesses,
entrust these to faithful men who will be able to teach others also.
II Timothy 2:2

7
PARALLELS THAT WORK

I entered Basic Training with a healthy dose of fear and trepidation.

Even though I volunteered to serve, I had also heard all the horror stories. I set a personal goal to follow orders and not draw undue attention to myself. I did not want to be anyone's public example of what not to do.

Fresh off the bus at Lackland Air Force Base in San Antonio, Texas, we met our Technical Instructors (TIs). Sergeant Molina was a short, tightly-packed, Hispanic woman, and Sergeant Ratcliff was a wiry "redneck" who loved tractor pulls and probably chewed tobacco off duty. They played "good cop, bad cop" roles, and were securely in charge at all times.

They locked away our civilian (life) luggage and assigned us uniforms, minimal toiletries, a bed and a small locker in an open-bay, 50-bed barracks. It mattered little whether you liked them or not. We quickly learned that life went much smoother when we obeyed and functioned as a team. The goal was training – and making it out of there without undue delay.

The bugle sounded at 5 a.m., and within minutes, we stood dressed in formation on the concrete pad below our barracks. It was barely light as we ran and exercised. That began each day, and the TIs controlled every aspect of life, day and night, in the long weeks ahead.

Going into the military with an education degree and a keen interest in psychology, I was actually fascinated with the training process as it progressed. I observed clear objectives, order, and strategy – vital principles for military (and spiritual) development. In the nearly three decades of service following basic training, I came to appreciate many other training principles.

The fundamentals of military training (and their spiritual parallels) were covered in the previous chapter. This chapter offers more training principles that are very effective in the military – and could vastly improve the quality of spiritual training.

Committed

When I signed my recruitment papers, I made the commitment to train – to do whatever was required to fulfill my role in the United States Air Force. It was part of the package. The Air Force was also committed to our training – investing millions of dollars to produce military personnel capable of accomplishing the multitude of missions required for offensive and defensive goals.

Because so much is at stake, everyone involved has to be "all in."

Imagine the new recruit who lounges in bed when the rest of the flight is down on the pad at 5 a.m. Ridiculous. Unthinkable. You would ask, "Why did you even join?"

The military member puts all of life on hold to pursue initial training. Further down the road, they have to put other priorities on the shelf to fit in continued training. It's required – continually. Like it, or not. You are committed, so you do it.

Commitment is not often considered as a training principle, but training seriously breaks down when either the student or the teacher (or both) is not committed to the process. Throughout my military career, commitment to training was never in doubt. In fact, the military was so serious about continued training, if required courses were continually neglected, it resulted in forfeiture of pay, discipline, or possible discharge.

In the spiritual application, commitment to training is often minimal. We sign on as a disciple of Jesus Christ, but often never restrict the "details of life" long enough to pursue training of any significance. In his book, *Multiply*, Francis Chan addresses this lack of commitment. "Many people in the church have decided to take on the name of Christ and nothing else. This would be like Jesus walking up to those first disciples and saying, 'Hey, would you guys mind identifying yourselves with me in some way? Don't worry, I don't actually care if you do anything I do or change your lifestyle at all. I'm just looking for people who are willing to say they believe in Me and call themselves Christians.' Seriously? No one can really believe that this is all it means to be a Christian," Chan writes.[1]

Jesus commanded His first disciples to make disciples – to continue to learn, and to train others. They did this faithfully, and all but one died a martyr's death in the process. That is commitment.

Chan describes commitment to training this way: "Realistically, this will require a lifetime of devotion to studying the Scriptures and investing in the people around us. Neither of these things is easy, nor can they be checked off of a list. We are never really 'done.' We continually devote ourselves to studying the Scriptures so that we can learn with ever-greater clarity what God wants us to know, practice, and pass on."[2]

Greg Dyson concurs with Chan's assessment. As Dean of Students at Word of Life Bible Institute (and intentional mentor), Dyson admits that training isn't quick.

"Limit the people you disciple. Train deeply. Be deeply committed," he advised. Dyson also observed that many mentors are not committed long enough to see results.

Ron Luce, author of Battle Cry for a Generation, asks the commitment question bluntly, "Did you join or enlist?"[3] He contrasts a club member (who joins) and a soldier (who enlists) in some of the following ways: "pursues a common interest versus a common mission, consumes some free time versus dedicates whole life, gathers acquaintances versus gathers fellow warriors, passes the time versus seizing the day, considers preparation optional to staying alive versus considers preparation crucial to staying alive."[4] Luce writes that a club member has to be cajoled into staying involved, but the soldier is told to go home unless willing to give it all.

How does our commitment to spiritual training stack up against our other commitments? Have we ever considered training as a mandate? What civilian "luggage" might need to be locked up for a season to better concentrate on training?

Sequential

Education, at any level, cannot be random. We start in kindergarten and progress through the grades with an orderly building of information – or at least, that is the goal. In any given subject, you generally start at the beginning of the book and work through principles that build on prior principles.

Similarly, from "day one" in the military, there is a carefully planned training regimen – that spans a career – however long that may last. The military assesses skills before you enlist, and maximizes skills as long as you serve.

As a supervisor, it was my job to monitor training of all subordinates. Each military member had a training folder that tracked progress, and all training folders were inspected by higher headquarters on a regular basis to ensure training was applied effectively. Each folder had a long-range plan that detailed training several years ahead so the member knew where they were headed, and how to get there. At each skill level (3, 5, 7, 9) specific tasks were deemed critical. Many of these tasks were tackled through career development courses or schools, and the remaining tasks were done through on-the-job (OJT) training. A time frame was established in which to accomplish each level of training, and competency of each task had to be measured and certified by the trainer. If the time frame was not met, reports were forwarded up to the commander – which was never good.

Sequential training is critical to growth and military readiness. When mission success depends on well-trained people, it gets a lot of attention, and so it should. It's the only approach that makes sense.

"Of course it does," you say, yet that same logic often translates poorly in the spiritual parallel.

As a teacher-in-training in college, I wrote dozens of lesson plans. Each plan began with a clear objective, listed the sequential steps to achieve the objective, and ended with a method to evaluate the success of the lesson. Teachers approach training much like the military.

Yet, as a Bible study leader, I often ask participants to initially rate their current approach to spiritual study. On average, 80 percent admit to scattered habits, reading devotionals here and there, randomly opening their Bible and reading whatever is before them. Most cannot tell you how the Bible is put together, how the books inter-relate, how to follow a topic throughout the Bible, or even how to study at all. When teaching women how to study inductively, seasoned believers of 30 years tell me they have never been taught how to study their Bible. Sadly, this should be a very early part of the most basic spiritual training.

Overall, there appears to be very little sequential, purposeful training.

As a disciple of Christ, what does your training look like? Is there a clear path to maturity? Is it sequential and building on prior principles? Or is it random, and difficult to pull all the strands together into a cohesive biblical worldview?

In the military, training never ends. The same thing should be true spiritually. Sequential training should end when we do.

Singer Eartha Kitt wasn't exactly a spiritual role model, but she sums this idea up well: "I am learning all the time. The tombstone will be my diploma."[5]

Repetitive

I don't remember many of my grammar school teachers, but I remember my 7th-grade English teacher – a tall, ruddy man with little creativity. He would take students into the hallway to reprimand them. He apparently emphasized his disciplinary points by vigorous gestures with his fountain pen because a few students returned to the classroom with a splattering of ink across their shirt fronts. He also assigned the same lessons repeatedly. When we brought the oversight to his attention, he would admonish us with his deep baritone voice: "Repetition is the mother of all learning."

While that phrase is actually attributed to the White Mountain Apache Indians, (and possibly overused by a lazy teacher) it is obviously an adage also adopted by the military. There is a firm belief that "practice makes perfect" because many areas of training are mandated yearly – even if no content has changed.

Repetition is also linked to a theory called "muscle memory." The idea is that if you repeat a correct movement often enough, eventually it will be performed without conscious effort – and will create maximum efficiency within motor and memory systems.

In a fascinating article called, *The Brave Among Us*, Jeff Wise explains the science of muscle memory. Wise says that fear originates in the amygdala, and the intense emotion sends signals to the prefrontal cortex which is the reasoning part of the brain. Interestingly, Wise cites intense training as the key to overcoming the paralysis of fear because it stores the information in another part of the brain. "When you practice an act again and again, the responsibility for performing the action switches from the brain's outer cortex, where it is experienced consciously, to the basal ganglia, which executes the action automatically and isn't affected by fear," writes Wise.[6]

Armies have understood this principle for thousands of years, deeply imbedding the fundamentals of combat into a recruit's brain by relentless repetition. "That way, when intense fear shuts down a soldier's rational brain, he or she will still be able to function on autopilot," says the science writer.[7]

Steve Allen is a fan of repetitious training – particularly with weapons. "Every delay has a price," said the nuclear radiologist who spent eight years as an Army doctor, including a deployment to Somalia with the 101st Airborne division. He said that initial training is not enough because skills become rusty over time. "Down the road... you need that skill, and now you have to think it through. That could get someone killed," he said. "It has to be automatic muscle memory, and that only comes through sustained repetitious training."

Allen thinks that the military tends to do a good job with in-depth, initial training, but doesn't train as frequently as it should to retain a high enough proficiency in some skills. In making the spiritual parallel, Allen said that even our initial training is typically faulty, and then we lack consistent training from then on.

If "rusty" skills can get us killed in a physical battle, how much more injury occurs when we are not even initially trained for spiritual battles?

For the military, repetitious lessons are a way of life. You have no choice, but at some point, you have to believe that there is a good reason for the repetition. As Christians, we often resemble preschool students in an Algebra class, bored and convinced that no possible relevance exists – or college students in kindergarten, with a dismissive, been-there-done-that attitude.

Obviously, there is a balance to repetition. Too much is clearly redundant and counterproductive, but the right amount of repetition builds proficiency and an up-to-date readiness for success in the mission.

Repetition is an important element of Christian discipleship – to review the old and move to the new. Refresher training is helpful because we tend to forget things in our loud and crowded culture.

It is also an essential practice to a deeper understanding of biblical instruction. I used to rush through Bible reading until I began to study inductively, which requires repeated reading of Scripture. My study tends to be fairly superficial the first few times through a section of Scripture, but details and insights become fascinating and more profound on my 10th, 15th, or 20th read-through. It never fails to amaze me.

What is our attitude toward repetition? Are we confident with concepts just because we heard about them once? Are we always looking for something new and entertaining? Is repetition even necessary?

Comprehensive

The military also illustrates the comprehensive nature of training. There is a commitment to sequential, repeated training – but the scope is broad.

As stated earlier, basic training provides foundational lessons in all areas. After basic training, members attend technical schools which provide instruction pertaining to the job they will perform in the military. Once a member begins to work at a base, he or she must continue to develop in military principles and their career specifics. But, they also receive instruction in other areas like: survival skills, fitness, how to care for each other, social issues, administrative topics, and leadership.

You can't just know about the military and your job – you have to know how to survive to do your job and how to work with others to get it done. It's a lot to learn – but it is all important.

The church, by contrast, often has training gaps. Believers' lives have many facets that present various training needs. In the context of biblical doctrine, they need to learn about church life, family life, work life, community outreach, and how to think biblically about the issues of the day. I may learn how to conduct myself as an individual, and in the context of my family, but not understand my role in the church or how I should interact with those that believe differently. I may understand my complex roles, but have no training in how to survive to pursue those roles. Do I know how to keep someone else spiritually alive?

Gaps in training are most evident in battle. The same is true in the lives of believers. Unfortunately, the same battles that expose the gaps often frustrate the very training deficits they reveal. We're too stressed out to train. By contrast, the military cares less about the capacity for training than it does about the critical need for training – on every level that may affect the ultimate outcome. The church needs to be mindful of the same – which is challenging without the commitment previously cited.

Cooperative

After Basic Training, my next stop was the Defense Information School at Fort Benjamin Harrison, Indiana. My classmates were Air Force, Army, Navy, Marine, Coast Guard, and a few civilians. Together we learned the ins and outs of photojournalism and the principles of internal and external communication in the military. It is one of the few technical schools that brings all military branches into one "schoolhouse." It makes sense to put us all together if the military wants to be consistent in the relay of information.

As each decade of my military service passed, the changing global landscape required more "joint service" endeavors. Through Operations Desert Storm and Enduring Freedom, the intense missions required greater cooperation among military branches. The option of being territorial makes no sense. It erodes the overall mission. The escalation of terrorism after 9/11 heightened the need for cooperative efforts and training among allied nations and their militaries. The Boston Marathon bombing that killed three and injured more than 250 others propelled an inter-agency effort combining local, state, federal, and some international agencies to track down suspects and assess continued threats.

The church also has an extremely important mission, but tends to weaken its effectiveness by neglecting "inter-agency" training and serving. Too often, denominational factions, in-fighting within denominations, territorial interests, and doctrinal differences keep the church from serving God's mission with unity, strength and power. (Doctrinal differences should matter if they are so great that you can no longer be considered to be on the same side – the side of the fundamental truths of the gospel of Jesus Christ.)

Every branch of the military service brings strengths and weaknesses to the table – and the same is true regarding churches. It's not always easy to blend the differences. It takes strong leadership and much humility to bring the best ideas to the table and let various strengths prevail for a stronger whole. It's not easy, but it is imperative as the church faces possibly the most perilous times ever.

A great example of cooperative training is found in Florida around the issue of foster care. When newspapers in Broward County reported a shortage of foster care facilities and parents, Calvary Chapel of Fort Lauderdale took the lead by forming "Churches United for Foster Care" initiative in 2002. In the early stages, Calvary Chapel planners realized the task was great and the effort had to reach beyond church walls. One planning member set the tone well with his comment, "We need to leave our logos and egos behind if we are going to meet this need."

The program, now called 4KIDS of South Florida, works in tandem with the community and other churches to build residential homes, staff them, and train potential foster parents. According to their website, every day, seven kids, needing care are removed from abusive homes.[8] More than 17,000 kids have received care through their program, and hundreds have been adopted.[9] Their combined efforts have been very effective and serve as a model for other communities.

When tornadoes blew through Massachusetts communities in 2011 (including ours), churches combined efforts to provide community clean-up. More recently, it was encouraging to attend a women's conference held at one of the larger local churches – with more than 500 women attending from 105 churches. Local churches also take turns staffing an area homeless shelter by each providing meals one night each month.

Cooperative training on a spiritual level can take many forms. Training across church walls makes each church more effective than it can possibly be on its own, and provides an attractive show of unity and relevancy to the community.

How readily do we reach across denominational lines to train and co-labor with other churches? Do we humbly access the strengths of other churches to shore up our weaknesses? Do we offer our strengths to others? What steps would allow us to train cooperatively? Food for thought.

Simulated practice

For years, I covered various war exercises which simulated situations that could likely occur in a real war environment – including enemy snipers, bombings, security breaches, chemical weapons, plane crashes, etc. I gained a much deeper understanding of the training, however, when I was assigned to be an exercise evaluator.

What I originally saw as somewhat random events were actually carefully planned for thousands of strategic reasons. Exercise planners collected data from every career field in the unit and created a comprehensive list of Mission Essential Tasks (METs). They then created battle scenarios filled with problems, challenges and opposition to test every participant in the exercise.

As an evaluator, it was amazingly informative to help with the year-long planning – and a little heady to have access to the master scenario before it even began. I knew what was going to happen next, and it was my job to rate how well public affairs members responded according to pre-set expectations. The experience gave me a glimpse of God's perspective on training as He knows exactly what to bring into each of our lives to test and train us for future victories.

It also illustrates the value of simulated training – to provide situations as close to the real deal – so you get to practice for optimum skill when the real deal happens. Additionally, the closer the real deal is, the more simulated training occurs. The best example involves deployments to Iraq and Afghanistan. To prepare soldiers for combat deployment, they must complete intensive simulated training just before heading to the Forward Operating Base (FOB). Mock FOBS are created stateside or in forward locations closer to the deployed location. Military members live, work and train in these environments to prepare themselves for life in a real FOB. "Just-in-time" training is specific instruction scheduled as part of pre-deployment preparation.

Colonel Philip Wright has served as Army chaplain in deployed locations. He worked with a Ranger battalion required to execute difficult missions with a small force – with very little margin of error. "They rehearse, rehearse and rehearse," he said. "You train for the unexpected."

The military simulates battle challenges to prepare soldiers for survival and mission accomplishment. How could believers do the same? A few examples show the possible value of simulation.

As believers, one of our missions is to be salt and light to the culture. The apostle Paul showed great skill in engaging the culture with the truth of the gospel (especially in the book of Acts), but many Christians today are untrained in defending their faith or presenting a biblical worldview on cultural topics. While teaching high school comparative worldview classes, I would regularly present students with simulated "encounters." Two "volunteers" would sit in front of the class – one asking the prompt question and the other fielding the question. Being put on the spot is never easy, but that is often how it happens in real life. Students tried to "think on their feet" on the topic presented. After the student fielded the question as thoroughly as possible, we debriefed the topic together. By simulating real conversation questions, they gained greater skill in conversing biblically in actual situations.

The same simulation works in a women's worldview study, with much humor, but also much learning. After one particular topic question simulation, I received an e-mail from one of the women telling me that the very next day, she was asked the exact same question at work, and felt more skilled. "I had such peace, and the conversation went really well," she said.

Simulations get us thinking about all of our options before we encounter real situations. It helps students to learn in "safe" environments, and can increase victories in actual, often-hostile environments.

Like any other training principle, simulation loses effectiveness if overused, or poorly planned. Like the war exercise planners, it's important to know exactly what skills the exercise is expected to teach, and the simulation should be realistic enough to be relevant.

Deployment

In the earlier years of my military service, we trained for "contingencies" but saw very little of them. In the early 80's, things were fairly quiet and the Reserve forces were rarely called into significant involvement. All that changed with Operation Desert Shield in 1990, with activations and deployments becoming a more regular occurrence. This changed the intensity of training because the likelihood of direct involvement was very high. Whether you agreed or disagreed with defense initiatives, there was a general acceptance: "This is what we train for."

In the decades that followed, the Reserve forces were regularly integrated with active duty military as a seamless force. Gone was the expectation that you served only for contingencies. You trained for war.

So, imagine the futility of continually training a soldier for deployment, and never actually sending them anywhere. What would be the point? The need is there, but the soldier is not.

That, of course, was not the case. Thousands of members left home and family for six-month to year-long deployments. In most cases, there was great satisfaction in working the "real deal." On deployments, they used their learned skills – and deepened their expertise considerably. They returned with new insights, new appreciation of home and family, and they became valuable trainers for those yet to deploy.

The military trains for a purpose, and expects its members to fulfill their purpose, with diligence and skill.

There are amazing examples in the church of many who do the same, but there are also examples of those who are constantly learning, but never implementing what they learn.

I heard a great analogy from Pastor Harvey Carey who spoke at a Global Leadership Summit I attended in 2010. He likened the church to a football team who constantly "huddles" on the field of life, but then goes back to the bench without executing the play. "Who would want to attend a game like that?" he asked.

As senior pastor of Citadel of Faith Covenant Church in Detroit, Michigan, Carey is a dynamic speaker and an effective, creative trainer. He chides the church for collecting too many conference binders and not practicing what they learn. He also has a very interesting "deployment" strategy for his inner city church.

With no shortage of needs in his community, he will often "deploy" his congregation on Sunday mornings. On unannounced Sundays, he will give a short training message on what they are to do – then they leave church and travel to parts of the city to use their training right away. It may be sharing their faith, ministering to the homeless, reaching out to those caught in prostitution, praying for others – or whatever needs might be presented. Groups of men in his church have actually "camped out" in front of crack houses to help break the cycle of drugs in the inner city. They are winning battles in an urban "war zone" because they deploy to act on what they learn. People commute in from the suburbs to be a part of his effective strategies – to be a part of something that is actually making a difference.

His motto is simple: "You need to learn how to just go and do what Jesus said to go and do."

He was my favorite speaker, and I welcomed the squirming conviction he brought to the conference.

I found a similar conviction tucked into the book of Exodus. In chapter 3, God speaks to Moses from the burning bush. God identifies Himself clearly, and then tells Moses that He has heard the cry of the Hebrews suffering in Egyptian slavery. "I am aware of their affliction…and have come down to deliver them…," God says to Moses. He then points to Moses and tells him that He plans to use Moses to bring the people out of bondage. Despite God's clear declaration of His power and plan, Moses recites a litany of reasons why he is unfit for the job – eventually incurring God's anger. Moses didn't understand that God had trained him so far, and his deployment back to Egypt to free the Hebrews was part of both further training and the mission itself.

Studying those passages gave me the same squirming conviction as Harvey Carey's admonition to the church. "What afflicted groups has God heard crying out to Him – and plans to deliver them – by using me?" I find myself praying that personally, and challenging others to do the same. It may be in my own church, my community, or overseas. The question is, will I study, study, study – but never be willing to deploy?

Pastor Dave Young, of Westfield, MA, did his doctoral thesis on spiritual "deployments" when he wrote on the value of short-term missions regarding personal discipleship. "Jesus used 'field training' as part of building disciples," he said, and added that the word "missionary" actually comes from the word "missile" which means "something launched."

"In short term missions, the 'going' is what produces so many results," Young said. He said it brings believers into environments that challenge them to act on what they believe. "Away from home, without normal distractions, they are generally more dependent on God, they witness different cultures, and often develop a greater love for God and for people," Young explained. Like the returning soldier, they come back with a deeper appreciation for what they have, and are often challenged to make changes in their lives consistent with what they learned. The goal of both is growth, change – and a testimony to encourage and train others.

Pay it forward

"Pay it forward" has become a popular adage – meaning the beneficiary of a good deed repays it to others instead of to the original benefactor. The concept compounds kindness – and is also an effective principle to enhance and multiply training.

The military intentionally incorporates this principle all through a member's career in the form of mentoring. In fact, the process is assigned and mandatory. Once a member completes initial training and is assigned to a base, mentoring is a regularly-scheduled event. A typical mentoring session assesses short and long-term goals, strengths and weaknesses, strategies to strengthen weaknesses, increase strengths, and maps out plans to reach goals.

In a mentoring relationship, it is important that the mentor exemplifies the skills and qualities desired in the mentee or subordinate. Often "more is caught than taught," so the mentor's appearance, bearing, conduct and performance of duty should be worthy of imitation. The mentor has been previously taught by someone else, and they pass on their training to others.

Mentoring enhances learning at every level, and ensures training throughout a particular population. Leaders become accountable for effective training, and the depth and breadth of training increases exponentially. Training becomes everyone's responsibility. Training is part of the culture.

This is true in the military, and often in corporate environments, but is not well-developed in the church even though mentoring examples abound in Scripture.

Good mentoring examples are found through Moses and Joshua, Elijah and Elisha, and Paul and Timothy. Failed mentoring is found with Eli as his sons Hophni and Phinehas, were described as worthless men that their father, the priest, did not rebuke. (I Samuel 3)

The book of Titus lists the credentials of a godly leader/mentor – and also outlines why there is such a critical need for careful discipleship. There is a mandate for older men and women to be models of maturity and for them to pass on sound teaching to younger generations. As a seasoned leader mentoring Titus as a leader-in-training, Paul encourages him to "be an example of good deeds, with purity in doctrine, dignified, sound in speech which is beyond reproach..." (Titus 2:7-8)

The mentoring relationship is more than the mere passing of knowledge – it is relationship. The depth becomes clear contrasting the Greek "didaskolos" (teacher) with "matheteuo" (disciple). Dr. Spiros Zodhiates describes it as: "more than mere academic impartation of information; one is doing more than simply instructing a pupil in a particular field of study or aiding a student in developing a certain vocational skill. Rather, the word suggests the deep shaping of character and the cultivation of a world-view through a close, personal relationship between the mathetes and the didaskolos."[10] He goes on to say: "The teacher is a mentor par excellence who seeks to stamp his image on his disciples and thereby enable them to participate in his life. For the goal of discipleship is not simply the attaining of information but the experience and enjoyment of fellowship."[11]

Using the Word as the Manual, both the mentor and the mentee allow Scripture to teach, show error, show how to correct errors, and how to walk in what is right, in the pattern of II Timothy 3:16.

While the subject matter of our training is diverse (knowledge of God, the cross, His commandments, holiness, righteousness, etc.) the pattern of mentoring is specific – sound content and a good example.

Sadly, both the military and the church have examples of poor role models who taught one thing and lived contrary to what they taught. It caused others to stumble and brought ill repute upon respective institutions.

But, both have a higher calling – especially the church – with Christ as the Model.

Ezra, the teacher/scribe ministering to the returning remnant after Babylonian exile, illustrates a good mentor. "For Ezra had prepared his heart to seek the law of the Lord and to do it, and to teach in Israel statutes and judgments." (Ezra 7:10. He lived what he learned and passed it on.

With a correct pattern of mentoring, there is exponential growth because both parties should continue to learn and mature – sort of "two-for-one" instruction that pays forward to future generations – keeping the church vibrant and strong.

Deliberate

Life is demanding. Training is often the first casualty in the tyranny of the urgent – but it is also often the difference between surviving and thriving.

The idea that reverberates through this book is the predictable consequences of an untrained soldier. It is lazy, crazy and dangerous to ignore training. May that reality encourage us to consider some of these principles and implement them in our churches, our families, and in our own lives – on purpose.

CHAPTER 7: PARALLELS THAT WORK

Most important "take-away" thought(s):

1. As a disciple of Jesus Christ, do you feel that you have a good grasp of personal spiritual training goals? Rate on a scale of 1-10, then explain why you chose that rating

2. What type of education did you pursue to equip yourself for your job goals? Were you committed? Was it sequential? Why? Have you approached your spiritual training the same? Why or why not?

3 The military uses simulated training to prepare soldiers to face the "real deal." How could simulation be used in spiritual training? What difference could it make?

4. What good would it be if a soldier trained for war, but never deployed to accomplish the mission? What is the mission of the church? I what ways might we "deploy" to accomplish God's mission for us?

5. Has anyone mentored you spiritually? Are you mentoring another believer? Name at least two mentor relationships in the Bible. Are we mandated to mentor? Explain.

"When you go out as an army against your enemies, you shall keep yourself from every evil thing."
Deuteronomy 23:9

8
THE SOUL OF THE SOLDIER

Hundreds of men sat among their tanks and Humvees in the quiet, desert night – camped on the Kuwaiti border waiting orders to cross into Iraq. All the training of the First Battalion, Fifth Marine Regiment, would be put to the test when they crossed the threshold into real battle.

Chaplain (Lieutenant) Carey Cash observed the Marines in their flak jackets and helmets, each carrying a rifle and knife, surrounded by high-tech gear and vehicles. As he watched each soldier contemplating the invasion mission, Cash observed that technology had changed the face of war, but not the face of the warrior. Each seemed lost in thought. Cash couldn't help but compare their looming battle to the battles Joshua faced in the Old Testament, and how Joshua understood that the real battle lay not with weapons and armor, but in the realm of faith.

"In those few quiet moments, I pondered where we were in the world and what our president was about to call us to do," writes Cash in his book, *A Table in The Presence*.[1]

He continues: "I began to see that for us, as for Joshua, the real battle would be won or lost before we even crossed the line of departure into Iraq. Each of us had to find courage, faith and quiet resolve, and to experience a peace that surpasses understanding – these were the real victories that had to be won in each of our lives."[2]

In their final preparation, just hours before the crossing into Iraq, Cash held a service for the men, shared his Joshua meditations, and offered Joshua 1:9 as their spiritual marching orders: "Have I not commanded you? Be strong and of good courage; do not be afraid, nor be dismayed for the Lord your God is with you wherever you go." Cash writes that the power of the ancient Hebrew Scripture washed over them like a flash flood in the desert. "Every man there knew he had his rifle, his ammunitions, his food and water, but those things seemed to pale in comparison to his need for God."[3]

This sentiment has been understood through centuries of war as leaders intuitively knew that proficiency in training fails without inner fortitude and solid core values.

Marine Major General J.N. Mattis, quoted the late Army General George C. Marshall, in a letter sent to chaplains prior to the Iraqi war: "The soldier's heart, the soldier's spirit, the soldier's soul are everything. Unless the soldier's soul sustains him, he cannot be relied upon and will fail himself and his country in the end."[4]

Trained Barbarians

History is filled with chilling examples of military proficiency devoid of principles – valor without values – might without morality. Hitler perhaps provides the most recent example easily understood by many. Hitler was an intelligent, influential speaker with great military prowess, but he left a cruel legacy most powerfully remembered by graphic images of emaciated corpses piled in heaps.

Hitler is only one of many brutal dictators who used well-trained soldiers to implement twisted objectives planted in the soil of unprincipled ideas. Each left legacies of mass graves.

Trained armies of old often added rape and pillaging to the initial conquest, completely devastating people already victimized by war. Ancient Assyrians waged psychological terrorism through physical torture, impaling village leaders to die agonizing deaths at the village gate, and piling skulls outside the gate as gruesome reminders to anyone who dared oppose their ruthless rule.

In these instances, training produced military prowess, but the absence of values like human dignity, integrity, just-cause war principles, and basic compassion, produced trained barbarians. The results were typically catastrophic. This ability to inflict harm, with a conscience devoid of principles, is a danger to an army, a soldier, a nation, a culture, a neighborhood, a home, and a human heart.

Divided allegiance

The absence of loyalty in just one person can be a value breach even more dangerous than an entire unprincipled army.

Recent history chronicles the damage done by individuals who swore allegiance to their country but betrayed their oath through subterfuge and deceit. John Walker, Jr., was a well-trained Navy communications officer with serious ethical flaws. In 1967, he began selling secrets to the Soviets and padded his pockets for 17 years in the treason business – using his training to promote national harm rather than national security.

Edward J. Snowden put an entire nation at risk by leaking thousands of classified documents, surveillance systems, and security strategies, to the public via Wikileaks. Despite the controversy surrounding Snowden's actions, his ethical breakdown, that served personal interests at the risk of public safety, is still an example of training gone awry. Personal and corporate morality have become increasingly relativistic – breaking down the common-core moral truth from which all training should originate.

Military and technical skills become risks rather than assets without a solid ethical core. Both of these examples show how people with divided loyalties could be in the work station next to ours – and we could be totally unaware. They appear to be on the same side, working for the same objectives, while they are actually opposing us. The Bible repeatedly warns us to be on our guard, spiritually, for the same thing. Spiritual traitors may be in the same community as us, the same church, or same pew.

In the small book of Jude, its single chapter gives multiple warning of divided allegiance and how much harm it can hold. In verse 4, Jude warns that "certain men have crept in unnoticed" turning God's grace into opportunities for lewd sin and denying the authority and deity of Jesus Christ. He warns believers that such men have crept into churches, pretending to be authentic (and blend in because they are unnoticed). Jude gives great clarity as to their true motives and gives examples from both the earthly and angelic realms of similar deception – and their ultimate judgment. Jude culls through the Old Testament and highlights the deception of Cain, Balaam and Korah as examples. Verses 16-19 detail the moral attributes and actions of seemingly trained believers whose core has rotted. Jude ends his short letter admonishing believers to walk in authentic faith with love and compassion – and from that solid core – to help rescue others.

Our loyalty to Christ is always under attack. From Genesis to Revelation, we are exhorted to singularity of purpose to God, and are shown the cause and effect when such loyalty is breached. A shocking example of God's "no-kidding, serious" take on disloyalty is found in Jeremiah 21.

King Zedekiah (of Judah) sent representatives to the prophet Jeremiah because the Babylonians were attacking them. In verse 2, Zedekiah wanted God to deal with Judah's enemies "according to His wonderful acts so the enemy will withdraw from them." Jeremiah, however, sent back very bad news to the king. Because of Judah's disloyalty to God, and their sinful immersion in the pagan culture around them, God was not only turning His back on them, but He was using a pagan nation to discipline them. Verse 5 is extremely sobering as God speaks through the prophet: "I Myself will war against you with an outstretched hand and a mighty arm, even in anger and wrath and great indignation."

Wow! Not a good thing to have God warring against us, rather than warring for us. Our loyalty to Him, shown by our actions, is critical. Our lives constantly present us with loyalty choices. In verse 8, Jeremiah gives this stark contrast to the king: "...Thus says the Lord, 'Behold, I set before you the way of life and the way of death.'"

Near the end of the Bible, James warns believers that "a double-minded man is unstable in all his ways." (1:8) The Christian walk is one of constant "reset" in this area. James gives us the reset process: "Draw near to God and He will draw near to you. Cleanse your hands, you sinners; and purify your hearts, you double-minded." (James 4:8)

"I pledge allegiance" is a core component for an authentic soldier – and a true believer.

Core values

Because training without core values is predictably perilous, military service branches all promote character traits in the creeds they live by – and fight by. The Air Force core values are: *integrity, service before self, and excellence in all we do*.[5] The Navy and Marines list: *courage, commitment, and honor*.[6] The Army expands their list to: *loyalty, duty, respect, selfless service, honor, integrity, and personal courage*.[7]

It is interesting to note that core values did not have to be specifically taught as new concepts until the last few decades. I have seen this change during the scope of my own career. In the 70's, core values were still relatively entrenched in the general society, so they were assumed as desirable societal character traits. As the culture became more relativistic, and moral boundaries crumbled, the subset culture of the military could no longer assume long-standing character traits were defined. Now they had to be taught.

Now, integrity, service before self, and excellence in all we do, are virtues included in mandatory Air Force training. As decades pass and the culture continues to slide, military moral efforts and topics keep expanding. The military needs a solid moral foundation to fight well and win often, but the greater culture can no longer define any clear moral targets with confidence, and it leaks into the military.

Predictably, despite greater efforts to teach the importance of core values, incidents of moral failure within the ranks continue to rise – with rising concerns about its effect on the military mission.

A quick example of the cultural moral slide bleeding into the military is in the area of sexual behavior. In the 80's, character training focused on issues of fraternization, which is any type of unprofessional relationship between officers and enlisted ranks. In the 90's, sexual harassment became the training emphasis. The new millennium brought the upgrade to mandatory training regarding sexual assault which was becoming more widespread. As society has embraced more forms of sexual behavior previously thought deviant, the most recent decade now presents staggering numbers of military rape cases.

I will never forget the day I sat in a mandatory sexual assault prevention class. I felt very uncomfortable sitting in a mixed audience as the training video showed a simulated date rape after military members had partied at a local bar. Even more troubling was the simulated interview with the rape "victim" after her experience. "I've had sex with other men, but this was different," she said, supposedly to highlight the moral point of the video. Her moral admission of promiscuity (which was presented as "normal") undermined any moral framework to build a more solid case against sexual assault. I wondered why they used an immoral example to teach a moral concept. It stands as one more example of our moral confusion – ignoring morals in one venue – while appealing to it in another.

Training is diluted in the absence of absolutes.

A moral freefall in the general society bleeds into societal subsets, with the military and the church being the most critically affected. Both have overarching, critical missions where core value breaches ripple throughout their populations – crippling credibility – and hindering the success of the mission.

While the military has had its share of ethical embarrassments, the church has its own "hall of shame." Private moral failure among high-visibility spiritual leaders has brought the best theologically-trained pastors to a place of public ridicule, and even prison. Sin implodes a church from the pulpit down – and presents a distorted picture of true Christianity to a watching world.

Examining examples of moral failure, most were models of integrity and strength until a storm blew through their lives exposing a hidden vulnerability. I saw a display of this principle when a tornado blew through our neighborhood a few years ago. Surveying the debris and damage an hour later, it was amazing to see huge oak trees felled in the tornado's swath. On closer inspection of the felled oaks, either the root system was flawed, or there was hidden disease within the trunk. When just the right storm hit, the tree succumbed to the wind and crashed through roofs, crumpled cars, and leveled landscaping. What was meant for beauty, shade and protection caused great destruction when they fell. The same is true with soldiers – and believers in Jesus Christ.

Andy Stanley nails the idea of flawed root systems in his book, *Enemies of the Heart*. Proverbs tells us to "guard our hearts with all diligence for out of it flow the issues of life." (4:23) Stanley explores four areas of "heart rot" that weaken our walk and ruin our relationships. They are guilt, anger, greed and jealousy. They operate undetected until just the right circumstances expose them. Stanley uses the book of James to illustrate the battle within the human heart that causes us to waste our energy battling each other rather than fighting the real enemy. James poses the question: "What causes fights and quarrels among you? Don't they come from your desires that battle within you?"

"James seems to think that our external conflicts are the direct result of an inner conflict that has worked its way to the surface," writes Stanley.[8] Any soldier, military or spiritual, must pursue "core training" to pursue true victory in the external battles of life.

In his book, *The Enemy Within*, Kris Lundgaard also draws from the book of James (1:14-15) to show the steps that precede moral failure. Lundgaard lists them as: "1.The dragging away of the mind from its duties; 2.The entangling of the affections; and 3.The capturing of the will in consent to sin."9

Moral failure is not an event, it's a process. It is a process that no one is exempt from if great care is not taken to prevent it. Training for warfare is lacking if it does not emphasize core values that promote the use of our skills within a moral framework.

Moral integrity matters, and without it, sheer competence will never be enough.

Integrity

Integrity is a comprehensive word that merits a closer look.

British author, Samuel Johnson says it like this: "Integrity without knowledge is weak and useless, and knowledge without integrity is dangerous and dreadful."10

The book of Proverbs offers this nugget on the topic: "The man of integrity walks securely but he who takes crooked paths will be found out." (10:9)

Webster defines integrity as "an unimpaired condition, soundness; firm adherence to a code of especially moral or artistic values; the quality or state of being complete or undivided."11 In general terms, it means that truth is "integrated" into every aspect of your life. A culture that divides the "public and private" person – as if they were two different people – invites a lack of integrity. Do we have character in our home, our work place, our place of worship, our play, and in all our relationships? True integrity permeates all of life.

In Chuck Swindoll's message, "Plea for Integrity," he says, "Ours is a day of freely bending the rules and rationalizing what is wrong."12 He says that a growing number of Christians have bought into the mentality that says, "Grace covers everything, so go ahead and do whatever you want."

"The results fall somewhere between embarrassment and downright scandal," he continued, and added that marital commitment, sexual purity, intellectual honesty, ethical fairness, and financial accountability are [now] all options – rather than character traits to be embraced.13 "We desperately need to return to integrity," he said.14

British philosopher, C.S. Lewis noted that a mere knowledge of right and wrong is powerless against a person's appetites. He said: "Rather reason must rule the appetites by means of a spirited element – that is loyalty to a transcendent good higher than oneself."15 Lewis likened reason to the head, the appetite to the stomach, and the spirited element to the chest. "We remove the organ and demand the function. We make men without chests and expect of them virtue and enterprise," he wrote. "We laugh at honor and are shocked to find traitors in our midst."16

Training for war without integrity is, by implication, an impaired condition, lacking soundness.

My best military example of integrity is the Third U.S. Infantry's Honor Guard whose job is to protect the Tomb of the Unknown Soldier at Arlington Cemetery. After completing a class at the Pentagon some years ago, our group was invited to participate in the wreath laying ceremony. After the ceremony, some of us were invited beneath the stone structure to the Honor Guard offices. The unit First Sergeant explained the remarkably high standards for any "Old Guard" applicant. There were height, weight, and fitness requirements, as well as a spotless record. Training was grueling and each applicant had to make an extremely high moral commitment – both on and off duty – and for life. Anyone breaking the moral requirements could no longer wear the coveted Honor Guard wreath medal.

The Honor Guard creed starts with: "My dedication to this sacred duty is total and wholehearted. In the responsibility bestowed on me, never will I falter. And with dignity and perseverance my standard will remain perfection. Through the years of diligence and praise and the discomfort of the elements, I will walk my tour in humble reverence to the best of my ability..."[17] Integrity is so prized in this elite unit that the tough, seasoned First Sergeant actually teared up recounting stories of his unit's dedication to duty.

This unit demanded integrity both on duty and off, in every aspect of life. I was impressed by this up-close and personal look at such high standards in a "loosy-goosy" culture. The life of a believer should model the same – and present biblical integrity to a wayward, watching world – showing more credentials and less criticism.

Fortitude: courage and bravery

Training is important. Core values are important. But, both are insufficient if we lack the courage to implement them. Someone once said that bravery is not the absence of fear, but pushing through it.

Our culture is enamored with "extreme sports" where people take enormous risks to push the bounds of physical endurance and/or accomplishment. Others attempt foolish feats to show how brave they are. But, perhaps the greatest example of bravery is found in those who risk everything to stand for what is right.

Martin Luther King lost his life taking a consistent stand against racial inequality. William Wilberforce tirelessly toiled against slavery, relentlessly facing opposition until near the end of his life.

Core values are embedded in the definition of "hero." Dictionary.com defines a hero as: "a man of distinguished courage or ability, admired for his brave deeds and noble qualities."[18]

A hero often stands alone, but can have a radical affect on others. Billy Graham says: "Courage is contagious. When a brave man takes a stand, the spines of others are stiffened."[19]

The ultimate Model of courage in the Bible is Jesus Christ, but many that served Him are included as examples to follow. We usually think of Joshua, mentored by Moses, as a model of courage as the Israelites embarked on battles on the border of their long-promised land. "Be strong and of good courage" is repeated three times in the early chapters of the book of Joshua – which of course implies that great fear was their default.

Or we think of David as he stands up to giant Goliath – finding great courage through God's strength – and his past encounters with a bear and a lion.

Perhaps less obvious examples of raw courage are found in Noah who acted in brave faith to build an ark in an atmosphere of ridicule and no rain, or Abraham's scary obedience to raise the knife to slay his long-awaited son Isaac.

Job had the courage to endure in faith as he faced devastating loss. The prophets were brave enough to warn stiff-necked rebels who showed their appreciation with deadly stones or beheading. Paul spoke boldly to any audience God gave him, despite a painful track record of beating, prison cells and stoning.

Courage takes faith – faith in the One who bore more than any other, and left a perfect example to follow.

Where would we rank on a bravery barometer? Where is fear keeping us from using our training to serve God's kingdom? Maybe the first act of new bravery is the courage to answer the hard questions.

Identity

Most probably, the core of core values lies in our identity. Just who do we think we are?

Most of us have been asked that question in a more negative venue – when we act in pompous, selfish ways. In that venue, the question is meant to bring us to humility. Sadly, few of us have been asked that question in the best possible way.

The fact is, we act according to our perceived identity, and it can go either way, which is why it is so important. If we perceive ourselves to be brave, we act bravely. If we believe we are shameful, we act shamefully. If we believe we have a high calling, we walk carefully.

Our purpose is intrinsic to our identity. Who are we, and why are we here? Our purpose should drive our identity, and our identity should fuel our purpose. There should be a cohesive link between who I am and what I do. A break in that link breaks down integrity.

The military understands this principle and works hard at instilling identity and purpose (mission). In fact, in light of the changing culture, and the emphasis on self-identification over corporate purpose, they are working even harder at this concept. It is not unusual to see an Air Force assembly standing at attention reciting the Air Force creed in unison:

Airman's Creed

I am an American Airman.
I am a warrior.
I have answered my nation's call.
I am an American Airman.
My mission is to fly, fight, and win.
I am faithful to a proud heritage,
A tradition of honor,
And a legacy of valor.
I am an American Airman.
Guardian of freedom and justice,
My nation's sword and shield,
Its sentry and avenger.
I defend my country with my life.
I am an American Airman.
Wingman, Leader, Warrior.
I will never leave an Airman behind,
I will never falter,
And I will not fail[20]

The Air Force creed is a deliberate attempt to encapsulate the identity and mission of every Airman within its ranks. It brings unity to diversity, and clarity to purpose, even though each member plays a different role. There is great value in taking the time to establish a creed, which is a system or codification of a belief.

The business world gets this concept, too. Most of us are familiar with vision statements and mission statements. Business CEOs know that employees are unified and more productive when they understand the bigger vision and how they fit into the mission.

Many individuals get it. Mission and identity are key components of personal effectiveness in the well-known 7 Habits™ established by Stephen Covey. The first time I took the course, it was life changing for me to clarify these foundational principles. While facilitating the 7 Habits™ in the Air Force, I watched people wrestle through aspects of their identity and mission – taking the time to seek out the deeper answers of purpose.

All too often, the church doesn't. As a result, believers get their cues about identity and mission from the culture instead of the Word of God. They form their identity by default – often not even realizing what it is – yet they act on it. Their focus is temporal instead of eternal. Their identity is dysfunctional and their mission clouded. They flounder instead of flourishing.

Creating creeds

During the Trench Buddies conferences, after the military creeds are read, each group is asked to create a creed by the end of the day. What does the Word of God say about who they are and why? There is something powerful about these creeds. It has been delightful to see what groups create as they search the Scripture to determine their identity and purpose. Some groups marched to the front and said the creed together, others incorporated impromptu songs, and others created slogans. No two were the same. It was a rich activity. The Bible has so much to say about our identity in Christ and why we exist.

This exercise became even more personal as an assignment for a 9th-grade comparative worldview class I taught. Students had to write a personal creed based on their Scriptural study of identity and mission. It was powerful to hear these young adults articulate a Biblical identity and an abiding purpose. To emphasize the importance of their personal creeds, a co-teacher and I typed and framed each one for the students to remember and display. The experience was very moving. While I had taught the principle, I was convicted that I had not actually worked out my own creed. I admitted that to the class, and asked them to make me accountable to write my personal creed. It was so clarifying. I still find it hard to recite my creed publically without deep emotion.

Our identity and mission define the core of our existence. As a believer, I find both in God, and they are exercised, with power, through God. Soren Kierkegaard takes this concept of identity to a core level. He is quoted in Tim Keller's book, *Reason for God*:

"Sin is: in despair not wanting to be oneself before God... Faith is: that the self in being itself and wanting to be itself is grounded transparently in God."[21]

Keller rephrases Kierkegaard, "Sin is the despairing refusal to find your deepest identity in your relationship and service to God. Sin is seeking to become oneself, to get an identity, apart from Him."[22] This is a profound concept few of us grasp. It answers the heart's cry, "What are we here for?"

Throughout Scripture, God displays His identity before He shows us our purpose, because our true identity is found in Him. Isaiah and Ezekiel saw visions of God before being called to bring foreboding prophetic news to God's people. In the New Testament, God revealed Himself to both Paul and John to prepare them for God's call on their lives. But, Moses is the example that rocks me the most.

In the book of Exodus, chapter three, Moses receives his call to deliver God's people from Egyptian bondage. During the most mundane task of tending sheep, Moses encounters a burning bush. God speaks through the bush, and Moses finds himself on holy ground receiving a holy calling. Moses obeys, and enters into God's "basic training," moving from Midian back to Egypt. Initially, Moses experiences what seems to be one failure after another. He seems to struggle with his identity and mission until a turning point occurs in Exodus 3 and 4.

Here, God clearly defines the mission, He defines Himself, and then He brings Moses onboard. Moses argues with God based on his natural identity which he feels disqualifies him from God's call. Moses has murdered a man, failed at what he thought was his initial purpose, he's been an exile, a filthy shepherd – and who knows what else. He was clearly not God's man for the job – or so he thought.

God is clear that His call is based on who He is – not based on who Moses is.

Moses was a slow learner – as many of us are. Chapter after chapter chronicles Moses' struggle to emerge as the leader God identified him to be, for the mission God gave him. His progress encourages me because I struggle with the same thing. My identity is not my failures, but who God is in me, and how He defines me.

In Christ, I am redeemed, forgiven, loved, adopted, called, equipped, cleansed, etc. etc. etc.

The "I AM" determines who I am – and what I do. This is a powerful concept worthy of our attention.

Walk worthy

The military is a calling – either involuntary or voluntary. There are expectations of behavior that are clearly defined in the Uniform Code of Military Justice. In addition to behavior, the military strives to instill heart attitudes that will sustain the soldier and bring him/her to noble, heroic deeds. Military creeds encourage soldiers to walk worthy. The Bible does the same for us as followers of Jesus Christ.

Towards the end of the Book filled with diverse heroes, the apostle Paul writes to believers in Ephesus from his prison cell: "I therefore, the prisoner in the Lord, beseech you that you walk worthy of the calling with which you are called, with all lowliness and meekness, with long-suffering, forbearing one another in love, endeavoring to keep the unity of the Spirit in the bond of peace." (Eph 4:1) Paul shows that they all have different gifts and functions, but a common mission. He warns them to be careful – to walk in the newness in Christ – and not as the nations around them in the vanity of their minds, and darkened understanding. In the rest of the chapter, Paul reviews core values, listing what to avoid and what to embrace. Paul knew that rotted values ruin callings.

Paul encourages the believers at Colossee the same way: "...walk worthy of the Lord to all pleasing, being fruitful in every work and increasing in the knowledge of God, being empowered with all power, according to the might of His glory, to all patience and long-suffering with joyfulness." (v.10-11) Paul's letter to the Colossians points us to the Manual to increase in the knowledge of God, but promises the power for the walk as well. Paul tells the Thessalonians to "walk worthy of God" (I Thess 2:12), but clarifies our calling ultimately "to His Kingdom and glory." Core values allow us to finish strong.

The believer's core values should be heavily influenced by the indwelling of the Holy Spirit and the very character of God – as it is revealed through all of Scripture. The discipline of the Holy Spirit within us should reflect love, joy, peace, long-suffering, kindness, goodness, faith, meekness and self-control. (Galatians 5:22-23) Think about that for a minute. We get so familiar with this power in us that we don't apply it – or appreciate its impact. Consider each "fruit" and how important it is to the heart of a good soldier. This does not produce "sissy soldiers" but rather noble men and women who can be trusted with power to use it rightly.

Clean hearts

Lieutenant Cash cited Joshua to encourage Marines facing imminent combat, and Joshua's words can also underscore the importance of core values as we face spiritual battles. As the Israelites stood at the brink of their battle for "promise," Joshua knew training was not enough. They needed clean hearts. As the armies mustered for battle, Joshua knew the real key to victory. He encouraged comprehensive self-examination. Were they right with God? Joshua commands them: "But sanctify the Lord God in your hearts, for tomorrow the Lord will do great works among us."

God did do great works among them in the days to follow, emphasizing the basic truth of this chapter: "Right core – God does more."

Good time for inspection?

CHAPTER 8: THE SOUL OF THE SOLIDER

Most important "take-away" thought(s):

1. Our mission and our identity are linked. If you were to write a creed, list out the details of your identity as a God's child.

2. What are some of the purposes we have individually, and as a church, that the Holy Spirit will empower us to accomplish?

3. Describe a person in your life that modeled integrity. What were the characteristics and what impact did they make in your life.

4. Describe ways that Christians live in opposition to their identity in Christ. Why do you think this happens? Explain.

5. We have a great God and a high calling. What personal character weaknesses do you battle? What strategies can you implement that will draw you to God with a pure heart?

*"Rejoice always; pray without ceasing; in everything give thanks;
for this is God's will for you in Christ Jesus."*
I Thessalonians 5:16-18

9
CAN YOU HEAR ME NOW?

Ten men hunkered down in the jungles of Vietnam, battle-weary, separated from their unit. An enemy ambush had scattered them in all directions. The enemy was still out there, but where? Some of the men were hurt, but there was no way to radio for medical evacuation. Supplies were low. They sensed enemy movement, but had no way to call for reinforcements. They no longer had access to intelligence reports from Command and Control. They were on their own – driven by survival instincts. With no way to contact their unit – or anyone else – life had become a "blind battle." The war strategy no longer guided their actions. Now it was, "just make it through today."

The absence of communication brought in a paralysis of sorts. Thoughts of enemy capture – and subsequent torture – were ever-present, creating a seedbed of fear.

This is so easy to imagine. It has happened throughout history, and the results are sad. A breakdown in communication is devastating to a soldier, to a unit, to an army.

It is equally devastating to a believer in Jesus Christ, to a church, and to Christianity universally. No one is exempt. This breakdown breeds confusion, in-fighting, fear, frustration, hurt and defeat. However, these symptoms are seldom traced back to a basic communication failure, and are therefore seldom corrected.

Communication in war

So, what is the role of communication in war? How does the enemy hinder it? What are the common barriers to effective communication? It's easy to see that communication is vital to any war effort. It unifies, fortifies and edifies. Clear, continual communication points people in the same direction, reduces confusion, and brings wider resources to the fight. Coordination is impossible without communication.

Imagine coordinating Army, Air Force, Marine and Navy resources towards a pivotal battle strategy. A lack of central command and control would have the Navy in the wrong sea, air coverage on the wrong front, and battalions at the wrong battle. It takes copious communication for even one successful mission.

Military communication also happens within a clearly-defined chain of command. The mission goals begin at the top and eventually must be relayed down to each relevant individual to successfully implement the mission. All training and talents are wasted without clear command directives – and the willingness to follow them.

Communication must be dynamic, fluid and constant. Any seemingly insignificant person left out of the loop can make or break a mission. What if you had aircraft, but no fuel? Parts, but no mechanic? Medics, but no medicine? There has to be continual "top-to-bottom" and "bottom-to-top" communication – from command level to the "boots-on-the-ground."

Communication in war is also vital for intelligence – coordinating all scraps of available information to produce the most reliable assessment of the big picture. What exactly is going on? What are we responding to? How has it changed since we started? Good intelligence determines the threat, monitors enemy movement, drives the strategy, and keeps the mission in real time.

Communication (connection between resources) drives tactical troop and weapons system placement, mission supplies, cooperation, unity, and other intangibles like morale, confidence, and commitment.

The cost of poor communication can't be overemphasized. A lack of communication creates confusion, frustration and alienation. Vital resources are wasted and the mission fails. In worst case scenarios, friendly fire may even cost lives. When the advantages of communication in war are clearly defined, the perils of poor communication become equally clear.

Connecting the dots

Establishing the importance of communication is fairly easy. Covering it as a very broad topic is not. Perhaps the best approach is directional: down, up and around.

Former Marine Communications Officer, David Frakes, sums up this directional approach: "The end goal of communications is connectivity – between superiors, subordinates – and laterally, as well. Our job was to make the connections and keep them working."

Communication from on high

Those connections up and down the chain of command actually happen up and down from the heavens. Modern communications rely heavily on satellites moving at about 7,000 mph at roughly 22,000 miles above the earth. According to Frakes, who holds a masters degree in communications, the military connects through phone systems, radios, and computers – all satellite-driven. He explained carrier signals, uplinks and downlinks, and the importance of transmitters and receivers to make it all happen. Frakes said that all satellites are built for certain frequencies and certain band widths. "Wrong frequency – no uplink or downlink," he said.

Communication is a concise process – not just the information transmitted – but exacting coordination with all equipment involved. Modern satellites provide a global range to communication which was previously impossible or was dependent on cumbersome cables laid across land and sea.

Satellites also provide global surveillance and critical global positioning systems vital for navigation through the battles. Imagine any modern army waging war without these essential pieces of information – all available from "on high."

Hopefully, your mind is already spinning with the spiritual parallels related to this – as there are many. The most obvious parallel to satellite communication is prayer – we are the transmitter and God is the Receiver—with God driving the process.

According to Frakes, who also holds a seminary degree, "prayer is the most direct link." He said we don't need a radio, phone, or computer for transmitters, but we do need to be on God's frequency. "God, as the Receiver, is always perfect. The problem is never at His end, but on ours," said Frakes.

Prayer

Prayer has always been a mainstay in the military. As the saying goes, "there are no atheists in foxholes." There is something about facing death in war that clarifies our priorities. In Charles Sasser's book, *God in the Foxhole*, President Franklin Roosevelt issued a D-Day prayer prior to the invasion of Normandy in 1944:

> "Almighty God, our sons, pride of our nation, this day have set upon a mighty endeavor.... They will be sore tried by night and by day, without rest until the victory is won. The darkness will be rent by noise and flame. Men's souls will be shaken with the violence of war... They fight not for the lust of conquest, they fight to end conquest. They fight to liberate. They fight to let justice rise among all thy people. They yearn for the end of battle, for their return to the haven of home. Some will never return. Embrace these, Father, and receive them, Thy heroic servants into Thy kingdom."[1]

There is urgency in war that brings us to the end of our finite resources and points us to supernatural resources, and the Source of comfort so desperately needed.

Lieutenant Carey Cash prayed with soldiers before battle in Iraq in the early 90's:

> "Of course our prayers were simple, but they were exactly what we all needed. We prayed for protection, for courage, for victory, for faith in difficult moments, for the assurance that we were not alone, for help in making tough decisions, for grace to endure, and for strength to overcome.... We called out to God as children, as men in need, as brothers facing trial. We relied on the power of the Psalms, the will of God, the teachings of Jesus, and the promises of eternal life. We clung to hope, trusted in God's love, and believed in a divine power and plan behind it all."[2]

After their pre-battle prayer, Cash said the men asked him deep, vulnerable questions about God. "They were desperate. And desperate men do not hunger for trivialities," he writes. "They hunger for someone to point them to the One who is the Way, the Truth, and the Life. They long for relationship with God."[3]

Men and women throughout human history have cried out to God in the trials of life – and many are recorded in the Bible.

Prayer is a major biblical topic – occurring in 350 different portions of Scripture. The Old Testament contains 10 different Hebrew words for prayer, and the New Testament contains seven different Greek words. In the Bible, people prayed at all times of the day and night in diverse circumstances. Prayer was often the pivot point where God's provisions were brought to bear on critical issues.

Powerful weapon

"Prayer might be the most powerful weapon God has given believers. Power falls where prayer prevails," said Bible teacher and pastor, Chip Ingram, in his teaching titled *The Invisible War*. "We are commanded to pray strategically, biblically, intensely, and powerfully in such a way that God does supernatural things," Ingram said.[4]

E. M. Bounds describes prayer as "a specific divine appointment, an ordinance of heaven, whereby God purposes to carry out His gracious designs on earth, and to execute and make efficient the plan of salvation."[5] Bounds says if prayer puts God to work on earth, then prayerlessness rules God out of world affairs – leaving man's circumstances with all its sorrows, burdens, and afflictions – without any God at all. Sobering stuff.

Bounds also presents the up-to-down approach to communication through prayer. "Prayer affects three different spheres of existence - the divine, the angelic and the human. It puts God to work, it puts angels to work, and it puts man to work. It lays its hands upon God, angels and men. What a wonderful reach there is in prayer! It brings into play the forces of heaven and earth," he writes.[6]

The Old Testament is filled with examples of fervent prayer (often with fasting) that brought about stunning victories in physical wars against overwhelming odds. One great example is found in II Chronicles 20 when a great multitude came against the people of Judah. King Jehoshaphat proclaimed a national fast, and went to God in prayer. He exalted God, described the threat, and cried: "For we have no power against this great multitude that is coming against us; nor do we know what to do, but our eyes are upon you."

As the people looked to God in prayer and fasting, God's answer came through a prophet in their midst named Jahaziel, son of Zechariah: "Do not be afraid or dismayed because of this great multitude, for the battle is not yours but God's." The people bowed and worshipped God in response to the proclamation. In an unusual battle pattern, the singers and worshippers actually led Judah's army to the fight – and they watched in amazement as God caused the enemy to fight against each other – destroying every last man. In verse 22, it says, "Now when they began to sing and to praise, the LORD set ambushes against the people of Ammon, Moab, and Mount Seir, who had come against Judah; and they were defeated."

Conversely, Joshua 9 shows us how a lack of prayer can be devastating, as the Israelites failed to consult the Lord before agreeing to a treaty to protect the Gibeonites. As a result, the Israelites fought a war against five kings that would have been otherwise unnecessary.

Jesus models prayer

God is the Source of victory in the Old Testament examples. In the New Testament, victory is found in the person of Jesus Christ, through the power of the Holy Spirit. Jesus modeled prayer throughout His earthly ministry.

He sought God's protection when facing crisis (Luke 3,6,9), focus in success (Matt 14:23, John 11:41), God's direction (Luke 4:42, 5:15-16, John 6:15), God's comfort (Matt 26:36-46, John 12:28), and God's will as He breathed His last (Luke 23:46). On the eve of His death, Jesus prayed with His disciples – especially Peter (also called Simon). In Luke 22:31-32, Jesus knew the spiritual battle Peter would face before and after the resurrection. Jesus said: "Simon, Simon, behold, Satan has desired you, that he may sift you as wheat. But I have prayed for you, that your faith fail not..." Peter did fail miserably in the days to come, but emerged as a faithful leader – just as Jesus prayed.

Jesus' disciples prayed in prison, prayed for wisdom, and prayed in persecution – always knowing that constant communication with God was the key to fulfilling their call.

Ingram says, "Whenever you see God's power fall in supernatural ways that transforms lives, institutions and churches – and God opens doors and does things no one can explain – somewhere, someone, a handful of people, or a whole church is praying."[7]

Lieutenant Cash acknowledged the same concept: "While we fought the physical battle against flesh-and-blood enemies, it was our mothers, fathers, wives, children, friends, churches, schools, Girl Scout troops, and countless others who were fighting the spiritual battle on our behalf."[8]

Battle for battle prayer

Regarding the difficulty of prayer, Ingram sites Elizabeth Elliot in her "Notes on Prayer. "Seldom do we realize the nature of our opponent and that is to his advantage," Elliot writes. "When we do recognize him for who he is, we have an inkling as to why prayer is never easy. It is the weapon the unseen power dreads most."[9]

Few argue the importance of prayer, yet many struggle (including myself) to establish regular prayer habits – a habitual connection with God that affects every aspect of life, particularly our battles. A closer look at military satellite communication may provide some helpful clues as to why prayer is such a hard discipline.

Where are we vulnerable?

Satellite communication offers huge advantages, but also dangerous vulnerabilities.

Every component in the connectivity chain can be subject to error, malfunction, or enemy attack. Because communication is a vital part of warfare, the enemy seeks to break our connections and we try to do the same with theirs.

On a spiritual level, Satan is well aware of the power of prayer. He does all he can to break our connection with God. To achieve victory in any war requires an assessment of where we are vulnerable to the enemy, and to minimize those vulnerabilities as much as possible.

Referring back to satellite communication, Frakes talked about some of the variables subject to breakdown. He cited one incident where communication was lost simply because of a shortage of batteries. "Even the smallest details matter when it comes to communication," Frakes said. The same could be said of us.

There are some aspects of physical and spiritual communication that fall under personal responsibility. A few are: Priority, Power supply and Positioning.

Personal priority

Where does prayer fall on our to-do list? The military knows communication is vital so they ensure that connectivity is a 24/7 priority. I saw this in person while working a civic leaders' flight to Colorado Springs some years ago. We visited the Air Force Space Command at Peterson Air Force Base. As technicians were explaining how they monitor satellite status, an alarm sounded. We watched in respectful silence as they went into full action mode to diagnose and correct the problem. Their guests were no longer their priority – communication capability was the number-one priority.

Prayer priority is my personal challenge in the demands of everyday life. Prayer gets crowded out by deadlines, work, family, media, crisis, illness, and any number of competing distractions. Tulsa pastor and Bible teacher, Dr. John Barnett teaches that a lack of prayer will contribute to disobedience, spiritual weakness, blindness in God's Word, foolishness, and spiritual poverty. In his teaching, *The Power of a Word-Filled Life*, Barnett suggests we should set a time for prayer, choose a place to pray, pray systematically, pray as often as possible, and pray for and with people. He talks about incorporating prayer into every activity: reading prayer as we read the newspaper, watching prayer as we watch television, talking prayer as we speak with people, listening prayer, and writing prayer.

If prayer is a priority, it will permeate every area of life 24/7. That goal of constant connection is what the apostle Paul calls ceaseless prayer in I Thessalonians 5:17.

Personal power supply

All the communication technology in the world is useless without a power supply – as illustrated by Frakes' example of a lack of batteries.

What does that look like in respect to prayer? At the most basic level, it involves our physical stamina. Every day has the same amount of hours but many options as to how we use them. What saps our energy? Do we give every other activity priority so that we are too exhausted to pray?

Any teaching on time management tends to include Charles E. Hummel's phrase "the tyranny of the urgent" as a common stumbling block to achieving true priorities. Life is full of broken people, relationships, health, cars, appliances, etc. that can easily sap our energy and keep us from the most empowering coping activity – prayer.

Besides my personal stamina, am I tapped into supernatural resources that bring power to prayer? God is the ultimate power, but our actions can enhance connection. The early disciples gave us a pattern of habits that access supernatural power: they gave themselves to the apostles' teaching, fellowship, and prayer. As a modern believer, there is still no substitute for time in the Word. It is our Manual for connection: teaching us how to know God and his will as we petition Him. Fellowship with other believers around the Word is also an effective power supply that brings encouragement, comfort, and more communication connections through intercessory prayer. When the busyness of life crowds out the Word, church and fellowship; the power for prayer is greatly diminished.

Personal positioning

Positioning is an important aspect of satellite communications. Position either enhances the signal or blocks the signal. The same is true for the believer in prayer.

People pray in all sorts of physical positions, but God seems to place less emphasis on the physical position and more emphasis on the heart position when it comes to prayer. Many of those heart positions fall within our realm of responsibility.

An obvious heart position is reflected in our relationships with other believers. Scripture tells us to leave the altar if we have something against our brother, or our brother has something against us (Matt. 5:23-24). Strained relationships put us in a position that blocks God's communication reception. He wants an uncluttered connection so He admonishes us to do what we can to reconcile, and then restart the "uplink." The apostle Peter speaks to husbands, in particular, when he tells them that their prayers are hindered if they are not rightly related to their spouses. (I Peter 3:7-9) James says to confess our sins to one another and pray for one another – in the context of the effectual prayer of a righteous man that accomplishes much. (5:16)

Any type of sin not confessed, forgiven and cleansed places us on a frequency not compatible with God's. (I John 1:9) The Bible is filled with factors that hinder prayer and many involve our behavior choices. Lack of forgiveness, bitterness, or selfishness can actually put us on the enemy's frequency! On the other hand, thankfulness, paired with prayer (Philippians 4:6), and coupled with compassion (Proverbs 21:13), are key components to a clear connection.

Just as military personnel at the Air Force Cyber Command are vigilant and diligent to troubleshoot any signs of satellite communication breakdown, believers would greatly benefit from careful self-examination for issues that hinder our connection to God.

Enemy sabotage

The military does all it can to enhance satellite communications from their end of things, but they also have to avoid enemy attacks. The enemy can intercept, scramble, or otherwise hinder communication channels, and in some cases, destroy equipment completely.

It is critical that we distinguish between enemy and friendly communication transmissions. In the military, any hint of a threat prompts full authentication procedures. Army Field Manual 24-33 describes this basic threat: "Proper use of authentication prevents the enemy from deceptively entering our nets... The enemy has skilled experts whose sole mission is to enter our nets by imitating friendly radio stations."[10] The manual lists several conditions which might indicate how the enemy is posing as a "friendly," and lists types of transmissions that require extra discernment.

Authentication is a biblical principle presented throughout Scripture. Perhaps the most relevant verse is found in I John 4:1: "Beloved, do not believe every spirit, but test the spirits to see whether they are from God, because many false prophets have gone out into the world." A believer must exercise great care in every communication venue – from their own thought life, to external media, to conversations. Every area of receptive communication should be carefully examined according to the truth of Scripture in order to authenticate where it comes from – and then respond strategically if the communication proves hostile.

Besides masquerading as friendly forces, the enemy employs other strategic methods to break down communications. According to Frakes, enemy interference happens most commonly through jamming, satellite-to-satellite signal intercept, and satellite destruction.

Jamming

"Jamming is an effective way for the enemy to disrupt our command, control, and communications on the battlefield. All the enemy needs to jam us is a transmitter tuned to our frequency with enough power to override friendly signals at our receivers."[11]

Frakes defines jamming as "directed electromagnetic interference by a strategic transmitter." It means that radio frequency energy targets communication channels. The fact that all of this happens in an unseen realm makes the analogy all the more applicable to prayer. There are unseen forces strategically focused on breaking our connection with God.

The Army manual lists two types of jamming: obvious and subtle. Listed in the obvious are interference signals like random noise, stepped tones, sparks, random pulses, wobblers, and recorded sounds. Basically, they are all "noise" added to normal signals that either degrade or disrupt the signal or frustrate the operator. One particular signal caught my attention, simply called "recorded sounds," that distract operators and disrupt communications. These include "music, screams, applause, whistles, machinery noise and laughter" as examples.

We live in an increasingly noisy world. With modern technology, studies show that the average person is "plugged into" some type of electronic device at least eight hours per day – creating a constant flow of media noise.

Dr. Archibald Hart has done much research on this social condition and has written a book called: *Digital Invasion: How Technology is Shaping You and Your Relationships*. He reviews issues like stress overload, social alienation, and declining IQ scores. Hart says that the constant barrage of "noise" reduces the ability to think deeply on subjects because new information is constantly being added at such a rapid pace.

Like the type of subtle jamming signals, our cultural noise comes in all different forms: music, texting, video games, social media, television, radio, movies, and more. These assault our available mental bandwidth with a cacophony of beeps, call tones, music, screams, etc.

Hart, a clinical psychologist and psychophysiologist, says he is not a technophobe. He cites all the advantages of technology, but is alarmed at the pathologies it presents as well. He cites both parents and their kids as equal offenders and says technology promotes too much time in virtual worlds instead of in real, nourishing relationships.

"Clearly, this will have an effect on their ability to spend any significant time in prayer, let alone reflect on Scripture or pay attention to a deep sermon. In addition, these consequences must inevitably affect their spiritual practices as well," Hart writes.[12]

"Take time to be quiet, as God whispers and the world is loud," hangs in my hallway as a reminder to cultivate quiet to hear the voice of God – and also to be able to plumb my own heart for the things I need discuss with Him. How much noise is normal "signals" and how much noise is enemy jamming? Can we discern the difference? Do we even think in those terms? Not typically, so our spiritual enemy is often very successful in jamming our prayer life. Do I have protocol in place to intercept and reduce enemy signals that resemble what the Army calls "obvious jamming?"

The Field Manual also mentions subtle jamming that doesn't use noise, but simply creates a stronger enemy signal that effectively squelches incoming friendly signals. As it applies to prayer, we simply need to ask what signal, or form of communication is strongest in our lives. Are the world's messages stronger than the Word's messages? Whatever we feed on more will ultimately be the stronger of the two, and effectively squelch the other.

We can strengthen our "God signal" through consistent spiritual disciplines and constant connection through the Holy Spirit. During seasons of intense spiritual battles in my life, I may listen to five to ten Bible teaching messages a day! I listen in the morning, while I cook or clean, in the car, before I go to bed – intentionally creating a high volume of God's frequency to squelch the enemy signals that seek to destroy me – and I severely limit any media source filled with ungodly content. By increasing my godly signal volume, there is little room left for enemy signals to make it through communication channels. I sustain this habit as long as it takes to gain equilibrium – and victory.

Finally, the last aspect of jamming is unintentional and not always enemy-driven. Certain atmospheric conditions can interfere with satellite communications. Storms can cause significant interference in communications just as storms in life can challenge our prayer life. We are especially vulnerable when life feels "maxed out" by high-velocity storms, or by a series of bad storms. We can't often control these storms, but understanding our vulnerability should prompt us to seek additional communication channels through other believers to shore up the temporary interference.

Satellite-to-satellite

Some interference is accomplished from satellite to satellite, according to Frakes. He says that enemy satellites can actually try to intercept signals – to capture them, or delay them. The spiritual example of this "battle in the heavenlies" is found in Daniel's prayer in Daniel 10:13. Daniel had prayed and his prayer was immediately heard, but it took 21 days of heavenly battle before a return message could be transmitted. Daniel modeled patience in prayer.

Satellite destruction

The third type of enemy interference Frakes mentioned was sending distortions in transmissions to destroy the receiver, or taking out the satellite by explosion or other means of rendering it inoperative. Spiritually, no transmission can possibly destroy God as the Perfect Receiver. Our transmissions may be distorted or faulty, but God has given the Holy Spirit to translate our prayers according to the will of the Father. In Romans 8:26, it says that the Holy Spirit gives utterance to prayers that we cannot even form.

No type of attack on God as Receiver will ever be successful – which should give us great confidence in the area of prayer.

Sabotaging the enemy

The military goes to great lengths to protect our systems and has a strategy for communication countermeasures as outlined in Field Manual 24-33. What are our countermeasures to shut down the enemy on a spiritual level?

Resistance is a common electrical term, and also a key term used in James 4:7 to shut down the enemy. First, we "submit to God" wholeheartedly, then "resist the devil" and he has to flee. Ephesians 4 echoes this strategy. We are told to put off the old man (the frequency of the enemy) and be renewed in our minds (to God's frequency). We are to be rightly related to each other. Verse 26 speaks of sustained anger, and verse 27 says, "neither give place to the devil."

To sabotage the enemy, we think rightly, act rightly, and serve God fully – blocking any access.

Air superiority

The majority of this chapter has dealt with heavenly communications using the satellite analogy, but it's time to head a little closer to earth. As a believer in Jesus Christ, I feel a deep affinity with infantry soldiers – the "ground grunts" who engage the enemy in regular, often unpredictable battles. They have a hard job – and much rides on their success or defeat. Fortunately for them – and us – they have access to resources above and beyond themselves which provides great courage and comfort.

The greatest friend to any infantry soldier is the confidence of air superiority – the certainty of air cover providing broad protection and significantly more fire power. The soldier is no longer limited by their own resources. Prayer coverage is much the same for the believer.

Two aspects of prayer/air coverage are found in warning systems headquartered in Oklahoma and Georgia. The Boeing E-3s located at Tinker Air Force Base provide air surveillance through the Airborne Warning and Control System (AWACS). Robins Air Force Base in Georgia, hosts the Joint Surveillance and Target Attack Radar System (JSTARS). The Boeing E-8C aircraft is filled with banks of computers designed to monitor all ground movement. Both types of air coverage provide comprehensive intelligence information vital to war efforts keeping the military from "blind battle" scenarios that could prove disastrous.

Imagine the advantage of "surveillance" provided through prayer as we petition God for wisdom in our battles. Would we be like Elijah – who prayed – and then his servant saw the landscape lined with horses and chariots of fire previously invisible to him? (II Kings 6:17) Or, would we see beyond our "flesh and blood" battles to discern the principalities and powers behind them as the real enemy? (Ephesians 6:12)

Once we have the advantage of discernment through prayer, how comforting to know that we have "air cover" once we engage in battle? Air superiority has turned the tide in many a battle. It was instrumental in WWII. Joseph Goebbels' conversation with Hitler was noted in Goebbels' diary on March 21, 1945: "Again and again we return to the starting point of our conversation. Our whole military predicament is due to enemy air superiority."[13]

An infantry soldier would find great comfort hearing an F-22 Raptor roar overhead as he marched into battle. The F-22 is capable of strategic strikes far beyond the resources of a single soldier. How emboldening to know – whatever the outcome – that every possible resource is brought to the fight?

That is only possible through communication – before, during, and after the fight.

It's easy to see how air superiority is crucial to land battles, but it is too often a forgotten topic when it comes to life battles. Next time, think planes, then, plan prayer.

Fog of war and friendly fire

The last level of communication is at ground level – on the horizontal plane of the battlefield. This level involves the most people, has the highest level of failure – and many needless casualties. Those in the thick of the fight, especially if long-term, face the most daunting atmosphere for communication – the fog of war.

During the revolutionary war, lines of opposing soldiers would open fire at each other, creating huge clouds of musket smoke that obscured visibility. In this "fog of war" it was unclear how many bullets hit their mark. Did the enemy continue to advance? The confusion caused by this fog of war has continued into more modern battles. Musket smoke has been replaced by the profusion of information coupled with the traditional elements of fatigue, stress, and injury. Technically, fog of war is the uncertainty in situational awareness experienced by people in military operations.[14] War is messy and it can mess up our connections with each other.

What affects armies also affects churches in much the same way. Things like back-to-back battles, loss of a clear battle objective, shortage of resources, and costly errors provide an atmosphere ripe for ruin.

One of the most common tragedies of fog of war situations is friendly fire – we fire on each other – instead of the actual enemy.

Communication confusion has prompted sad samples of friendly fire. A recent example happened in Desert Storm as convoys were racing across the deserts of Iraq. Command and Control had ordered communication blackouts as the tank convoys advanced in order to avoid enemy detection. In the absence of communication, the forward tank group began to take fire – but it was actually from their own troops. The forward tank group had advanced so rapidly that the greater distance caused the rear tank units to mistakenly detect their movement as an enemy advance. Once command and control recognized what was happening, they immediately ordered communication to resume and the firing stopped before any serious damage occurred. Simple mistake. Consequences could have been tragic.

Loss of life in any war is a grievous loss, but how much more egregious when inflicted by your own side. Communication breakdown and the fog of war cause much of the infighting found in and among churches today. They drain resources and keeps us from a united strategy toward the real enemy. Jesus said to take care to not bite and devour each other. (Galatians 5:15) We could expand the bite-and-devour list to include stonewalling, slandering, condemning, hating – or just ignoring the many biblical instructions regarding how we should communicate with each other.

In the fog of war, prayer keeps us focused on the right information with the right attitude. Awareness of the fog of war should prompt us to exercise greater caution in the fight, and grant greater grace for those we fight beside.

Closing questions

What parts stood out to you most as you reviewed these principles? What areas need attention to enhance your heavenly connectivity? What noise needs to be silenced that is jamming your connection? Do you have any conditions in your life that set up fog-of-war? What can you do to abate them? Are people being picked off by friendly fire? What can you do about it?

CHAPTER 9: CAN YOU HEAR ME NOW?

Most important "take-away" thought(s):

1. Military communication follows a chain of command. How is this applied spiritually? Give examples.

2. Our lack of connections with God in prayer is never God's lack of connectivity with us. In what ways do we break the connection? Be specific.

3. In what ways does the enemy "jam" your communication in prayer?

4. Prayer provides "air superiority" in our spiritual battles. What difference does this make during a believer's battles?

5. Describe a situation you've encountered in relationships (or in church) where communication breakdown resulted in "friendly fire."

"My people have gone into captivity, because they have no knowledge." Isaiah 5:13

10
TAKEN CAPTIVE

Lieutenant Charles Brown looked tired and gaunt as he walked off the C-9 Nightingale aircraft at Westover Air Force Base on April 1, 1973. But, it was a jubilant homecoming for the B-52 pilot who had been shot down over North Vietnam and held prisoner in Hanoi for 101 days.

Capture is always a possible peril of war, but it's also the last place a soldier ever means to be. The POW experience changed Brown's life – and the day I met Brown, it changed my life.

As a young airman at Westover in 1985, I worked an awards ceremony for former POW's receiving the newly authorized POW medal. Ushering WWII and Vietnam War former POWs to their seats, I heard their stories while we waited for others to arrive. There was an easy camaraderie among the white-haired heroes. I listened with the wonder of a child as they spoke of the initial shock of capture, the squalor of confinement, the uncertainty of survival, the torture, seeing comrades die, and their own eventual release. The collective stories of these brave men awakened a new appreciation for their service.

After the ceremony, I watched a tender moment as Brown knelt by his sons and showed them his medal. I thought of how captivity of a loved one can be hard on everyone. Over the years, I did several more interviews and it deepened my understanding of the POW experience.

But, the most compelling POW story I've heard to date is the remarkable survival story in Laura Hillenbrand's book, *Unbroken: A World War II Story of Survival, Resilience, and Redemption.*

The main character, Louis Zamperini, was an Olympic runner in the 1936 Berlin games, and enlisted in the U.S. Army Air Corps in 1941. His B-24 Liberator crashed into the Pacific during a search-and-rescue mission in April 1942. Zamperini and crewmate "Phil" Phillips survived the open seas for 47 days and made it to the Marshall Islands, only to be taken captive by the Japanese. He endured three years of unbelievable cruelties as a POW until his eventual rescue in August 1945.

It's hard to comprehend the horrific experiences of those taken captive in war. Captivity is a place of isolation, deprivation and manipulation. The enemy's goal is simple: to break your will to resist or even to stay alive. Only the toughest survived – and those that did never lost sight of liberation, freedom, and hope. It took grit and creativity to avoid being broken by the enemy's tactics.

In all the POW stories, I've yet to hear of a POW who did not know he had been captured. They all knew with frightening clarity how grave their circumstances were. Every waking moment was a mental battle against discouragement, defeat – or, God forbid, cooperation with the enemy.

By comparison, in the nearly three decades since I met the now-retired Colonel Brown, I've met many, many Christians taken captive in the spiritual realm – but they are completely unaware of their captivity. This ignorance subsequently robs them of any rescue/escape strategy, and the mental diligence necessary to survive until rescued.

Who of us has not watched once-vibrant believers gradually or suddenly snatched away to live under the cruel tactics of our spiritual enemy? How many have unknowingly defected and now live under the oppression of sin, claiming their "freedom" as the reason to do so? Many think they are valiantly in the fight, blind to the invisible bars of their captor, Satan himself, the enemy of all that God is.

The prophet Jeremiah saw ahead of time that the whole nation of Israel would fall blindly into spiritual, and then physical captivity. He tried to warn them: "But if you will not listen to it, my soul will sob in secret for such pride; and my eyes will bitterly weep and flow down with tears, because the flock of the Lord had been taken captive." (Jer. 13:17) The Bible contains tragic cycles where God rescues His people from captivity only to see them drift back into captivity.

We are equally susceptible.

As our spiritual captor, Satan is an unprincipled foe who discards all the rules. Our military is governed by the Geneva Convention which established the humane rules of war. Satan has no such limitations. He exploits all advantages. Satan brings no compassion or dignity to our captivity.

Who gets captured?

There is no foolproof way to avoid enemy capture. Charlie Brown was one of 60 B-52 crew members that flew that December day in 1972. Why him?

Brown was obviously at greater risk because of his location in enemy territory. He needed to be there for the mission. It was a calculated risk because of the anticipated benefits. The more troublesome situations occur when aircraft or people "wander" into enemy territory due to carelessness or flawed navigation.

Because the military understands the importance of reliable navigational systems, they have safeguards in place to ensure correct information. For example, since the C-5 Galaxy aircraft is a huge target in the air, it is equipped with four inertial navigation systems to constantly check against each other to detect even the slightest variance. If one of the four disagrees with the other three, it grabs the attention of the flight engineer for an explanation. True readings are not only vital to reach the destination, but also to prevent drifting into enemy airspace unaware.

The spiritual implications of this are staggering when viewed in relation to our present culture. In an age straining against absolutes, our moral compass forfeits a true north for successful navigation through life. All life coordinates are up for grabs – family, sexuality, business practices, relationships, etc. Without a biblical reference for true north, enemy coordinates are loosely defined and therefore very easy to "wander" into. Today, the boundaries between right and wrong constantly change.

When the boundaries were clear, believers were less apt to be taken captive. The steps into enemy territory were more intentional. Now, believers are regularly taken captive spiritually, but their moral compass still reads that they are in free air space. Reliable, pinpoint-correct navigational aids are important in military maneuvers but seldom even on the radar screen in the day-to-day spiritual experience.

Besides wanderers, who else is at risk for captivity? A few categories may prove helpful to understand and, in some cases, possibly avoid captivity. What category might you fit in?

Fearless

It took extremely brave men like Charlie Brown to fly directly over an enemy city they knew was well-armed. There was simply no other way to take out strategic targets. Those in the thick of the battle – closest to enemy lines – are in the greatest danger. That is why military training includes what to do if captured. It's an occupational risk.

Thinking through these concepts increased my appreciation of POWs like Charlie Brown and caused me to change the way I view spiritual captives. Some are in spiritual captivity because they fearlessly fight for the cause of Christ. Think of John the Baptist sending messages to Jesus from prison. John fearlessly served his Lord and one of the ramifications was a physical prison – and ultimate beheading. It moves me to compassion. It provokes an admiration for his tenacity and should provoke me to similar service.

I have a "spiritual Special Forces" friend. Over two decades, I have watched her fearlessly tread in the enemy territory of abortion, pornography, homosexuality, and addiction – seeking to rescue those the enemy has taken captive in these insidious areas. I have seen the enemy manifest himself in her life in very scary ways – seeking to take her captive at every turn. She has been a spiritual Louis Zamperini, prevailing and helping others in the midst of her own extreme pain. Her life has been an object lesson illustrating the risks of fearless faith. She has learned to take every thought captive so she won't be. Besides being a great example to me, she has also challenged my role to support the fearless. Fearless (but wise) believers need great prayer support, compassion, and diligence on our part. How can we be a Trench Buddy to those in peril? It involves "messy ministry" that simultaneously reaches out but maintains personal strength. Trench Buddies seek to rescue those in the clutches of captivity, but avoid capture themselves.

Foolish

Some people are captured because they are just plain foolish. In fact, some people in this category walk right through the front gates of the POW camp. Others stumble behind enemy lines with no mission-related reason to be there. They just wander in with no compass to guide them. Still others see all of life the same and see no distinction between "safe" and "non-safe" territory. They see life as one vast "demilitarized zone" devoid of threats.

Fortunately, I have no real military examples of this category, but I unfortunately have numerous spiritual examples – many of which have prompted a deep burden for this type of book. I have repeatedly witnessed the agony and pain of those who, against all warnings, have run into spiritual enemy territory. They take unnecessary risks all the time. They swagger like a highly-trained soldier but have invested little time in real training. In their false confidence, their lust lures them to the snares buried in their pleasures. Like the proverbial mouse chomping on the cheese, the bar snaps down and they're stuck.

In their captivity, they look emaciated, fearful, and hopeless. They are broken. Some have even formed deep alliances with their captors in what is known as the Stockholm Syndrome. Captivity becomes their new normal. Rather than plan strategies for a way out – they settle into their captivity for the long haul, thinking this is just the way life is. Like a wounded dog, they snarl at anyone who risks a rescue attempt.

I have also watched the residual suffering in all their loved ones as they anguish over their capture and wonder if rescue will ever come. In their pain, the ones anguishing over a loved one are too often sidetracked from their own mission. That pain is in my own family. I know it all too well.

So what is our response to the foolish spiritual POW? What does a Trench Buddy look like here? This topic is presented in more detail in section five, but a few quick tips fit here. First, let the situation serve as a warning to you. Whenever I see captivity happening in others, I recognize my own vulnerability and take greater care in my own life. Secondly, pray. Pray for them, and pray for wisdom in your rescue attempts. Military missions exploit the best possible scenarios for success, avoiding anything that looks like a suicide mission taking even more lives. Often, it's prudent to wait – to watch and pray. Third, I enlist help. In the hardest of rescues, the military creates joint operation teams – taking the best from each branch to combine them for the best team.

Finally, no matter how foolish a captive has been, stay compassionate and never give up hope. Regardless of how a person gets into captivity, we don't want them to die there.

Feeble

Just as lions target the weakest in a herd, Satan prowls about as a roaring lion seeking to devour in the same way. This category covers a broad spectrum of weak including the wounded, the sick, the young or very old, or those just plain tired from back-to-back battles. Their defenses are compromised due to disability, age, or just a lack of training. The enemy always targets those who lag behind their unit, or who are isolated from their unit altogether.

Here again, Trench Buddies can be "messy ministry." It takes time, energy and wisdom for believers to break through the barriers that hide vulnerability to be captured. Does the risk of being real trump the risk of enemy capture? Just the opposite should be true.

I have seen all these categories of feeble fall captive. Most of us have been wounded in church relationships, and some leave the church as a result – only to be taken captive in their self-imposed isolation. The sick and very old are often in long seasons of isolation and loneliness – separated from their "unit" and therefore highly vulnerable.

An alarmingly-large category of weak are the Scripturally-feeble believers. A good chunk of any church is scripturally ignorant, and lacks the training to use scriptural truth strategically. Failing to fall under God's authority due to ignorance and disobedience to the truth brings them unwittingly into the devil's compound.

Jesus spoke about freedom to Jews who denied they were in any captivity. In John 8, Jesus said, "if you continue in My Word, you are my disciples indeed. And you shall know the truth, and the truth will make you free." (v.30-31) The Jews answered him, "We are Abraham's seed and were never in bondage to anyone. How do you say, You will be made free?" (v.33) Jesus addresses their spiritual captivity by saying, "Truly, truly, I say to you, whoever practices sin is the slave of sin." (v.34) Ultimate freedom is captured in verse 36: "Therefore if the Son shall make you free, you shall be free indeed."

Surviving captivity

"Free Indeed" is the mantra for every POW. It is the thought they feed above all others. It is what keeps many of them alive in captivity. They picture life after rescue. They talk about what they will do when they get home. It brings buoyancy to an otherwise shattering experience. Those that make it speak of comrades who didn't. Once hope was abandoned, they just shriveled up and died.

How do you survive spiritual captivity? Besides relentlessly embracing hope, there are a few jewels gleaned from former military POWs. The first is pivotal: Don't dialogue with the enemy.

Don't dialogue with the enemy

What are the three things a prisoner is allowed to tell the enemy captor? Right – "name, rank and serial number." Other than those few details, they are to divulge no other information, even though the enemy uses painful tactics. POWs spoke of regular torture and beatings to get them to talk. Deprivation was also a common tactic to provoke a soldier to compromise in order to get food or medical treatment. Captors would commonly make empty promises they never intended to keep once a combatant cooperated. If maltreatment didn't work, sometimes psychological methods proved effective – feigning friendship and compassion to encourage wrong loyalties.

In the previous chapter on communication, we learned the importance of information and the need to guard it from the enemy. Those surviving captivity must also guard something much more precious – their heart. I pondered the three scant pieces of information POWs are allowed to divulge.

To state your name is to remind yourself of who you are. You are not who the enemy treats you like. Your name gives you the stability of a sound identity, and reminds you of your family back home who are waiting for you to return.

Rank reminds you of your position in the mission. The mission doesn't end with captivity.

While in captivity, Louis Zamperini took every opportunity to sabotage enemy equipment, efforts, etc. He was relentlessly stubborn in his mission as Lieutenant Zamperini throughout his confinement – and often suffered for his efforts.

Finally, a soldier's serial number signifies his singular standing in his country. He is a citizen of a country and is not alone. Thousands of others currently fighting the war in his absence – and planning for his rescue. These three aspects of a soldier's identity are allowable to the enemy – and an important reminder to a soldier's soul as well.

How does this relate to a believer in captivity? In a real POW situation, any negotiations take place far above the POW's level. Leaders generally talk to leaders. The same is true spiritually. We are not to dialogue with the enemy but let God work on our behalf.

Any time I feel imminent capture in an area of my life, I confess my identity. I am a child of God, I have been given an important mission, and I serve for a greater good beyond myself. I have found this to be a very powerful tool as these aspects of my identity are transcendent. They will never change and they do not depend on me to be true. My "rank" also reminds me of the Authority I submit to– and that no other authority has true access to me.

Never give up

Hope is critical in confinement, but determination and diligence bring hope to fruition. Hope is an active process. It is vital in captivity to take every thought captive. As a POW, your body may be captive against your will, but your mind must be completely captive to your will, which is subjected to God's will. It is determination and diligence that keep your mindset free and hopeful in the midst of circumstances you cannot control.

Viktor Fankl was an Austrian neurologist, psychologist, and Holocaust survivor of Auschwitz concentration camp, and two other camps affiliated with Dachau. Frankl's POW lessons became part of Stephen Covey's *7 Habits* course. Frankl observed that the last human freedom was the freedom to choose. He said men could take away virtually every other freedom, but they could not take away our freedom to choose. He saw hundreds of people subjected to the same torture, but some responded differently, and never allowed their circumstances to change their values. He particularly noted captives that were days away from personal starvation still sharing their minimal portions with others. He marveled at the power of mental choice in the midst of such suffering. They chose kindness in the face of extreme cruelty. They chose not to allow the enemy to make them hard and bitter.

Believers have much to learn from POW survivors. The survivors I spoke with never succumbed to life as a victim even though it would have been very easy to do so. They learned to take every thought captive unto the obedience of their mission, and to cling to a hope that they would live to see freedom. They never saw the enemy as their friend, and they never stopped resisting.

You often cannot choose your circumstances, but you can always choose your response to the circumstances.

Help fellow captives

As we choose our responses to our circumstances, one of the best responses is to help others that share our suffering. In the majority of POW interviews I conducted or read, helping others was part of their daily routines. Whether it was tending to wounds after a beating, or tapping codes on concrete walls, the intention was to make it out together. Charlie Brown explained the communication code they tapped on the prison walls because the guards did not allow them to talk to one another. The tap code utilized the Polybius Square which placed the Latin alphabet in a five-by-five grid. It was a tedious process so they often abbreviated words to make it easier. According to Brown, two common tap abbreviations were GBU for

"God Bless You," or GBA for "God Bless America." Other POWs encouraged each other just by lightening the atmosphere however they could. Zamperini reportedly regaled his fellow captives with elaborate Italian recipes they could enjoy once they were free.

It is said that friendships made in battle trenches run very deep, and POWs experience something very similar. For the duration of captivity, they become your family. They are all you have.

The essence of Trench Buddies is the same thing. Whether in battle or captivity, trench buddies come alongside and minister to the soul. Sometimes, trench buddies minister when the rest of the world has given up. They are usually people transparent about their own pain – and brave enough to walk through pain with others.

Too often, as believers, we are too consumed with our own agendas, or our own pain, to reach out to help others. We try to maintain a personal comfort zone that ignores the needs around us. POWs have the "advantage" of no comfort zone to hide in. The pain is raw and obvious – so the response choices are stark and immediate. Will I help or avoid?

Those who emerge from their captivity with the greatest overall health are the ones who chose to help others. And, like Frankl observed, we all have that freedom to choose.

Plan for the future

Any successful survival story involves planning for the future. One such survival story that easily rivals any POW tale is Sir Ernest Shackleton's two-year saga after their ship was crushed by ice during an expedition to Antarctica in 1914. Alfred Lansing unfolds their riveting experience in his book, *Endurance: Shackleton's Incredible Voyage*. When their plight became clear, Shackleton formed the 28-man crew into a level team – all portions equally important. Shackleton was an impressive leader, always strategizing the next step to rescue. Every new obstacle was tackled with ingenuity and toughness. Through Shackleton's leadership and team tenacity, the whole crew miraculously emerged alive after a two-year struggle for survival.

POWs strive to stay in a forward-thinking mode, and it is a powerful motivator.

These heroes teach us that if we don't look beyond our current circumstances to a potentially better future, we are severely handicapped in our present state. The enemy always tries to demoralize prisoners by getting them to believe their current state will have no end. "This is the way it will always be," is the incessant whisper. The overcomer is the one who silences those words and replaces them with thoughts of future victory.

What is the application on the spiritual level? Scripture tells us to "set our affection on things above, not on the earth." Paul tells us to focus on that which is eternal and not that which is temporal.

Despite Paul's severe trials, he remained resolute to "press on," to finish well no matter what. Believers struggle when they get stuck in their current circumstances. Wallowing in where we are only allows us to sink deeper, and makes it harder to move forward. The Bible presents a balanced view of processing our present (learning to "stand") but pressing on from our trials. Jesus presents the best illustration of this forward thinking in present trials. The book of Hebrews (12:2) describes Jesus as the author and finisher of our faith – and suggests that we follow His example: "who for the joy set before Him endured the cross, despising the shame, and has sat down at the right hand of the throne of God."

If Jesus looked forward to finish His race successfully, how can we do less?

Moving on

Looking forward energizes our present, and moving on quiets our past. Louis Zamperini endured untold suffering in three years of captivity. After his liberation in 1945, Zamperini struggled to move on and enjoy his freedom. He struggled with Post Traumatic Stress Syndrome and relied on alcohol to cope. He would have nightmares involving one particularly sadistic prison guard named Mutsuhiro Watanabe (nicknamed "The Bird"). It wasn't until Zamperini came to faith in Jesus Christ at a Billy Graham crusade in 1949 that Zamperini could successfully move on.

A critical component of moving on for Zamperini was forgiveness. He actually visited some of his former guards and communicated his forgiveness. In 1950, he visited the Sugamo Prison in Tokyo and shared the gospel with some of his former tormentors. After that point of intentional forgiveness, Zamperini not only survived his captivity, but began to live as a free man – and thrive.

Brown and others move on with life, but they live out lessons learned in captivity. They sustain a keen appreciation for loved ones because they didn't have them for a season. They remain humbled by their experiences. As Brown progressed through the ranks at Westover, he retained a gentle humility – always a strong leader, but ever the advocate for those who worked under him.

I am happy to report that I have encountered many followers of Jesus Christ that have redeemed their captivity experiences for the glory of God. While I see some believers acting the victim after trivial trials, I see many others that have been through unimaginable suffering, yet move on to great ministry. They are not stuck in pain, but have pursued healing in Christ, and move on in power.

Moving on is not easy, but necessary. The apostle Paul was a POW, imprisoned and beaten for his faith. He lists his suffering in his first letter to the Corinthians (chapter 11) and then offers a remarkable perspective in chapter 12: he cites his weakness as an asset because it made more room for Christ's power. He knew it was "for Christ's sake" that it all happened and he was able to move on. He maintains this attitude in 12:10: "Therefore I am well content with weaknesses, with insults, with distresses, with persecutions, with difficulties, for Christ's sake; for when I am weak, then I am strong."

Wow. That is moving on. That is a healthy perspective.

Liberation/Freedom

Toward the end of Zamperini's captivity in Japan, he sensed something was changing because the guards were more agitated than usual. He wasn't sure if that was a good thing or a bad thing because, as the war wore to an end, some prison guards opted to kill the prisoners rather than see them rescued. Zamperini knew this had been happening, and it made sight of allied planes flying over his Japanese POW camp all the sweeter. Rescue was imminent – and hope soared.

In both Japan and Germany, allied forces were shocked at the sight of the emaciated, ghost-like captives they rescued. Prison guards fled the camps prior to the rescuers arrival. Victors had won the right to rescue the POWs. The Allies had persevered to win World War II, but not without great cost, in both lives and money.

War is costly, and victory always demands a price.

This is a profound principle when applied to spiritual captivity. Prior to the cross, the Bible says that we were all spiritual captives to our own sin. In a war that began in the Garden of Eden, it took God Himself to fight for our rescue in a battle that culminated with the cross of Jesus Christ.

The cross is the central theme of the Bible, and is the ultimate victory symbol for all spiritual POWs. Jesus Christ came to set captives free. Because of the cross, the enemy has no legitimate grounds to hold a believer captive. That is a life-changing, amazing truth. Sadly, we are all too often "willing captives," dwelling in cells that are no longer locked.

Imagine how awful it would have been if the Allied forces marched into concentration camps to liberate POWs, and the captives refused to leave. The cost of war waged for their release would be nullified by their refusal to leave their tortuous captivity behind. The freedom they dreamed of for years was now a reality, but they could have refused to believe it – and actually live free. As ridiculous as that sounds, it describes the experience of many a believer.

The simplicity of the gospel is that sin held us captive but the cross broke its power to hold us. In the book of Romans the cross broke the power of sin – it has no true authority over us. (Chapter 6) If war is about who gets to be in control, the cross clearly vanquished any challenge to God's sovereign, loving control. We have every resource we need to walk spiritually free, but the enemy relentlessly pursues us to get us to believe otherwise. He looks for any opportunity to steal our freedom and get us under his control and authority.

We must be extremely vigilant in our daily battles to avoid enemy captivity and control. John Bevere reviews this vigilance in his book, *Enemy Access Denied*. Like military training to avoid capture, Bevere teaches the believer to be aware of enemy activity and possible capture. According to Bevere (and the Bible), any sin in our lives gives the enemy (Satan) access to our souls. In choosing to sin, we submit that part of our lives to Satan and invite his authority to rule over us. Only full and steady obedience keeps us firmly under God's loving and safe authority – and ultimately living lives of sweet freedom. The cords of sin can no longer entangle us, the weight of guilt and shame can no longer torture us. There is healing for prior pain and suffering, and we wear robes of righteousness instead of ragged, foul, prison garb.

To understand the full implications of the cross is to exult in its exquisite glory. If we understood its full meaning, we would worship with the exuberance of a POW spotting rescue aircraft. We would understand the full extent of rescue – and like Charlie Brown and all the POWs he represents, our lives would never be the same. We would be shaped by our suffering, but would never again take our freedom for granted. We would also become better trench buddies.

So how does this all relate to believers and being a better Trench Buddy? On the most basic level, the goal is to avoid capture yourself, and try to keep others from the same fate. Training helps. The military mandates yearly anti-terrorism training to minimize the risks of capture or harm, so some spiritual tips may be equally helpful for some summary Trench Buddy applications.

Don't go it alone

Don't try to live the Christian life alone. No soldier lives, trains, or fights alone. They make good use of a "buddy system," and so should we. Is there someone who has your back, providing cover for you? Do you play that role in at least one other person's life?

The chainmail armor of old linked small metal rings together to form an impenetrable mesh. A break in the link created a vulnerability. As believers, we should be linked together as a body of believers in local churches and small groups to provide a protective spiritual covering. I am infinitely safer when I live an open, honest life before and with other believers who care enough to battle hard for my soul.

Prayer

Pray often, for and with others. There is a power and connection to prayer that is not found any other way. Because our spiritual captor is invisible, prayer is the protection that covers that realm, and brings angels to the fight.

I learned this the hard way in the process of writing this book and presenting conferences on the content. For more than three years, I battled spiritual warfare on many fronts. At times, I was taken captive spiritually, bound by defeat, discouragement, fear, and doubt. I allowed the enemy to take authority in areas Christ had already purged and cleansed. In my captivity, I was weak and tired, and made very little progress. Finally, I had my "duh moment" and realized that my battle plan lacked the prayer reinforcement necessary for the freedom and power to complete this project. Casting aside pride and the fear of what people would think, I began to form an extended prayer team. I enlisted the support of a few local pastors, and asked individuals and prayer teams from three different states to join me in my mission. Within a few months, it was like a weight had lifted – probably the bars of captivity. Something very oppressive was gone, and I began to make serious, unhindered progress. Through prayer, God also provided specific portions from other believers to shore up weaknesses that were crippling me.

Prayer is often our last resort instead of our first line of defense and/or offense. I am sad it took me so long to realize this, but glad to realize the wonderful benefits. As with so many other things, once I see the value of prayer for myself, I am even more motivated to provide it for others as well.

Study the Word

The Word of God is the ultimate Manual for life. It is of little use if not read, studied, learned, and applied. Studying the Word helps me recognize God's voice above all others, and conversely helps me recognize the enemy's voice (because it disagrees with all that God says). The Bible shows me numerous examples of people taken spiritually captive and how it happened. It also shows me valiant warriors who remained free, or became free, and accomplished much for the kingdom. Studying the Word with other believers brings unity and corporate readiness for battle. There is no substitute for the Word of God as protection from captivity. It is the only reliable navigational aid to keep the believer from wandering into a spiritual POW camp.

There are many other tips that could be inserted here, but this entire book is really a manual of sorts to avoid spiritual capture. I offer these last few tips from the final chapter of Ray Pritchard's book, *Stealth Attack*:

- Be alert
- Don't be naïve
- Be bold
- March in tight formation
- Live without fear[1]

Always a risk

Spiritual captivity will remain a real risk for any believer in Jesus Christ. It comes with the mission. The apostle Paul provided an interesting juxtaposition as a final lesson. He knew the perils of spiritual capture especially knowing how deeply he was deceived before becoming a disciple of Jesus Christ. He repeatedly warned other disciples to be on their guard – to constantly be on the lookout for false teachers who would take them captive. Paul shared his own strict vigilance with the Corinthians: "But I buffet my body, and lead it captive, lest proclaiming to others I myself might be rejected." (I Corinthians 9:27 MKJV) Basically, he takes himself captive, so other won't spiritually.

During Paul's ministry, there were several times when he was taken captive physically, but it is interesting that he uses his physical captivity to proclaim his spiritual state. In Paul's letters to the churches, he repeatedly calls himself, "a prisoner of Jesus Christ." He couldn't choose his physical state, but he was resolute that the only one he would ever be captured by is Christ. He was so captivated by Jesus Christ, no other force – physical or spiritual – could truly confine him.

Like Charlie Brown, a gaunt and tired apostle Paul finished well, jubilant not to be rescued on a physical plane, but to be "flown" to his eternal home to the truest freedom man will ever know.

DIGGING DEEPER

CHAPTER 10: TAKEN CAPTIVE

Most important "take-away" thought(s):

1. Have you ever been a spiritual POW? How did you get captured? Explain. Give at least one instance of someone else that has been, or still is, a spiritual POW.

2. What are the enemy's goals regarding captivity? How does he lure us, and what does he do to us once captive?

3. What are some examples of enemy territory in our times? How can we keep ourselves from wandering into enemy territory?

4. How does our approach to a spiritual POW change based on how they got there? (Fearless, Feeble, Foolish) Be specific.

5. What is the sin (or sins) in my life that gives the enemy the opportunity to capture me? What strategy do we have to help each other? Be specific.

THIS PAGE INTENTIONALLY LEFT BLANK

Section

2

WEAPONS

WEAPONS: A Personal Profile

Jane had lost track of how long she lay on the carpet in prayer.

Her tears had run dry and she felt something she hadn't felt in years – hope. It was time to change. She needed healing and restoration.

She had tried everything else. It was time to pursue God – for real, this time.

Looking back, the Bible has always been a part of Jane's life. She knew all the stories and had even memorized a bunch of verses in Sunday school classes. Her parents had done all they could to equip her in the Word. What went wrong?

With the help of a godly mentor, Jane spent months unpacking what set her up for spiritual ambush. It seemed to start in Jane's teen years. With an independent bent, Jane bristled against the spiritual disciplines her parents had encouraged. Christianity was really her parent's faith – but she had never truly embraced it as her own. Jane read the Bible out of obligation, but as she listened to others talk about the "inconsistencies" in the Bible, she began to read looking for loopholes. She no longer read the Bible to build faith. She was reading to fuel her doubt.

By the time she got to college, her faith was dangerously weakened. The people she thought were intellectual poked fun at the Bible, and discounted Christians as foolishly mislead and ignorant. Jane had never really learned why the Bible was true and reliable, so she had nothing to say. Soon, she distanced herself even more from her childhood faith.

Marriage and kids challenged Jane's independence. Without the Word, she now got all her cues from the culture. It bred dissatisfaction and simmering rebellion.

As Jane progressively questioned her faith, she also began to question God. As sin increased, God felt more and more distant. Her prayer life was soon non-existent. Why pray to a God that may not even exist? Besides, she had asked Him for things in the past and God seldom answered the way she wanted. Why bother?

In hindsight, Jane could see the enemy active at every turn of events in her life. Satan executed his cold, hateful, systematic strategy against her. Without the Word and prayer, she was defenseless against his schemes. She had been under attack – but out of ammo.

With God's help, never again.

"There He broke the flaming arrows, The shield and the sword and the weapons of war. Selah."
Psalm 76:3

11
THE WEAPONS OF OUR WARFARE

War and weapons go together. If one side of a conflict has no weapons, then it is not war, but just oppression and capitulation. To put it simply, in a world where evil is ever-present, weapons are necessary for good to triumph over evil – or at least for good to fight back.

Entire books have been written on the philosophy of war, so I will leave that discussion to those with heavier brains than mine. But, as a general statement on weapons, can we agree to say that war is a reality, and weapons matter in the outcome?

Types

So, what exactly are our weapons? The Department of Defense acronym DIME summarizes them: **D**iplomatic, **I**nformation operations, **M**ilitary (including physical weapons of force) and **E**conomic strategies. When we think of war, we automatically think of bullets and bombs, but unconventional weapons can also be powerful.

In our technological age, we have a growing variety of weapons at our disposal. This awareness is either scary or comforting, depending on who has the weapons and what they plan to do with them. In theory, anything can become a weapon, but for the purpose of illustration, we will review generally-accepted categories of weapons.

Conventional

Conventional weapons run the gamut from knives to fully-equipped, multimillion-dollar aircraft. There are pistols, rifles, grenade launchers, guided missiles, drones and tanks. The choice of weapon is often determined by the threat, or simply by what is available. Big threat – use a big weapon.

These are the physical weapons most combatants expect to encounter in war, and their impact is somewhat measureable.

Non-conventional

War is a complex thing with huge ramifications on a nation, its people, and resources. Diplomatic efforts seek to put all these topics on the table, determine possible outcomes, and agree on mutually-beneficial solutions. Diplomacy is a defuser, using the talk phase to its greatest advantage.

I had the rare opportunity to learn some real-world implications of diplomatic efforts during a joint-service exercise for a major command. As a reporter at a mock press conference, I interviewed an admiral involved in a volatile part of the world. He described the efforts made to build one-on-one relationships with political leaders in that area of the world– to constantly pursue relations that maintained benefits to both nations. It was fascinating to observe the finer intricacies involved in foreign policy. Diplomatic dialogue can be a weapon in the best possible way.

As stated in the communication chapter, information is power and therefore a weapon that can be used for good or evil. Economic sanctions, or provisions, are also weapons brought to potential or full-blown conflicts.

At the most basic level, parents illustrate these unconventional weapons in family conflicts. They seek to control their children's behavior, limit harm, and promote best outcomes. Parents may withhold finances if a child doesn't do chores, or financially reward a child for outstanding behavior. There are times when a child's behavior warrants an old-fashioned spanking. Sometimes it takes a diplomatic conversation, and other times it might take a little "investigative work" to gain more information or to provide resources to bring the right information to a child. It is an ongoing battle to raise healthy, responsible kids. It takes loving control, and a variety of weapons to win battles for their sakes. The same is true for nations, and the same is true for the church.

Spiritual weapons

The Bible, particularly the Old Testament, introduces us to traditional weapons of war. Ancient soldiers used swords, spears, javelins, catapults, chariots – and even the lowly slingshot. The Bible is full of battles. God's people won some and lost some.

God emphasizes the need to be ready for war. After the Israelites' long bondage in Egypt, Moses was instructed to take men 20-years and older from each tribe "who were able to go to war." A census revealed that this army numbered 603,550 men! (Numbers 1:46) At the end of the book of Numbers, the people of Israel were finally on the other side of their wilderness of sin, and needed to face the Midianites in battle. "Arm men from among you for the war, that they may go against Midian to execute the Lord's vengeance on Midian," Moses said. (Numbers 31:3)

God's battles only

Before we address spiritual weapons, it's important to note that both physical and spiritual weapons in Scripture are to be used to fight battles *the Lord brings us into* – not the ones we devise on our own. A classic example of this is found in the book of Deuteronomy. Moses recounts the time God's people were told to go up against the Amorites and God would fight the battle for them. This was God's battle at the right time. God said He would fight for them. But, the Israelites shrank back in fear and invoked God's judgment for their lack of trust and disobedience. After their rebuke, the Israelites took the battle into their own hands, even though Moses warned them that God was not among them – same battle, but no longer God's timing. In their rebellious presumption, the Israelites were crushed before their enemies, and wept bitterly in their defeat. (Deuteronomy 1: 41-46)

We need to use great care with weapons, making sure that God is directing the battle. This can be tricky because our motives are not always clear or honorable.

God is not against war. Indeed, David says in Psalm 144:1: "Blessed be the Lord, my rock, who trains my hands for war, and my fingers for battle." Isaiah prophesies: "The LORD will go forth like a warrior, He will arouse His zeal like a man of war. He will utter a shout, yes, He will raise a war cry. He will prevail against His enemies." (Is. 42:13)

All through Scripture, God's people experienced great victories when they were in His will. But, when they were not right with God, physical weapons were useless in war, and their disobedience actually incited God to open His armory and use His "weapon of indignation" against them. (Jeremiah 50:25) It can be a scary thing to consider that God has an armory – or it can be the most comforting knowledge. It just depends on where we are in our relationship to God.

The ultimate "spiritual just war" is one that God leads, and is consistent with His purposes and timing.

God's battles – God's weapons

We also lose so many battles because, even if it is a battle that God calls us to fight, we tend to fight our way instead of his. That's why Paul tells the Corinthians that "the weapons of our warfare are not carnal, but mighty through God to the pulling down of strongholds." (II Corinthians 10:4) This verse reveals much about weapons and why we use them. It would appear, from Paul's exhortation that our default choice of weapons is carnal – fleshly, by sight, in our own strength and human reasoning. In many of our battles, we are reactionary. We've been hurt or threatened in some way, and we lash out, cause physical harm, or manipulate by withdrawal.

The main reason for most of our incorrect reactions is that we believe our battle is with people. The verse does not say "to the pulling down of people." Paul revisits this theme with the Ephesians. In the often-quoted chapter six of Ephesians, Paul says, "for our struggle is not against flesh and blood, but against the rulers, against the powers, against the world forces of this darkness, against the spiritual forces of wickedness in the heavenly places." (6:12) When we focus on people as our primary adversary, we fail to recognize the deception and lies behind the conflict. We can't help but fight the wrong way because we are focused on the wrong target.

It helps me to think of people sometimes like marionettes. They are the ones doing the hurtful actions, but someone else is actually pulling the strings. Spiritual warfare is not physical warfare. How easy to forget that pivotal point!

Personal weapons assessment

Fortunately, there are helpful lists in Scripture that help me assess my involvement in spiritual battle – and my choice of weapons. I find two lists particularly helpful because they reveal when my weapons have become carnal.

Ecclesiastes 9:18 says that "wisdom is better than weapons of war…" but this presents a choice between carnal ideas and spiritual wisdom. The book of James gives the contrast between godly wisdom and earthly wisdom. If I have bitter jealousy and strife in my heart, and glory and lie against the truth, James 3:15 tells me that this wisdom is "earthly, sensual, devilish." By contrast, wisdom from above (or godly wisdom) is "first pure, peaceable, gentle, easy to be entreated, full of mercy and good fruits, without partiality and without hypocrisy."

May I be "exhibit A" for a moment? God has caused me to walk through much of the material for this book over a period of several years – to write from experience rather than theory. I remember a particular argument with my 20-something daughter a few years ago. I don't remember the topic, but I do remember that it got very heated. Tempers flared, voices rose, and feelings were hurt. As I stomped away from the tirade, my heart was arrested by the wisdom lists in the book of James. I wasn't very peaceable, definitely not gentle, and I generally failed to meet any of the other godly wisdom criteria. I realized that I wasn't fighting my daughter, but there was much more going on. My weapons were carnal, and I lost sight of the strongholds that needed to be pulled down.

In a rare moment of instantaneous obedience, I turned back to my daughter and confessed my sin. I shared my "wisdom list" and admitted that I had not been gentle, or any of the other things. I asked her if we could start over with the right criteria. Instantly, things changed. I experienced a clear victory in spiritual warfare that day. Unity, harmony and peace were restored. Wisdom won.

The second helpful list is found in Galatians where Paul contrasts the works of the flesh (carnal weapons) with the fruit of the Spirit (spiritual weapons). The works of the flesh are: "adultery, fornication, uncleanness, lustfulness, idolatry, sorcery, hatreds, fightings, jealousies, angers, rivalries, divisions, heresies, envying, murders, drunkenness, and revelings." Imagine how battles flare when our weapons are carnal or fleshly like these. Paul then lists a contrasting set of criteria. Galatians 5:22-23 lists the fruit of the Spirit as: love, joy, peace, long-suffering, kindness, goodness, faith, meekness, and self-control." Now, imagine the outcome of battles with these spiritual weapons. Likely, a much better outcome. These lists continue to be an effective diagnostic tool to pick the right weapons in my daily battles.

God's ways are not our ways

God's ways are not our ways. Sometimes they are downright odd.

In one instance, God has musicians lead armies into war (Jehosophat). In another instance, God's people took the great city of Jericho by marching around it in silence seven times, and then sounding trumpets. The great walls crumbled and the city was theirs for the taking. Other times, God's people were just told to stand and watch while God brought complete confusion to the enemy. God is not limited in any way when it comes to war, but we are when we chose our own way instead of His.

Even though God is not always predictable, He does recommend some primary spiritual weapons that we should use often. By far, the most common spiritual weapons in Scripture are prayer, fasting, and the Word of God.

Prayer

Many a battle has been lost because of lack of prayer. As mentioned in the communications chapter, prayer brings power to the fight – air power. There is a story tucked away in the book of Judges (19-20) that shows the progression of battle when spiritual weapons are added. In a rather bazaar beginning, a concubine is abused and left for dead on the doorstep of a Levite. The woman is cut into pieces, and pieces are sent to each of the 12 tribes to highlight the crime and request 10 percent of soldiers from each tribe to battle the perpetrators – the sons of Belial. Four hundred thousand men of Israel armed for war go up against 26,700 Benjamites. False confidence and no spiritual weapons bring about a sound defeat in round one of the battle. Bruised and shaken, the Israelite soldiers add prayer to their spiritual arsenal and are once again routed in battle. Finally, battered and humbled, they cry out to God in prayer, fasting and offerings. Finally, they are adequately prepared for war and they soundly defeat the enemy.

Fasting

Fasting is simply defined: "to abstain from food, or to eat sparingly or to abstain from some foods."[1] Jentezen Franklin describes biblical fasting as "refraining from food for a spiritual purpose," and says that fasting has always been a normal part of a relationship with God.[2]

Johosaphat fasted when facing battle in II Chronicles 20:3, and it brought God's favor and fight to the war. Nehemiah was a cupbearer to King Cyrus when he learned that Jerusalem was in shambles. "When I heard these words, I sat down and wept and mourned for days; and I was fasting and praying before the God of heaven," says Nehemiah in 1:4. He poured his heart out before they Lord, and God supernaturally gives him full passage, provision and protection to return to Jerusalem to rebuild the wall. When the Jews faced national extermination through wicked Haman, Esther proclaimed a fast. (Esther 4:16) Prayer and fasting opened a way for Queen Esther to speak to the king, and through a bazaar twist of events, Haman was hung and the Jews are saved.

In Scripture, even unbelievers saw the value of fasting. Wicked Jezebel called for a fast in I Kings 21:9, and the king of Nineveh proclaimed the most severe fast in the Bible that included even the animals in Jonah, chapter 4.

There were also counterfeit fasts done with wrong motives that brought nothing to the fight. Isaiah warned the Israelites that they "fast for contention and strife and to strike with a wicked fist." (Isa. 58:4) Then Isaiah went on to describe activities we generally do not associate with fasting like "loosening the bonds of wickedness, setting the oppressed free, feeding the hungry, inviting the homeless poor into your house, and clothing the naked." (verses 5-6) When fasting is done right, Isaiah tells them that "the glory of the Lord will be your rear guard." (v.8)

While I don't pretend to understand the full impact of fasting, there is something powerful about denying the desires of the flesh to access more of God. Personal testimonies (and biblical examples) link fasting to greater spiritual power, focus, ability to hear God more clearly, authority in the supernatural realm – and victory. Jentezen uses Paul (Acts 9), and Peter (Acts 10) as examples of how fasting brings fresh vision and clear purpose to these men. A lack of fasting may be a contributing factor as to why so many Christians live weak lives of faith.

Jentezen warns that our fasting must be authentic, and highlights two other primary weapons to the fasting process. "Without being combined with prayer and the Word, fasting is little more than dieting," Jentezen writes.[3]

Sword of the Spirit – the Word of God

The sword is the most common weapon in biblical times, and the sword of the Spirit is the most common spiritual weapon as well. The "sword of the Spirit" is the Word of God. The outstanding power of this weapon is grounded in Jesus Christ Himself. John 1:1 says, "In the beginning was the Word, and the Word was with God, and the Word was God."

The Word of God is more than merely a manual for war. It manifests God in all His truth and glory. It shows us the amazing work of the Father, Son, and Holy Spirit on behalf of mankind. It shows us His plan from beginning to end, how He won our victory on the cross, and how we find victory in our own battles. Two verses link the Word to our victory: "...faith comes by hearing and hearing by the Word of Christ" (Romans 10:17); and "...this is the victory that overcomes the world, our faith." (1 John 5:4b)

This makes perfect sense. Since the enemy is a liar and the father of lies, his greatest weapon is lies. Thus the truth of God's word would be the best counter weapon. Every single spiritual battle must be fought with Scripture.

Consider the essence of most spiritual battles. Imagine that someone is shooting at you. You have a gun, but it is useless because you have no ammunition. As a result, you have several choices – none of them good. You can retreat, hide, get wounded, or die. If you're fortunate, maybe someone else has ammunition and is willing to fire back for you. This is the picture of too many believers who own a Bible, but aren't trained to use it. When the enemy starts shooting lies at them, they are unable to "discharge their weapon" to declare particular Scripture to deflect the lie. They have not learned Scripture to build the shield of faith detailed in Ephesians 6.

When applied strategically, the Word becomes active and powerful. It always is. We just don't train with it enough to realize what an amazing weapon we have at our disposal.

Jesus models this weapon with the greatest skill. In Matthew 4, Jesus was led into the wilderness to be tempted by the devil. Jesus had fasted for 40 days and was hungry. Capitalizing on His "weakness," the devil began a three-prong assault. In each attack, Jesus simply said, "it is written" and then fired a Scriptural volley specifically aimed at the particular attack. Jesus didn't dialogue with Satan, but simply responded with the truth of the Word. Boom. Done. Verse 11 says, "The devil left Him and angels came to minister to Him."

There are a few other "weapons" that influence our level of authority in battle: love and obedience.

Love

Love is not a word commonly associated with war, but in spiritual warfare, it is a central principle. Even though it seems counterintuitive, the believer in Jesus Christ successfully battles only from the vantage point of love. It is love for God that prompts us to submit fully to His authority to gain access to His power for battles, but it is also love for God and others that provokes us to fight.

I used to think that hate was the opposite of love, but both hate and love invest a great deal of emotion. The true opposite of love is apathy. We love so little, we just don't care. It saddens me deeply to see so many struggling Christians, ambushed by the enemy on a regular basis, and no one battling for them. Their countenance is filled with pain. They are bleeding out spiritually, but we just want to give them a hug and a band-aid and send them on their way. Spiritual warfare is "messy ministry," but love demands our involvement.

In the familiar John 3:16 passage, we see that God so loved the world that He gave His Son. Love prompted the Father to send the Son, and the Son to send the Spirit – all for us. He died for us while we were still His enemies (Romans 5:10), which leads us to the most challenging part of spiritual warfare: God commands us to love our enemies.

In both Matthew (5:44) and Luke (6:27), God says, "But I say to you, love your enemies..." In Matthew he adds that we should pray for those who persecute us, and Luke adds that we should do good to those who hate us. Really? That seems impossible. Yup. That is the nature of spiritual warfare. It is impossible in the natural, so it propels us to God for the resources for supernatural battle.

While loving our enemies seems out-of-place in a conversation on war, I have witnessed the greatest spiritual victories when this advice is heeded. In our daily battles, we typically see people as our enemies, and so ignore the real enemy behind the battle. By loving our enemies, we focus on the real enemy – Satan. I have seen people injured by divorce, betrayal, rejection, abandonment, and other hateful behaviors. When the injured party stews in their resentment, it does nothing to the perpetrator, but it destroys the injured – adding manifold pain to the original injury. I have seen believers wither and die spiritually from a wounded heart that fails to love their enemy. In contrast, I have seen victims of the worst possible circum-stances remain tender, submitting to God's command to love and forgive. I am in awe of the strength they attain when they choose love over resentment – no matter how warranted their bitterness might be.

Loving our enemies does not release them from the responsibilities of their actions, nor does it release us from the responsibility to battle for them. Loving our enemies keeps us right with God, rational, and spiritually strong for the battles ahead. It also allows us to fight our enemy with greater wisdom.

Lastly, love is the weapon our enemy least expects us to use in war. We live in a fallen world full of pain and dysfunction. People are mean so we're used to meanness. We have built up defenses against all types of ill treatment. But, I've yet to meet a person with a strong defense against love. They simply haven't been loved enough to build one.

A number of years ago, there was one person that was a regular part of my life who made me miserable with his rude, proud, thoughtless behavior. We were at a stalemate for years, but when a series of events left this person in need, God challenged my injured heart to love. A loving gesture broke through his defenses. Tears flowed as he hugged me and said, "I don't deserve this, especially from you." Love breaks down the toughest opponent; they just don't know what to do with it.

Obedience

Obedience is not actually a weapon, but is listed here because of its importance in accessing victory through Jesus Christ and the Holy Spirit. Weapons provide fire power in a war, and our obedience is vital to accessing the power of God in spiritual warfare.

A few pages back we looked at the Word of God as a weapon of great force, and looked at I John 5:5 to learn that our victory comes from faith. The few verses before verse 5 bring out love and obedience as factors involved with faith and victory. Verses 1-4 say that if we love God, we keep His commandments. If we don't, we don't love Him, which puts us in the wrong motive for battle. Earlier in I John 2:3-4, John gives clarity between obedience and truth: "By this we know that we have come to know Him, if we keep His commandments. The one who says, 'I have come to know Him,' and does not keep His commandments is a liar, and the truth is not in him..." All spiritual battles are waged for truth with truth. Disobedience muddies the truth and brings confusion to the battle – which is exactly the weapon the enemy uses.

Obedience keeps us in truth, but it also aligns us with God's favor in the fight. The Old Testament is filled with if-then statements. If we obey, God helps us. If we disobey, God is not fighting for us, but actually may fight against us. Leviticus 26 gives frightening clarity to these polar opposites. "If you keep my statutes and walk in my commandments," God says that He will bless His people agriculturally, give them peace, protect them from wild animals and help them with their enemies (v.3-8). "But, if you do not obey Me and do not carry out all these commandments..." God promises to appoint sudden terrors, disease, stolen crops, and failure in war. (v.14-16) Listen to these sober warnings: "I will set my face against you so that you will be struck down before your enemies; and those who hate you will rule over you, and you will flee when no one is pursuing you." (v.17) God gives clear parameters for victorious living and it is rooted in obedience. Sadly, God's people rejected His statutes repeatedly and suffered greatly as a result. If anyone is tempted to test this truth, a read through the Old Testament confirms that God kept His word.

Obedience is important in spiritual warfare for one more reason: it maximizes the power of the Holy Spirit in us. When Jesus was on the earth, He attributed His power to the Holy Spirit. When He left the earth, He told His followers to wait for the Holy Spirit saying, "But, you will receive power when the Holy Spirit has come upon you..." (Acts 1:8) Wait they did, and when the Holy Spirit descended on them, a group of terrified believers were transformed into fearless warriors, many of whom ended their lives as martyrs. Paul prays for believers to have the same Holy-Spirit transformation. He prays "that He would grant you, according to the riches of His glory, to be strengthened with power through His Spirit in the inner man." (Eph. 3:16)

The Holy Spirit is vital for strength in spiritual warfare, but we can quench or grieve the Holy Spirit through our disobedience. When that happens, we are like Samson in the Old Testament. After enjoying extraordinary strength for years, Samson suffered defeat through his own carelessness and lust. Just after his fateful haircut, Judges 16:20-21 records the saddest statement. The "Philistine alarm" went off again like before, and Samson "awoke from his sleep and said, 'I will go out as at other times and shake myself free.' But he did not know that the Lord had departed from him. Then the Philistines seized him and gouged out his eyes..."

The prophet Zechariah speaks to Zerubbabel about the power of the Holy Spirit: "This is the word of the LORD to Zerubbabel saying, 'Not by might, nor by power, but by My Spirit,' says the LORD of hosts." (4:6) The Holy Spirit is the big guns of spiritual warfare, and our obedience either lets them roar, or our disobedience silences them.

After all this talk about weapons, what are they for?

Purpose

People use weapons for all kinds of reasons – some good, some bad. Our headline news is filled with examples where weapons are used inappropriately.

Because these events get most of the press attention, much of society has lost track of the true value of weapons – and their more noble purposes. It is precisely because of the malicious use of weapons that the right uses are all the more necessary.

We can unknowingly carry this weapons perspective into our spiritual battles. We can view war and weapons in such a negative way that we naively live our faith unarmed, and therefore without power or victory. Satan is a reality in our world, and evil dwells in us and others. Just as in the physical realm, if we don't believe in carrying weapons, it doesn't stop others from having them, and possibly using them for evil intent. Ignoring evil doesn't make it go away – it allows it to proliferate.

We need to be armed and ready. I love the picture painted in the book of Nehemiah. He returns from exile to Jerusalem with a burden to repair the walls around the broken, battered city. Their enemies do not want them to complete the wall. As a brilliant leader, Nehemiah kept his eyes fixed on the mission, but faced the enemy threat head-on. "All of them conspired together to come and fight against Jerusalem and to cause a great disturbance in it. But we prayed to our God, and because of them we set up a guard against them day and night." (Nehemiah 4: 8-9)

Nehemiah understood the value of weapons – to avoid war – and get the job done. I love this next part: "From that day on, half of my servants carried on the work while half of them held the spear, the shields, the bows and the breastplates, and the captains were behind the whole house of Judah. Those who were rebuilding the wall and those who carried burdens took their load *with one hand doing the work and the other holding a weapon*. As for the builders, each wore his sword at his side as he built..." (4:16-18)

Nehemiah was no warmonger. He was not looking for war, but he was looking to build. Weapons were the necessary deterrent so the enemy would not cause them to fail in their mission. We have a mission as believers. Weapons are vital to our warfare, our welfare, and the completion of our mission.

So, if weapons can be used for good, what are some of those good uses?

Protection

If evil people have weapons (whether gained legally or illegally) then good people must have weapons to protect themselves. Consider the father protecting his family against intruders, a city protecting the people from criminals, and a nation protecting its citizens against harmful threats through military force. All these are impossible without weapons in the hands of good people with noble intent.

Our spiritual warfare must also have noble intent— and not be self-serving. Who or what are we supposed to be protecting? Our primary battle is for our faith. The tiny book of Jude warns us to contend for our faith, and then lists the various types of ungodly attacks that we have to fight. Hebrews reminds us that "without faith it is impossible to please God," (Hebrews 11:6) so we must protect it at all costs. If our faith is so important, then battling for the faith of others is a close second. I have interviewed many young people who have wandered from their faith into some very dangerous territory. When they look back on their fall from faith, they will often share that they wish someone had chased them. I am always surprised to hear that because we are so influenced by our "mind-your-own-business" culture. We should battle to protect our family – especially when it comes to faith issues.

Control and containment

Weapons are also used to control and contain evil. Imagine a prison guard with no weapon against hundreds of hardened criminals. Evil people must be controlled and contained to prevent them from escaping to do more harm. When known terrorists are hunted down, weapons are used to keep them subdued and stripped of weapons they used to inflict deadly harm.

We see control as a mostly negative word because of "control freaks" we have encountered, but control is a good thing. We should have self-control so we don't behave in a harmful manner. Control yields a power that should be governed by good – otherwise control becomes yet another threat to be opposed.

Probably the most difficult thing we need to control in spiritual warfare is ourselves. Paul understood that with great clarity. He says: "but I discipline my body and make it my slave, so that, after I have preached to others, I myself will not be disqualified." (I Corinthians 9:27) We fight to control evil in our churches. The Bible teaches many disciplinary methods to control and contain evil within the church. Paul and Peter speak often in their epistles about controlling and containing false teachers among them.

True spiritual warfare is always aligns with what God protects, controls, etc.

Rescue

Rescue is necessary when protection has either been absent or has failed. Consider the person currently in the hold of evil and needing rescue. Weapons are used to overpower the enemy holding the captive, and also used to safely remove them from danger. Evil people do bad things – and don't generally give up without a fight. A fight necessitates weapons in order to win. Anyone who has been rescued is thankful that the good guys had weapons – and used them for good.

Rescue is something not often preached in the church. We regularly hear that God has rescued us through His Son Jesus Christ, but we are rarely trained in how to rescue each other. In the tiny book of Jude, Jude not only warns us to contend for our faith, but also addresses rescue. Jude tells us to "keep ourselves in the love of God, and have mercy on some who are doubting, save others, snatching them out of the fire; and on some have mercy with fear, hating even the garment polluted by the flesh." (1:23)

Save others. The word "snatch" is a powerful word that suggests strength and urgency. Matthew 18 also gives us good guidelines for spiritual rescue: If your brother sins, go and show him his fault in private; if he listens to you, you have won your brother." (18:15) Matthew continues and says that if the person doesn't listen to you, take one or two witnesses with you to be sure the facts are straight, and for a stronger rescue. Interestingly, Galatians 1:6 says that "you which are spiritual" should do this. Our faith must be firm before we seek to rescue others. Do we have the proverbial log in our own eye while we seek to rescue another with a mere mote?

Why are we so hesitant to rescue a falling brother? One valid reason may be that "vigilante-Christians" often do such a poor job of rescue. They are "spiritual police" ever on the lookout, but their efforts are not rooted in love, so they alienate the very ones they try to rescue.

Another reason we may not pursue spiritual rescue is that we fear we may be wrong, or that we don't know how to do it right. "What if I hurt them?" we say. This is the visual that I have presented to different audiences. I ask, "What if you were safely in the trench, and you saw a buddy injured on the field in front of you – he's bleeding out and likely in shock – would you leave the safety of the trench to rescue him?"

"Yes," they say.

"What if I break his arm getting him to the safety of the trench?" I ask.

"Do it anyway," they say.

"Really?"

"Yes! It's a matter of life or death. You may break his arm but you will save his life."

They are right. Although it's easy to figure out in physical warfare, it's not as easy in spiritual situations.

Survival

Finally, weapons are necessary for survival. People find themselves in different situations where they must kill to survive. It may be an "either-him-or-me" situation, or it may simply be hunting for food to survive. Either way, survival presents a legitimate purpose for weapons.

We need spiritual weapons if we are to survive in our own faith. The enemy, Satan, seeks to disarm us. He gets us to think the Bible is boring and irrelevant, gets us too busy for prayer, too comfortable for fasting, and too noisy for quiet and solitude. Without our weapons for spiritual warfare, we are beaten to a pulp and left in a faithless gutter with only distant memories of Jesus.

Just like the oxygen masks on the commercial aircraft, we must apply our masks first, then assist those around us. The same is true spiritually, and spiritual survival is impossible without the conscientious use of our weapons of warfare.

Summary

In Tim Keller's podcast, "Spiritual Warfare," he speaks about the proximity of evil. He says the hands are already around your throat by the time you know evil is upon you. Keller says that we have to fight, but in the strength of the Lord, and not in our own might.

I really appreciate his thoughts as he contrasts Christ's strength with Satan's strength because he nails the paradox of this whole chapter. Spiritual warfare is often counterintuitive.

"Christ's strength is utterly different than Satan's," he explains. Keller poses the "weak strength" of Christ. "He won by losing; He triumphed by serving," says Keller. "Jesus suffered, served, surrendered... It was 'My life for you' warfare."[4]

Satan's strength, according to Keller, is direct, and about power and control. Satan's approach is "your life for me." That's how we often try to fight spiritual warfare, and it doesn't work.

Keller cites Paul in II Corinthians 13:4: "For indeed he was crucified because of weakness, yet He lives because of the power of God. For we also are weak in Him, yet we will live with Him because of the power of God directed toward you."

"Strength and weakness live together in your heart," says Keller, "It takes incredible strength to be weak."[5]

Keller summarizes a spiritual soldier well. Because of who Jesus is, we are humbled. Because of what Jesus did, we are confident. We should take up our weapons with humility and confidence, willing to do a radically different warfare that typifies Jesus' approach of "my life for you."

CHAPTER 11: THE WEAPONS OF OUR WARFARE

Most important "take-away" thought(s):

1. Have you ever been in a spiritual battle that God had not called you to fight? What happened? What did you learn?

2. Turn to the list of godly wisdom traits in James 3:17-18. Rate yourself according to the list. Are you armed with true wisdom? Explain your assessment.

3. Of prayer, fasting, use of the Word, love, and obedience – with which "weapon" are you best trained? Which "weapon" needs further training?

4. Give specific instances where you would use spiritual weapons for: protection, control and containment, or rescue.

5. Jesus battled with a "my life for you" mentality. What is our default mode of battle typically? How can we change the default?

"The world is passing away, and also its lusts; but the one who does the will of God lives forever."
1 John 2:17

12
SHOOTING AT THE RIGHT TARGETS

Just before 8 a.m. on December 7, 1941, the first bomb dropped on Pearl Harbor. The devastating attack lasted two hours. Casualty assessments began at 10:30 a.m. Japan had hit the United States in a very successful, surprise attack.[1]

We were suddenly at war.

Japan was our enemy, but to embark on a successful war effort, the United States military had to define specific targets. Without clear targets for the right purpose, our weapons could hurt innocent people. We needed to target the assets that gave Japan the capacity to fight: ammunition stores, strategic leaders, communication centers, aircraft, naval resources, etc.

We have to ask: "what/who are you going after?" and "why?" Military targets are selected to neutralize the enemy's ability to wage war, to weaken their defenses, and eliminate the threat by causing them to surrender.

Without clear targets, war efforts become wasteful and weakened – wearing us out, rather than the enemy. As stated in Chapter 4, the military spends copious amounts of time on strategy – and strategy necessitates defining clear targets.

Spiritual targets

Yet, when it comes to spiritual warfare, we stumble around after surprise attacks wondering what just happened. We either lash out at people, or lash out at ourselves for being so stupid. Either approach makes the situation worse and tends to give more ground to the real enemy.

We've learned about using the right weapons. Now we need to learn to fight the right targets. Our primary verse is 2 Corinthians 10:4: "for the weapons of our warfare are not carnal, but mighty through God to the pulling down of strongholds" (KJV). Chapter 12 addressed the first part of this verse – carnal versus spiritual weapons. The second half of the verse brings us to the topic of targets.

Strongholds

Paul defines targets as strongholds. I searched commentaries to understand the theological ramifications of the word "stronghold" but instead was spiritually slapped on the side of the head with the simplicity of the word itself. A stronghold is whatever has a strong hold on us. Duh.

The dictionary offers similar simplicity, but adds a few nuances: "a fortified place, a place of security or survival, a place dominated by a particular group or marked by a particular characteristic."[2]

Before we explore strongholds, we need to re-establish the battle arena for spiritual warfare. The battlefield is the mind. Paul establishes this context in verse 5 of 2 Corinthians 10 when he introduces the topic of strongholds: "pulling down *imaginations* and every high thing that exalts itself against the knowledge of God, and bringing into captivity every *thought* unto the obedience of Christ." The mind is the gateway to the soul, and where our faith resides, so our thought life is where the battle rages.

In the many messages I have heard on this verse, one definition of stronghold has been used the most. Strongholds are any patterns of thinking that run contrary to the Word of God – the strongest ones usually being the ones formed before a believer comes to a saving knowledge of Jesus Christ. Remember our definition nuances? Our mental strongholds are "a place dominated by a particular group." When our thoughts are not dominated by God (Let this mind be in you which is in Christ Jesus, Philippians 2:5), then they are dominated by Satan. There are only two kingdoms that vie for mental domination, God's or Satan's. Webster inadvertently reinforces this by identifying a stronghold as "a place of security or survival." When our mind is "stayed on Christ" (Isaiah 26:3), we are in a place of spiritual security. In a very practical way, God is truly our High Tower (Psalm 18:2), and our "very present Help in time of need." (Psalm 46:1) When our mind is dominated by the evil one, life becomes a place of desperate survival rather than victory in Christ.

Imaginations

To apply "pulling down imaginations," I have to ask myself, "What do I allow myself to imagine?" What do I think about, especially in my unguarded moments? In a fallen world, my mind is too carnal to operate unrestricted. It needs clear boundaries. II Corinthians 4:5 gives us the boundary lines: "the knowledge of God."

Due diligence in spiritual warfare requires us to take every thought captive unto the obedience of Christ – which indicates that the Word of God is our only reliable boundary. Does a thought align with Scripture or go against Scripture? I can't cast down that which is against Scripture if I don't know Scripture.

As stated repeatedly, spiritual warfare is about who gets to be in control. Disobedience, or sin, feeds strongholds and cedes control to the enemy. David learned this by painful experience. Although God's man, he succumbed to sexual temptation with Bathsheba, murdered Uriah, and was ultimately a man "with bloody hands" who was not allowed to build God's temple. To know David's past is to appreciate the wisdom he offers in Psalm 119:10-11: "With all my heart I have sought You; do not let me wander from Your Commandments. *I have hidden Your Word in my heart, so that I might not sin against You.*" (MKJV)

Spiritual thinking always precedes spiritual living. The battle begins in the mind, and is won or lost there.

Our character and actions reveal who fuels our thinking – God or Satan. If there's any doubt about what dominates our thinking at any given time, check out the fruit of the Spirit versus the works of the flesh in Galatians 5 for a quick diagnosis. It has pointed out my errors more times than I care to admit.

So, if our battlefield is our mind, and strongholds are our primary target, where do these strongholds hide? Strongholds originate in the world, the flesh (our carnal side), and the devil. All spiritual attacks originate in one of these arenas; therefore, in spiritual warfare we have a tri-fold target.

The World

As a believer, when I saw the "world" as a threat to my faith – and therefore a target in my battle – it was too general a term to be effective. I was "in the world" but not "of the world." (John 15:19) What in the world did that mean? How could I live in the world and fight against it at the same time?

The Greek word for world is "kosmos."[3] Besides meaning "world or universe," it means "something ordered, or an ordered system."[4] The world as our target is not the physical world, or nature. It is a world system that is currently under the God-allowed, limited rule of Satan.

When Satan tempts Jesus, he offers Jesus all the kingdoms He can see if Jesus will bow down and worship Satan. Elsewhere, Satan is called "the prince and power of the air." When Ephesians 6 says we wrestle against principalities and rulers in high places, it speaks of the spiritual power of Satan and his demons on the earth. The world system as we know it is a system heavily influenced by evil. As we look around at all the violence and pain, we have to acknowledge that a kingdom other than God's is exerting authority on a regular basis.

Believers in Jesus Christ should not be overly preoccupied with demons, but they *should* be more discerning, able to test people and situations. To be at the proper level of alertness, we should be in the habit of evaluating everything through the wisdom of the Word and guidance of the Holy Spirit. Trained soldiers are not paranoid, but have learned that a good dose of caution can save their lives.

I was trained to do this in the military, but lacked similar training in the faith arena – until about 10 years ago.

Worldview thinking

In an effort to prepare my daughter for the spiritual rigors of secular college, I stumbled upon a curriculum that compared six major worldviews that influence Western thought.5 By "racking and stacking" worldviews side-by-side in the areas of theology, philosophy, biology, psychology, sociology, law, ethics, economics, history, and politics, I could better understand – and recognize – the worldviews that run contrary to a biblical worldview. After that year of study (and teaching the course for four more years), I could better discern between the world versus the Word. By looking at the foundations of different beliefs, I am better able to recognize when my thinking has strayed from my biblical worldview.

By studying various worldviews, I see the things of the world in a different light. Movies, music and media all contain content that merit scrutiny. There is a message in all media. What should I accept, and what should I reject?

For example, how do sitcoms portray the family (sociology)? What values do they promote (ethics)? How do they present mankind – as an animal, or made in the image of God (psychology)? What is their basis for science (biology)? What is their position on truth (philosophy)? Once we pinpoint world system strategies, we better develop counterstrategies to protect ourselves from mental manipulation.

Practical training

Teaching comparative worldviews gave me (and my students) another practical way to target the world system. My students and I would start by picking a topic, such as gambling, same-sex marriage, etc., and determine what the world said about it. Then, we determined what God's Word said about it, including specific Scriptures. It was practical training in strategic use of the Word in warfare.

What shocked me as I did this activity was how much of my thinking had been formed by the world and not by the Word. When I did not intentionally search the Scriptures to learn God's truth on current topics, I often defaulted into the world's thinking – without even realizing it. The more I did these activities with high school students; the more I realized that few Christians take the time to sharpen their biblical discernment on the issues of our day – and thus lose their place at the table of cultural debate. They are swept up in the cultural current instead of standing strong in biblical truth.

We are told in I Peter 3:15 to be ready to give a reason (or an answer) for our faith to anyone that asks, with meekness. The reason for our faith is Jesus Christ, but the implications of Jesus Christ filter into every area of life. He's not just the "reason for the season" at Christmas, but His Word brings reason to the thorny and often confusing issues of our day.

Sloppy thinking

When I wasn't teaching worldview classes, I noticed my own thinking and training start to get sloppy. In the military, I needed to keep training to stay sharp and ready; the same is true spiritually. Sloppy thinking puts me at greater risk of being a target instead of offensively pursuing targets that can harm me.

Maybe a quick personal example will clarify this. I had let down my guard for two hours – and the world system snuck in.

I watched the movie, "Safe Haven," about a beautiful young woman fleeing an abusive marriage to a psychotic, alcoholic police officer. While she is hiding out in an idyllic North Carolina harbor town, a handsome young widower befriends her. His tenderness wins her trust. She subsequently succumbs to a sexual relationship with him. My heart was moved by the plight of this woman, and I rejoiced that she found a "good" man who treated her right. I was rooting for this poor woman until the end, when her hostile husband was killed, and she lived happily ever after with the good guy. The damsel in distress is rescued – a fairy tale ending.

The next morning, the initial emotion of the movie had subsided. As I processed the movie as part of a world system that warranted scrutiny, biblical truth pulled back the curtain and revealed a fake wizard pulling the levers of lies. I was shocked at how many false messages I had embraced. Because the main character was portrayed as a victim, I inadvertently gave her a pass on her immoral behavior. I did the same with the more "virtuous" young widower. He was portrayed as tender and loving, but used her for sexual satisfaction without a marriage commitment.

The scrutiny mopped up my sloppy thinking and prompted the proper battle against the right target. It exposed all the subtle moral, psychological, sociological and theological mindsets in the movie that stood in stark contrast to what the Bible teaches.

This battle of the world system rages continually against our heart, more strategically than ever before. Ravi Zacharias evaluates this threat in his message, "Mind Games in a World of Images." He says technology has made images so graphic that they provoke powerful emotional conclusions without first passing through the filter of the intellect. Zacharias says that we are meant to see through the eyes with the intellect. The power of the media, he says, has us see with the eyes, devoid of the intellect.

Malcolm Gladwell comes to similar conclusions in his book, *Blink*. It is a fascinating read and explores how many conclusions we come to "in the blink of an eye." According to Gladwell, much of our thinking occurs instantaneously through visual influences we are unaware are there. Advertisers make full use of these concepts to get us to buy their products, but the world system uses them as well to shape our thinking – and in ways we are unaware.

There are so many ways we are mentally manipulated. It takes training to recognize and avoid them.

God's way – God's blessings

The world system presents a constant threat to every believer, and is therefore a constant target to watch for. It is also a theme visited throughout Scripture. God's people lapsed into the world system over and over, and it always got them into trouble.

The first five books of the Bible display this recurring cycle. God loves His people and gives them parameters for living so they can prosper under His care, but they get lured away by the world system and they live in defeat and oppression. Their oppression brings them to repentance. They begin to live under God's authority and His blessings, but then the cycle back to the world system begins again.

I am most impressed with Exodus, Leviticus, Numbers and Deuteronomy to illustrate our fight against the world system. God delivers His people from 400 years of cruel oppression in Egypt to lead them into the Promised Land He pledged to them through a covenant with Abraham. Moses musters God's people by Mt. Sinai and teaches them a clear set of rules to govern every aspect of life – so they can flourish in the land God wants to give them.

God, know the threats His people will face, so He gives them a complete set of boundaries to protect them from internal conflict and external oppression. At the beginning of one of the most graphic chapters in the Bible, God sets the contrast between how He wants them to live, and what the world system presents as choices. "You shall not do what is done in the land of Egypt where you lived, nor are you to do what is done in the land of Canaan where I am bringing you; you shall not walk in their statutes." (Leviticus 18:3)

God knew the culture they came out of, and the culture they would soon be driving out, so He gave ample warnings and training.

Moses gives refresher training some 40 years later as God's people are at the border of the Promised Land in the book of Deuteronomy. Moses is like the loving grandfather giving his children instruction, knowing he won't be with them when they face temptations. In Deuteronomy 12, Moses tells them to "carefully observe" God's statutes. Four times in one chapter, Moses tells them to "be careful." He tells them to "be sure," and to "beware." Moses had watched God's people fail and face the consequences, so he sets clear contrasts before them: do it God's way and you'll be blessed; go against God's way and you'll suffer.

The world system ravages us, but it also lures us to "other gods." Moses communicates God's thoughts on this in Deuteronomy 13. They are to be on their guard against other gods – even if a prophet lures them through signs and wonders. An entire chapter is devoted to this warning. Verse 13 says that worthless men have gone out from among them and seduced the inhabitants of the city, saying, "Let us go and serve other gods." Verse 14 prompts us to careful thinking: "...then you shall investigate and search out and inquire thoroughly."

God is so serious about our battle against the world system (and the other gods it represents) that He tells them to kill the false prophets. As New Testament believers, we aren't instructed to kill those peddling other gods, but, at the very least, we should recognize them and avoid their seduction. The apostle Paul predicts that things will get worse as time progresses. He warns Timothy: "But the Spirit expressly says that in the latter times some shall depart from the faith, giving heed to seducing spirits and teachings of demons...." (I Timothy 4:1 MKJV)

The world system is clearly a threat – and a target.

The flesh

"The flesh" is a Christian term that can sound very weird. It brings to mind cannibalistic images. What exactly does it mean? In the context of threats and targets, the flesh is simply the fallen, unregenerate part of our being that defaults to sin. God created man with body, soul and spirit. In the process of salvation, the spirit is regenerated, but the body remains fallen. The life of the believer is plagued by an ongoing battle between the renewed spirit and the fallen flesh.

The apostle Paul wrote extensively about this battle, especially in the book of Romans. Paul recognizes the godly desires in his spirit, but sees his flesh as an enemy to those desires. He says: "For the good that I want, I do not do, but I practice the very evil that I do not want. Paul adds: "but I see a different law in the members of my body, waging war against the law of my mind and making me a prisoner of the law of sin which is in my members." (7:19, 23)

Thankfully, Romans 8 presents a clear choice, and the power to win the battle over the flesh. In verses 5-6, Paul gives the choice: "But those who are according to the flesh set their minds on the things of the flesh, but those who are according to the Spirit, the things of the Spirit. For the mind set on the flesh is death, but the mind set on the Spirit is life and peace." The rest of Romans 8 puts our life in the context of relationship with a triune God as the Source of all strength, Who loves us unflinchingly.

When the Holy Spirit rules our spirit, we have life and peace. When our flesh rules, it brings corruption and death. Since war is about who gets to be in control, this war pits the spirit against the flesh. Do we allow our redeemed nature to rule, or our fallen flesh? That is the essence of battling the target of the flesh.

Paul repeats this principle with the Galatians. Paul tells them they need, by the Spirit, to put to death the deeds of the body. "But, I say, walk by the Spirit, and you will not carry out the desires of the flesh. For the flesh sets its desire against the

Spirit, and the Spirit against the flesh; for these are in opposition to one another, so that you may not do the things that you please." (Galatians 5:16-17)

Paul tells the Philippians that he worships in the Spirit of God and glory in Christ Jesus, and that he "puts no confidence in the flesh." (3:3) Because Paul knew what he was capable of in his own flesh, he tells the Corinthians that he disciplines his body and makes it his slave, "... so that, after I have preached to others, I myself will not be disqualified." (I Corinthians 9:27)

Paul, like Moses, saw the absolute value of being under God's control in every possible way. They had both seen the painful fallout of doing things outside of God's loving parameters. They battled for their own personal spiritual victories, and tried to train others to do the same.

Recognizing the flesh

We may be convinced we have to thwart the threat of the flesh, but can we recognize when it's in control? The apostle John gives us some helpful clues.

John breaks the battle against the flesh into three categories: "For all that is in the world, the lust of the flesh, the lust of the eyes and the boastful pride of life – is not from the Father but is from the world." (I John 2:16)

John categorizes what is present in the world system and brings it to bear on our flesh. Lust is a primary problem. Lust is typically defined as an "intense sexual desire or appetite," but it can also expand the meaning to "a passionate or overmastering desire or craving."[6]

Lust is usually related to sexual appetites, but it can also be cravings for food, drugs, alcohol, approval, fame, power, money, possessions, etc. It is a craving beyond the normal, God-given enjoyment of His provision. Lust becomes a controlling, obsessive desire that typically can never be satisfied.

Ravi Zacharias offers one of the best explanations regarding lust versus legitimate pleasure. Zacharias says: "Anything that refreshes you without distracting from, diminishing from, or destroying your final goal is legitimate pleasure."[7] By contrast, he says: "Any pleasure that jeopardizes the sacred right of another may well be an illicit pleasure."[8] And: "Any pleasure, however good, if not kept in balance will distort reality or destroy appetite."[9]

To best understand Zacharias' definition of legitimate pleasure, it's helpful to add the definition of sin that Zacharias ascribed to Susanna Wesley. Zacharias quotes her: "Sin is whatever weakens your reasoning, impairs the tenderness of your conscience, obscures your sense of God or takes away your relish for spiritual things; in short, if anything increases the authority and power of the flesh over the spirit – that to you becomes sin, however good it is in itself."[10]

Taken together, those two definitions are powerful and very instructive when it comes to battling the flesh. These definitions help us check our behavioral bent – towards God, or towards the enemy.

Disciplining the flesh

The Winter Olympics are airing as I pen this chapter. In the joys and sorrows of competition, one thing is clear: no Olympian athlete makes it to competition without great amounts of discipline and self-sacrifice. They have a goal, and like Paul, they beat their bodies into subjection daily to train.

These athletes have all the normal temptations to entertainment and ease that we do, but they have their eyes fixed on a goal. While all their friends are sleeping in, or hanging out, these athletes sacrifice years of their lives to train for excellence. From the comfort of our couches, we admire their fortitude.

These Olympians highlight lives of determination that should inspire believers to do the same spiritually. What are we willing to forego in the flesh to excel spiritually? What are we doing that sabotages our spiritual health?

Fasting was mentioned in chapter 12 as a spiritual weapon, and fasting also serves as a great way to get the flesh under control. Fasting is a practice of denial – bringing our cravings for food (or other things) under control to intensify our desire for God. Those that fast regularly report a spiritual strength they never before experienced.

All of us, like Paul, wrestle with what we know we ought to do, and what we actually end up doing. It's a frustrating fight to keep the flesh in check, but to cede control to the flesh is far worse.

Every time I see someone in the painful consequences of sin, I am reminded anew that it could very easily be me – and it will be if I stop resisting the pull of the flesh. I love the truth penned in I Corinthians 10:13: "No temptation has overtaken you but such as is common to man; and God is faithful, who will not allow you to be tempted beyond what you are able, but with the temptation will provide a way of escape also, so that you will be able to endure it." Jesus Christ was tempted in all ways and yet He never sinned. God understands the weakness of our flesh and has given us divine resources to win the battle over the flesh. He has also given us each other.

Trench Buddies battle for the soul of their buddy – and that includes their war against the flesh. A trench buddy can see our blind spots. He/she can notice subtle changes in our behavior. They can often notice when our flesh is in control – a lot sooner than we can. We should welcome their input, and actively seek it for protection.

As our trench buddies recognize our struggles with the "lust of the flesh, lust of the eyes, and the boastful pride of life," we must also recognize that those struggles may not just come from within us, but also as a calculated attack from the devil.

The Devil

We have seen that the world and the flesh can be difficult to define, and the same is often true of the devil. Many deny his existence, and others make him either too big or too small. In Christianity, some believe that the devil makes them do everything, and others think they are overwhelmingly wicked within themselves.

In reality, our Christian walk is one of personal responsibility (empowered by God), coupled with an informed view of Satan and his strategic methods of attack.

According to Warren Wiersbe in his book, *What to Wear to War*, "Satan is not merely a flesh and blood human or a concept of evil; he is a living, personal, literal being with power to control people and to perform many evil deeds."[11] Wiersbe says: "We are wrestling against an organized, demonic conspiracy – principalities, powers, rulers of darkness in this world, and spiritual wickedness in high places."[12]

The bad news is that the devil can do great damage. The good news is that we have a way to stop it. The devil is a formidable force to be reckoned with, but, for the believer in Jesus Christ, the reality of the cross gives us strength greater than Satan's. John's short epistles present great news in our battle with the devil. The reason Jesus Christ came to earth was to "undo the works of the devil." (I John 3:8 MKJV) In the next chapter, we are told that we can overcome "because He who is in you is greater than he who is in the world." (I John 4:4 MKJV)

We have the potential for victory in Christ, but few Christians walk in the reality of victory. Even though Satan has been stripped of his authority over the believer, he still devastates believers on a regular basis. Why? The Word gives us some insight.

Words from the Word

Two contrasting examples give us clarity about the devil's tactics: the one against Eve was a resounding victory. The other against Jesus was an epic failure. Both attacks were similar, but Jesus modeled the right way to fight back.

Eve's enemy ambush is recorded in Genesis 3. Satan gets Eve to take her eyes off the magnitude of her blessings to look at the one thing that is forbidden. "Has God said?" is his first tactic. Eve responds with an incorrect rendering of what God actually said, and Satan twists it even further from there. Satan attacks God's character by hinting that God is holding out on Eve, getting her to doubt God's love and care. Then Satan hits the three areas. "You shall be like God," appeals to the pride of life. "The tree was good for food and pleasing to the eye," appeals to Eve's lust of the flesh and lust of the eyes. She succumbs to the threefold attack and the ambush is a complete success. Eve eats fruit, and shares it with Adam.

How did this happen in a perfect environment with no knowledge of sin? Simply put, Eve did not know God's character, or God's Word. She was deceived. She did not fight back. The Old Testament is filled with similar deceptions using the same old tactics with great success.

In the New Testament, Satan tried it on the wrong person. This time it was a high-profile target, and the stakes couldn't be higher. This time, it was Jesus.

As he always does, Satan waited for the best time to tempt Jesus – after Jesus had spent 40 days in the wilderness on a complete fast. Hungry and weakened, Jesus was the perfect target for a tactical strike. Just like he did with Eve, Satan started with questions to promote confusion. "If you are the Son of God," was the first volley. Satan attacked Jesus' relationship and standing with God. (This is especially significant because the question came just a few verses after Jesus' baptism, and the Father's affirmation, "This is my beloved Son in whom I am well-pleased." (Matt. 3:17 MKJV)

Satan's first line of attack is to get our minds off of our identity in Christ so we can be led by our feelings. "In general, Satan doesn't control us with fang marks on the flesh, but with lies in the heart," says Tim Keller in his book, *Encounters with Jesus.* "He doesn't come in with all sorts of special effects; he suggests ideas to the heart that contradict God's Word, impugn His character, and destroy the trust relationship we have with Him."[13]

Next, Satan capitalizes on the hunger of Jesus, his fleshly needs. Satan tempts Jesus to turn stones into bread so he can satisfy the lust of the flesh. The next tactic is to get Jesus to throw himself off a high pinnacle, and the third is the promise of grandeur if Jesus worships Satan.

For each tactic the devil throws at Him, Jesus models successful spiritual warfare with three simple words: "It is written." Jesus quotes Deuteronomy 8:3, 6:16, and 6:13. Every time Satan throws down a challenge, Jesus quiets and banishes Satan with the authority of the Word.

Keller writes: "When you are in moments of pain or shock, the things that come out of your mind and mouth are the most primal things in your being. And when Jesus was in such moments, out came the words of the Bible."[14]

Keller says that we need to know Scripture to process all thoughts and feelings through a grid of biblical revelation. When God's assurances, summonses, promises and revelations are secured deep inside us, Keller says it's extremely difficult for Satan to get a foothold.

Keller offers this challenge: "If Jesus Christ, the Son of God, did not presume to face the forces of evil in the world without a profound knowledge of the Bible in mind and heart, how could we try to face life any other way? When we are under attack – tempted to sin, or to be discouraged, or to just give up altogether – it is then that we must wrestle the words and promises of the Bible into the center of our being, to 'let the message of Christ dwell among you richly.'" (Col. 3:16) [15]

Jesus is our High Priest Who knows our weaknesses, yet provides help in our time of need. We are not alone in the fight. "Let's not rely only on the Word of the Lord, but also on the Lord of the Word. We don't simply have a book, as perfect as it is – we have Jesus himself, who has been through fiery trials so intense that we can't imagine them."[16]

The will to fight

It's important to know where our spiritual threats come from – and therefore what our targets are. But, it is equally important that we are willing to fight. It should be our expectation. It should be normal for the true Christian.

I have interviewed many pastors in the course of writing this book, from different parts of the country. One pastor advised me not to use the term "spiritual warfare" because it puts people off. He said that he didn't really preach about the enemy, but liked to focus on obedience instead. I understand some of what he meant, but also think it represents the mindset of much of the church today. We like Jesus because we want him to meet our felt needs, but we want to avoid the doctrines that make us uncomfortable. We want to avoid war.

J.C. Ryle says it well: "True Christianity is a fight.... There is a vast quantity of religious current in the world which is not true, genuine Christianity.... There are thousands of men and women who go to churches every Sunday...but you never see any 'fight' about their religion! Of spiritual strife, and exertion, and conflict, and self-denial, and watching, and warring they know literally nothing at all."[17]

Imagine what would happen if the church were trained. What would happen if the Word of God were so deeply driven into our hearts and minds that we not only recognized spiritual attacks, but also responded strategically with the Word?

Maybe Satan would discover what the Japanese discovered in the days that followed Pearl Harbor. Japanese Admiral Isoroku Yamamoto purportedly said, "I fear all we have done is to awaken a sleeping giant and fill him with terrible resolve."[18]

May the same be said of us.

CHAPTER 12: SHOOTING AT THE RIGHT TARGETS

Most important "take-away" thought(s):

1 .What is a stronghold? What stronghold do you struggle with the most, and how does it contribute to defeat in your life?

2. In what way do you target that stronghold? Can you think of ways that you aimed at wrong targets instead of your stronghold? (Example: I blamed others for my wrong thinking... etc.)

3. In what ways do you navigate through life giving little or no thought to how things contrast with Scriptural truth? Define three ways the world system poses a significant risk to your faith. Explain your strategy to use spiritual weapons against these targets.

4. In your spiritual walk, what dominates most – your spirit or your flesh? How can you tell which one is in control at any given time? What strategy, if any, do you employ to battle the flesh for a fuller life of faith?

5. We live in a post-modern world that negates the reality of absolute truth. How does Satan's challenge "Did God really say?" play out in modern Christianity? In your own faith, do you question Scripture? How might this be deadly? Once Scripture is discounted, what do you default to instead?

"In pointing out these things to the brethren, you will be a good servant of Christ Jesus, constantly nourished on the words of the faith and of the sound doctrine which you have been following."
I Timothy 4:6

13
WEAPONS TRAINING

On June 1, 2011, a large convoy of military vehicles rumbled along in the scorching heat heading to the Khost-Gardez Pass in Afghanistan. Combat medic, Michael Azevedo's M-ATV (Mine Resistant Ambush Protected vehicle MRAP) was about midway in the 12-vehicle convoy when the ambush occurred. The lead vehicle hit an IED (Improved Explosive Device). With the other lanes in the narrow pass blocked, the convoy took on heavy fire. Rocket-propelled grenades (RPG's) rained down from the ridge to their left, and small arms fire peppered the convoy taking out the mechanical system in Azevedo's vehicle.

"Our protocol is 'Get out of the kill zone – and plan counterattack from a safer place,'" Azevedo said, but they had nowhere to go. With grenades exploding around them, often within 10 feet of their vehicle, fear was not an option. "It was 'game time;' time to dismount and do our thing."

They were tracking muzzle flashes and movement from the ridge 200-300 meters from their position. "When you're being shot at, you put down as much fire as you can," said Azevedo.

As they defended their position, an Air Force combat controller in their convoy radioed for air support. Fortunately for them, an Apache helicopter was in the general area, and within 10 minutes, was strafing across the mountaintop releasing hellfire missiles along the ridge.

"Everything turned at that point," Azevedo recalled. "The RPG's stopped and we gained more momentum. Within 45 minutes from the start of the ambush, all was quiet. Amazingly, there were only two wounded."

Azevedo was happy to be alive. He was also glad for the grueling years of training before his deployment to Afghanistan – especially weapons training.

During Army basic training, he had a month of concentrated weapons training, mostly with the M-16 and M-4 rifles. He learned how to take his weapon apart, clean it, and put it back together. He learned how it functioned, and how to fix it when it malfunctioned. He was range-qualified, firing at pop-up targets from 50-300 meters, longer range up to 500 meters, and in varied terrains. He trained on mounted vehicles performing simulated training from different positions.

He remembers the urban weapons training section as most valuable. As a small fire team they had to strategize battle in urban situations, studying all the SOP's (Standard Operating Procedures), preplanning, and rehearsing multiple times before the actual battles. "We had to know the plan, practice the plan, and think on our feet as we engaged the plan," said Azevedo. They trained on multiple weapons including the 240 machine gun, M249 Squad Automatic Weapon (SAW), the M203 grenade launcher, rocket launchers, and M9 pistol. Despite months of intensive weapons training, Azevedo said he still had not developed the "muscle memory" that makes the training automatic in the chaos of battle.

That muscle memory came in his pre-deployment training which was also intensive, but used live fire. "If you screwed up there, you could end up killing another soldier," the Army sergeant said.

All the training was worth it when real bullets were flying on the K-G Pass in Afghanistan. There was no time to think. It was "fight back well, or go home in a body bag."

Ambush of the soul

Over the years I've had my own K-G Pass ambushes, and have sat across the table from battered, spiritual war veterans whose faith was tattered and torn. Spiritually, Satan works much the same way the Taliban did on the K-G Pass – and we can learn some lessons from the military for our spiritual battles.

First, most vehicles are equipped with armor to withstand IED explosions and small arms fire. It doesn't eliminate the risk, but it minimizes the damage from attacks. As Christians, most of us have heard the armor of God preached from Ephesians 6. Judging by the damage I see in so many followers of Christ, I'm not sure we are putting it on or understand the full significance of its provision.

Secondly, a convoy implies a group of people going out on a mission. According to Azevedo, their convoy was unusually large because of the multiple missions planned. They had nearly 60 people, and he said the combined fire power was significant to the battle. "We had superior weapons and lots of them," he said. They had people with diverse job skills to meet diverse battle needs.

As believers, living a corporate versus individual life makes a huge difference in our spiritual survival rate. All through the Old Testament, God set up His meeting place for festivals so His people would experience corporate worship for greater unity and divine strength. There is strength in numbers. A solo soldier is often a dead one.

Thirdly, it was air power that transformed an ambush into a victory. We covered the significance of air power through prayer in chapter 9, but it's a good reminder that prayer changes the outcome of spiritual battles.

Training pays off

In the ambush account, Azevedo is right about our weapons being superior to the Afghani weapons, but superior weapons are of no use without the training to use them in battle.

Tony Evans addresses this problem in his message "The Weapons of Authority". "Many of us walk to church every Sunday with the Bible, we just never get around to using the Bible that we carry," he said.[1]

The well-known preacher adds these strong words: "No wonder you're defeated. If you don't know how to utter the Word of God, use the Word of God, take it and use it when you need it, you're going to be defeated... because he [the devil] can handle your word but he can't handle God's Word. If you never use it, even if you hear it preached, you're wasting your time." [2]

I think Evans is right.

Most of us have heard the humorous Sunday School Bible bloopers – real statements made from young students. Here are a few:

- Adam and Eve were created from an apple tree. Noah's wife was Joan of Ark. Noah built an ark and the animals came on in pears.
- Lot's wife was a pillar of salt during the day, but a ball of fire during the night.
- Samson slayed the Philistines with the axe of the apostles.
- David was a Hebrew king who was skilled at playing the liar. He fought the Finkelsteins, a race of people who lived in biblical times.
- Jesus was born because Mary had an immaculate contraption.
- The epistels were the wives of the apostles.[3]

What might be funny from a child in Sunday School, is not so funny when a lack of biblical training leaves Christians ambushed and defeated. Believers have a virtual armory at their disposal, but they lack the training to make good use of spiritual weapons.

How do we train Christians in the use of spiritual weapons – to mature in their faith? I realize that the question is nuanced and complicated. It is very difficult to put in concrete terms. In fact, considering it can flirt with legalism and tempt us to fight with formulas. The Pharisees tried that, never connecting with the Author of their commandments, and ended up siding with Satan in his plot to kill the Savior and destroy his disciples.

Primarily, it is God that matures us, but all through Scripture, there is also an emphasis on knowing God's commandments, His statutes, and His ways, because there is life and safety in them. Jesus tells His disciples to go into all the world and make disciples. Paul and Peter pound the importance of sound doctrine, and warn of false teachers. And, as we have seen in the last chapter, Jesus models the importance of the Word to achieve victory against the attacks of the devil.

John MacArthur underscores the importance of knowing the Word in his book, *The Truth War*: "This is cosmic warfare, engaging the armies of hell, which are arrayed against Christ. Their weapons consist of lies of all kinds – elaborate lies, massive philosophical lies, evil lies that appeal to humanity's fallen sinfulness, lies that inflate human pride, and lies that closely resemble truth. Our one weapon is the simple truth of Christ as revealed in His Word."[4]

Strategic Approach

As we already reviewed, the military has a very organized method of training. Why? Because the mission depends on it. It's too important to be random.

When I contacted churches in different parts of the country – both large and small – I found no example where both the church leader and church attendees have a clear training plan. Discipleship is on their radar screen, but it is randomly accomplished. It might happen through pulpit preaching, through Sunday school, Bible study, or small groups, but there doesn't seem to be a clear plan to build principle upon principle – or to show how all the teaching connects. Too many believers don't even understand where the Bible comes from, how it is put together, and what makes it such an extraordinary book.

I don't have pat answers. I simply suggest that we look for answers, because training deficits are killing us spiritually. What if the personnel traversing the K-G Pass had not had weapons training? What if the Apache pilot hadn't been trained on the weapons system? The outcome may have been very different. The same is true for us.

Ballistics and Bibles

Military weapons training is like Azevedo described it. On a basic level, you take the weapon apart and put it back together. This provides a general overview before the particulars like function, malfunction and use are taught.

As an educator, I discovered that learning is best accomplished when an overview is created before teaching the details. Education writer, Mary Pride, described it as building a file cabinet (the overview) to provide a relevant and orderly place to store the file folders (the details). When information is presented in a more orderly fashion, then retrieval of the information happens more easily, which translates into more effective learning.

Taking it apart and putting it back together

As an avid disciple of Christ for more than 30 years, it was at least a decade before I began to understand an overview of the Bible. What are the parts? How do they fit together? Can I take it apart and put it back together? I can, only if I see how the parts interrelate. Because a biblical overview was not part of early discipleship, my knowledge of the Word (through Bible study, Bible college courses, pulpit messages, etc.) was fragmented. I was learning lots of details and stories without understanding how they related to each other. The more I appreciate the parts – the taking apart and putting back together – the more I marvel in its exquisite design and purpose.

Chuck Swindoll was helpful to me in this area. Twice, over the course of 20 years, he has presented a Bible survey study. In one, he used Route 66 to highlight the 66 books of the Bible. He said that describing the United States from one of two states (like Alaska or Arizona) would give conflicting images of the country. It is only a drive (on Route 66) through the country that gives us the correct overview to understand what appears to be conflicting details. The same is true of Scripture.

As I have taught the inductive Bible study method, I always use a helpful chart from Swindoll's study guide to provide an amazingly simple overview.[5] He combines the books including: creation, fall, flood, patriarchs, bondage, deliverance, law, wandering, and Promised Land, and then moves to the progression of Samuel, Saul, David and Solomon. Then it shows how the kingdom of Israel split after Solomon, and then divides up all the prophets as to which kingdom they spoke to, when, and why – all leading up to the life, death and resurrection of Christ – and the ministry following.

The overview made the study of Scripture less frustrating because it gave me a roadmap while reading.

Once an overview is created, a careful study of the parts is important. Here too, discipleship is often lacking. Carefully studying the parts of Scripture is called Hermeneutics. It means: the science of interpretation, especially of the Scriptures.[6]

The study of hermeneutics presents many methods to study Scripture. Often left to seminary students, the basics of hermeneutics should also be taught to even children. For instance, when a topic is studied, when is it first mentioned? (First mention principle) What does it say about it elsewhere in Scripture? (Progressive Mention Principle) And, what does the whole Bible have to say about the topic? (Full Mention Principle) What type of literature genre is the text? Poetry and historical text are interpreted very differently. What is the cultural context?

The point here is not to exhaustively teach the science of hermeneutics, but merely to show that greater care in handling the Word of God would make us more proficient in its use. It would allow us to take it apart and put it back together with skill and wisdom.

Function/malfunction

Once I know the parts of a weapon, it is critical that I know how it functions – and what to do if it malfunctions. The whole point of a weapon is to be sure it works when you need it. The same is true of the Bible.

How does the Bible work? What is its function? The primary point of any weapon is to successfully discharge projectiles to neutralize a threat. The explosive, barrel and bore all affect the outcome. The parts all need to work together to produce the desired effect.

The primary function of the Bible is to reveal God – in the work of creation, fall, redemption, and restoration. It equips us for every good work (Ephesians 2:10), it sanctifies us (John 17:17), it instructs, delights, warns, keeps us from sin, etc. Very importantly, it carries an explosive authority to neutralize the devil's wiles and threats.

If the Bible is not working in our lives, that is a malfunction. Something is wrong. Out on a battlefield, a soldier needs to know how to correct a malfunction to get the weapon working again. He is taught how to fix common malfunctions.

Consider the average believer in spiritual warfare. He has not trained well on his weapon. The Bible lies on a dusty shelf and is not maintained. An attack comes, and his weapon won't fire. Rather than know how to fix it (by careful inspection and cleaning), he tosses it aside – and often surrenders.

The most common malfunction is caused by lack of use. The fix is simply to use the weapon. Pick it up and read it. Better yet, study it. Become intimately acquainted with the Bible (and the Author). Another malfunction is a jam in the barrel – most often, sin in the life of the believer. The conviction of the Holy Spirit and the blood of Christ clean the barrel of obstructions and remove any jammed cartridges.

Technically, the fault is never with the weapon in the case of the Bible. The analogy always points to issues with the operator.

Repetition

Weapons proficiency is never attained without repetition – and lots of it. Azevedo spent hours, and thousands of rounds of ammunition to gain skill and confidence with his weapons. If our response in an attack requires "split-second firing," the Word of God must be in our hearts and minds – deeply. Repetition and memorization are tedious, but there is no other way to become proficient with our spiritual weapons.

I presented a Trench Buddies overview to a group of women in the Boston area last week. One of the women was very impressed that I trained to use an M-16. It was a timely object lesson as I admitted that I was no longer proficient because I had not trained with an M-16 in such a long time. The same is true with my knowledge of Scripture. If I am not actively training, I lose ground. I am no longer battle-ready.

Marksmanship

As we continue to move down Azevedo's training list, there are clear parallels between his weapons training and our biblical training. In the marksmanship part of his training, it was all about the ability to hit the target – in many different battle scenarios.

He fired from different distances, in open fields, urban streets, from fixed positions or from moving vehicles. Every imaginable battle challenge is considered, simulated, and trained.

As a believer in Jesus Christ, we don't get to pick our battles. They come in every area of life – home, work, school, church, recreation, and in all aspects of culture. Some are frontal attacks, and others are hidden. Some are fixed, some are moving. The enemy changes his attack mode to catch us off guard, or he just keeps using the same one because it keeps working.

For the most part, the church teaches truth. We learn Scripture. We might even memorize verses. We just lack the tactical training to use our weapons in the array of battles we fight daily. When Azevedo trained, he learned SOPs created by experienced veterans for each situation. Military members practice them (over and over). But, battles don't always follow textbook examples, so soldiers have to think on their feet and strategize for in-the-battle moments – always drawing from their deep, hands-on training.

We learn most effectively when we actively apply what we learn. Hours and hours on the firing range bear this out. The military instructor connects the instruction to the action – and can appropriately determine proficiency. There is a passive component to Christian discipleship that disconnects what is preached from what is practiced. The pastor, or Bible teacher, provides the instruction and often has no idea if any proficiency is established.

I am a big fan of interactive training. One year I taught 9th graders, and the whole purpose of the class was to "use" Scripture. Looking back, it was a marksmanship course similar to military training. We addressed many life topics – often the ones they brought up. We studied the culture to see which non-Scriptural areas were infiltrating our hearts. We did specific Bible word searches, searched out biblical convictions, and did lots of role plays. We did spontaneous debates. It was often painful for them to see how untrained they were, but it was also exciting when they gained skill they could use in real life to gain greater victories. It was hard mental work. We wrestled out many hard topics. They loved it – and so did I.

There's another active training exercise I find to be revealing and helpful. A group of individuals is split into two teams sitting opposite each other. One side of the table is the "enemy" side, lobbing an "accusation grenade" at an individual on the other side. That individual puts her head down and her team has to fight back with Scripture on her behalf. Often, there's a great struggle to come up with specific

Scriptures to diffuse the accusation, and a healthy alarm at being in a spiritual battle without bullets. Yet there's also great excitement when a glorious, biblical truth is recalled to shatter the lie with the "sword of the Spirit". No lecture is needed to understand our lack of and need for training.

As we do these types of exercises in the Trench Buddies conferences, I hear this phrase often from veteran believers: "I thought I was really prepared; now I see I am not."

Target insight

God wants us to be prepared. Through the Word, we are taught, reproved, corrected, and trained in righteousness – equipped for every good work. (II Timothy 3:16-17) In addition, God has also given us another unbelievable Resource – the Holy Spirit. Jesus said that after He left, the Father would send a Helper – the Spirit of Truth, an Advocate, Comforter, and Counselor. The Holy Spirit is a divine Resource dwelling within us, and if heeded, brings unimaginable resources to the fight. The apostle Paul said that his ministry was "in the word of truth, in the power of God; by the weapons of righteousness for the right hand and the left." (II Corinthians 6:7)

As Azevedo explained his experience with weapons training, one cool weapon feature made me think of the Holy Spirit. Azevedo spoke of a PAC4 laser system. The system would emit a laser beam on a target that could only be seen with night-vision goggles. The laser illuminated the target for those with eyes equipped to see – but the beam was invisible to everyone else. The Holy Spirit gives us spiritual insight in our battles – even in the darkness. Amazing truth!

Rubber dummies

While it is true that the Holy Spirit illuminates our targets, it is also true that the devil tries to tire us out firing at false targets. The Allied Forces tried the same tactics with the Germans during the D-Day invasion by using straw-filled, inflatable rubber dummy parachutes as diversionary tactics. Explosive-rigged dummies were dropped in the area of Marigny, France and were successful in diverting the German's 915th Infantry Regiment toward a fake drop zone. The diversion temporarily weakened defenses in the actual paratroop drop area.[7]

Battles against "flesh and blood" are often rubber dummies diverting us from the real targets. "The worst person in your life is not your problem. They are only the vehicle through which the angels are getting to you," teaches Tony Evans. "Many of us have been fighting people when we ought to have been fighting angels. We wrestle against principalities and powers... the angelic world," Evans said.[8]

Satan can get us focused on differences with our spouse to distract us from training our children in faith. At the very worst, Satan gets us to battle against God instead of seeing Satan as the real enemy. He did it with Eve, and he's been doing it ever since.

We can also get caught up in causes instead of with Christ. I once heard a teaching that made me consider this topic of rubber dummies. A drawing had two structures, each on a foundation. One represented the church and the other the world. It showed the church aiming at all these "issue" balloons (like abortion, creation, pornography, etc.) tethered to the world structure. While these are worthy causes to oppose, they did not target the foundation behind each of these issues. The drawing showed the world structure shooting directly at the foundation of the church structure – attacking core belief systems.

This is why worldview study has appealed to me so much; it targets the core belief systems from which they spring. These core targets should be appropriately battled through exposure, prayer, and relevant debate.

Satan wants to be in control and actively opposes God's control in any given arena. We are merely pawns in Satan's battle against God. We should see Satan as our primary enemy, and battle any control he seeks to take in our lives and in the world around us.

Weapon safety

There are also set protocols when we use our weapons. The Airman's Manual offers a few tips that are also helpful to the believer:[9]

- Never point your weapon at anyone or anything you are not willing to shoot
- Consider all weapons as loaded
- Keep your finger off the trigger until you're prepared to engage your target
- Don't shoot anything you can't positively identify
- Know what's behind your target
- Keep weapon on safe until ready to shoot

By now, you are probably already making many astute observations concerning these safety tips. It is a delight to see these concepts serve as a springboard to multiple applications, so I won't belabor the explanations.

Primarily, we need to see the Bible as a weapon. We need great wisdom to use it correctly. The term "Bible Thumper" is often applied to believers who use Scripture as a machine gun – spraying truth indiscriminately without the right heart or the right target. There is no safety. There is no wisdom with the weapon.

The Bible is loaded with truth and wisdom – but timing is everything. There is a right time – and a right place to engage. More training may be needed before I am ready to engage. I also need to positively identify what I am shooting at – which means I have to patiently listen. Ravi Zacharias wisely says that many times Christians are answering questions no one is asking. He says we need to take the time to listen to people and then respond to their heart issues.

The Bible offers life to a dying world. But it can also be painful. In John 6, Jesus is teaching in the synagogue and the disciples were grumbling among themselves at his teaching: "This is a difficult statement, who can listen to it?" (v.60) Many disciples then withdrew and stopped following Jesus.

Jesus asked the remaining 12 disciples if they were leaving also. "Simon Peter answered Him, 'Lord, to whom shall we go? You have the words of eternal life.'" (v.68) The truth often hurts people, but like surgery, it can also heal people. The application of truth and medicine, takes training, practice, care, and wisdom. Carelessness costs lives in medicine and war.

Law of armed conflict

War is not without rules – even when strategic destruction is the goal. Every year, part of my military training included a refresher in the Law of Armed Conflict (LOAC). In an article by Ron Powers called "Rules of War", he writes: "LOAC arises from a desire among civilized nations to prevent unnecessary suffering and destruction while not impeding the effective waging of war."[10] Powers says LOAC is a part of international law that "aims to protect civilians, prisoners of war, the wounded, sick, and shipwrecked."[11]

The idea behind LOAC is that legitimate threats are neutralized while protecting human dignity. The Bible contains similar guidelines in our battles – particularly those that involve other people. When we offensively pursue targets, we should not be offensive in our behavior. Peter tells us to give an answer with meekness. (I Peter 3:15) The apostle Paul often reminded his mentees to be gentle when correcting others. (II Timothy 2:25) Believers are often belligerent in their conversations with those that disagree with them – forgetting the nature of the real target. They war without rules to guide the scope of their battles.

I love the guidelines Paul gives the Thessalonians: "We urge you, brethren, admonish the unruly, encourage the fainthearted, help the weak, be patient with everyone. See that no one repays evil for evil, but always seek after that which is good for one another and for all people. Rejoice always; pray without ceasing." (I Thessalonians 5:15-17) The Bible does not rubber stamp our responses. We must see the heart of the people we engage (through the help of the Holy Spirit) so we can respond appropriately.

Rogue warfare

Finally, our weapons must be used under the right authority. When Azevedo's convoy used their weapons on the K-G Pass that June day in Afghanistan, they were in every way operating under right authority. They were in the country on valid orders. They were on an authorized mission which was mostly diplomatic, providing humanitarian assistance. They did not provoke the attack. They followed strict protocol in their response. They were under Central Command's (CENTCOM) authority and followed all LOAC regulations. In contrast, a soldier not under authority is a rogue soldier –a "loose cannon" with independent motives. Rogue warfare is typically volatile and unpredictable – with questionable outcomes.

We have all seen our share of rogue believers – using the Bible without proper restraint, nor under the authority of God. They do great damage to others and misrepresent the true mission of the church. The prophet Isaiah describes the rogue soldier: "as for a rogue, his weapons are evil; he devises wicked schemes to destroy the afflicted with slander, even though the needy one speaks what is right." (Isaiah 32:7)

To be "strong in the Lord and the power of His might" is only possible when we are fully submitted to Him. We fight in the power of His authority only when we are cleanly under His authority. Even when spiritual bullets are flying, we can have confidence that we are on His mission, in His service.

"You face a conflict – take up your position in Christ rather than taking up the circumstances you are facing," says Tony Evans in his teaching on spiritual warfare. "We've let circumstances become God, and when circumstances become God, God can't be God."[12]

Weapons wrap-up

The Word of God is a powerful weapon in spiritual warfare, but only when it is used under the authority of God. Like any other weapon, we need good training to use it effectively. We must use it within appropriate guidelines, at the appropriate targets, at the right time, in the right way.

Life is full of K-G Pass firefights. You can't predict when they will happen, but you can be trained for when they do.

It may only be when the firefight is over that you really appreciate all the training it took to survive.

CHAPTER 13: WEAPONS TRAINING

Most important "take-away" thought(s):

1. "No wonder you're defeated. If you don't know how to utter the Word of God, use the Word of God, take it and use it when you need it, you're going to be defeated... because he [the devil] can handle your word but he can't handle God's word. If you never use it, even if you hear it preached – you're wasting your time." Tony Evan's words are convicting... On a scale of 1-10, how trained are you in the Word? Explain your personal rating.

2. Think of your most common spiritual attack. What lie is most often whispered to your heart? Quick! Fire five rounds from the Word to neutralize the lie. How did you do? If you struggled, why?

3. Is your training in the Word active? How do you purpose to apply what you learn in the Word? If you don't, list three ways you could begin to actively train in the Word – to intentionally apply the Word to practical areas in your life.

4. What "rubber dummies" tire us out in spiritual warfare? What "surface" battles are you fighting that mask the real battle? Give at least one example.

5. What should be some rules regarding a spiritual "law of armed conflict?" Name three ways Christians use the Word of God the wrong way in battle. In what ways have you used the Word the wrong way?

THIS PAGE INTENTIONALLY LEFT BLANK

THIS PAGE INTENTIONALLY LEFT BLANK

Section

3

Explosives

EXPLOSIVES: A Personal Profile

The more Jane studied the Word, the clearer she saw how the enemy had set her up – planning her ambush step by step.

Once Satan had stripped her of the truth of God's Word, the lies slipped in so easily. Without prayer, Jane felt no relationship with God – so she longed for other relationships to fill the void. Satan had also filled her mind with lies about her husband, so soon; Jane began to look elsewhere for relationships. The set-up was going just as planned.

The longer Jane stayed away from God's Word, the distinctions between right and wrong became blurred. Jane's moral compass now looked to the culture for bearings. Many of the verses she had memorized as a child whispered God's loving warnings to Jane, but she no longer trusted God's character. God was just too rigid." The Bible is so yesterday; this was today", she thought.

"Perfect," Satan whispered.

Jane remembered all the people that tried to rescue her – to warn her about the explosives planted in her path. Her husband, her parents, her in-laws, and her life-long friends had loved her enough to intervene. One-by-one, she rejected their counsel. "No one was going to tell her what to do," she thought every time she was confronted.

How could they be so judgmental and intrusive? She was finally having fun. Drinking made her feel good. Hanging around the clubs made her feel sexy again. She was bored with her 10-year marriage. She wanted to feel attractive – to feel excited again. It was flattering when men wanted to dance with her at the clubs. Her new friends thought she was great. They made her feel accepted.

"This is going very well," the evil one observed.

Jane danced around the explosives for a couple of years until the cumulative effect ignited the fuses into a full-blown affair, separation from her husband, and alienation from everyone that loved her.

"Mission accomplished," the devil gleefully proclaimed. "Ambush executed."

"Then when lust has conceived, it gives birth to sin;
and when sin is accomplished, it brings forth death."
James 1:15

14
GOING BOOM

April 10, 2012 started just like any other day for Army staff sergeant Travis Mills. The 82nd Airborne soldier was on patrol. It was his third tour of duty in Afghanistan, and just four days before his 25th birthday.

Stopping to rest, Mills pulled his pack off his back and dropped it to the ground – immediately detonating an Improvised Explosive Device (IED) planted in the dirt. Seconds after the blast, the former high school sports star from Michigan was bleeding out from all four limbs. His medic quickly secured four tourniquets, and Mills was sedated to be airlifted to a medical facility. He woke up on his birthday to learn that he had lost both legs just above the knee, his right arm just below his armpit and his left arm just below his elbow.

"It was a normal day at work turned ugly," said Mills, who is one of only five quadruple amputees to survive the Iraq and Afghanistan wars. Mills wasted little time on remorse, but poured his energy into intense rehabilitation efforts at the Walter Reed National Military Medical Center in Maryland. With the use of prosthetics, Mills is now walking and using his arms.

Mills is one of thousands that have been dismembered or killed by IEDs in our recent wars. According to Gregg Zoroya in a *USA Today* article, "...the homemade bomb has created more American casualties over a decade and two wars than any other weapon."[1]

"Somewhere between more than half to two-thirds of Americans killed or wounded in combat in Iraq and Afghanistan wars have been victims of IEDs planted in the ground, in buildings, or worn as suicide vests, or loaded into suicide vehicles – according to data from the Pentagon's Joint IED Defeat Organization (JIEDDO)."[2] Zoroya cites Army data for statistics: "...more than 3,100 dead and 33,000 wounded, with the worst of the casualties being the nearly 1,800 troops who have lost limbs, the vast majority from blasts."[3]

The military uses the slang term "going boom." That's what happened to three Arizona Army Guard engineers as their armored RG-31 rumbled down Highway 1 in

Zabul Province, in Afghanistan. According to the Zoroya article, the 8,000-pound roller they pushed was designed to detonate anything in the road before the truck passed over it. The roller did its job, but the shock of the explosion caused painful ear pressure, black, billowing smoke inside the cab, and a chemical smell that burned their nostrils. Specialist Leif Skoog, 23, was closest to the blast in the driver's seat and was stunned and disoriented. After the blast, Skoog was out of combat for two weeks as he struggled with dizziness, headaches, and concentration problems – all part of traumatic brain injury (TBI) so common in IED blasts.

Another young Army lieutenant kept a journal during his deployment to Iraq. "Someone tried to kill me today," he scribed on page 172.[4] Greg Foley heard a loud explosion. His Humvee was lifted into the air and then it fell into the hole created by the IED. "All I can remember is the explosion, followed by dirt and sense of falling," he wrote.[5] Foley said the ballistic glass saved his life, but he too struggled with what is now recognized as traumatic brain injury.

The U.S. government has spent billions of dollars on technology and armor to combat the threat of hidden explosives. Meanwhile, insurgents can build a basic IED for about $30 a piece. Afghanistan clearly does not have the fire power of the United States, but it uses explosive devices to relentlessly erode a greater strength.

Concealed explosives appear to be the weapons of choice for Al Qaida and other terrorist groups, not just in Afghanistan and Iraq, but around the world. Why? Because, explosives are very effective.

More bang for the buck

Conventional military munitions are typically used in a more overt delivery system while responding to an aggressive action. The military uses all types of bombs – from huge missiles to small grenades – to neutralize threats. They are costly because they require some type of delivery system, and the explosives themselves cost more. There is also more predictability to conventional explosives because the nations that use them are typically under international rules of warfare.

Terrorism and IEDs are much different. The cost is low, the delivery is creative, and there are no rules. This creates a combustible combination for the combatant – or the average citizen as we saw recently at the Boston Marathon.

Hidden explosives also create distinct advantages for the terrorist.

Planting fear

Unpredictability is one of the greatest advantages of hidden explosives. Like the term terrorist implies, IEDs create terror. The ever-present threat of explosion carries a fear which can be immobilizing to the soldier. What goes through the mind of a soldier out on a mission when they have witnessed a fellow soldier killed or dismembered on a previous mission? "Will it be me today?" Terrorists seek to mess with the minds of soldiers in order to diminish their will to fight, or to pursue the mission set before them.

I heard some of these stories during interviews with deployed military members. During one deployment to Iraq, a sergeant reported daily mortar attacks on their base. According to the sergeant, the aim was terrible, and they rarely did much damage, but the attacks served to unsettle the troops as they waited for the daily mortar round. A former student of mine was injured on deployment – not by the mortar attack itself, but in the chaos of seeking shelter.

The enemy's goal is to get soldiers to fear the enemy, rather than to fight the enemy. Relentless attacks exaggerate the enemy's force and wear down the soldier's courage and stamina to fight.

Often the cumulative effect of sustained threat and fear is not felt until the soldier returns home to a typically safer environment. This may contribute to the rising rates of Post Traumatic Stress Disorder (PTSD) prevalent in returning veterans. The fear lingers long after the initial attacks.

Limiting movement

The presence of IEDs or landmines in an area limits the military's ability to move about freely to accomplish the mission. Many missions, a great number of them humanitarian in nature, require troops to operate "outside the wire" – which is outside the relatively secure area within the military installation. The risk of injury outside the perimeter of the base rises exponentially. The military does all it can to minimize the risk, but even sophisticated, technical detection methods are not foolproof, and they slow movement.

Removed from the fight

The most obvious advantage the enemy gains from explosives is to take more soldiers out of battle. Slight injuries, like those suffered by Specialist Lief Skoog, temporarily take a soldier down for a couple of weeks. More extensive injuries, like the ones suffered by Travis Mills, take them off the battlefield permanently. And, death ends the war altogether for far too many.

Collateral damage

Just like explosives can cause collateral damage to those physically near the blast, explosives can also cause collateral emotional damage to those around them. Watching the pain of an injured soldier can influence the will to fight in others.

This happens not only on the battlefield, but also through the media. Terrorists like to publicly flaunt the damage they cause in order to embolden other terrorists. Unwittingly, our media coverage of war casualties – without the balance of all the good done through the fight – can collectively cause us to lose our will to fight as a nation.

It is not my intent to debate U.S. foreign policy or the rightness of our involvement in the Middle East. It is my intent to show the widespread effect of explosives on our thinking. Hopefully, a quick personal example will illustrate the point. For this chapter, I viewed many stories on IED deaths and the horrific damage done to our troops (and to civilians). I've also written many articles on military medical staff tending to the war wounded, both overseas and at home. It is very difficult to look at the cost of war. It would change my thinking if I stopped there. But, I have also done many stories on the humanitarian good done in these battle-torn countries – the building of schools, clinics, hospitals, roads, infrastructure, etc. Ultimately, it is the benefit of battle that keeps us in the fight, and the relentless barrage of homemade bombs can obscure the bigger picture. (This point will become more important as we develop the spiritual parallel.)

Evil control

The last advantage to explosives, especially the hidden ones, is to maintain or regain control. In most wars, at least theoretically, a good force is seeking to neutralize an evil force. In the case of terrorism, it would be hard to ignore the evil carnage in its wake. This type of war is terribly difficult, but the end game is to minimize or eliminate the terrorists' control. By littering the landscape with all types of landmines, the enemy seeks control, and the freedom to continue their agenda.

What explodes in your life?

The human carnage of explosives stuns us. It shocks us. It grieves us. It also paints a vivid picture of what happens around us – and sometimes in us – on a regular basis.

What we see in war, and in terrorism, is what we see spiritually as sin explodes around us and sin implodes within us. Explosives provide a vivid illustration of the doctrine of sin.

Like explosives, sin wounds, disables and kills. It limits our movement, hinders our mission, destroys our courage, and allows evil to be in control. It comes in all different forms and is delivered in different ways. It dismembers our soul, causes agonizing pain, and creates collateral damage to anyone nearby.

Like explosives, the most effective damage is done when no one is paying attention because of the element of surprise. The careless and untrained pay the biggest price.

Similar to sin, IEDs are effective because they look like everyday things – a soda can, a rolled-up towel, anything that blends in as a part of normal life. Landmines are particularly deadly because they blend in with the terrain where they are placed.

They are usually covered with something ordinary. They are hidden, but just the right amount of pressure causes them to blow. It is the same with sin.

Also, like explosives, sin has lingering effects. What traumatic brain injury is to the soldier's brain, sin is to the believer's soul. The classic symptoms of TBI are confusion, headaches, irritability and inability to think, which often results in a higher risk of suicide. These symptoms can last for weeks or years, depending on the severity and frequency of the blasts. Sergeant Joshua Hansen could be the poster boy for TBI as the soldier who experienced 9 IED blasts during his tours as he cleared travel routes of bombs. As team leader for the 2nd Platoon, Company A, of the Army's 321st Engineers, Hansen suffered eight consecutive concussions and continues to suffer from TBI. According to the article, up to 20% of deployed soldiers are affected by TBI, totaling approximately 145,000.[6]

Contrast the TBI symptoms to the aftershock of sin, and the parallels are fitting. The blasts of sin linger longer depending on the severity and frequency of the blasts. Hansen encountered the blasts seeking to protect others from harm, while many believers suffer damages seeking pleasure rather than protection.

Universal risk

Previous chapters have emphasized the inescapable nature of war – particularly spiritual warfare. In the cosmic battle between good and evil, God and Satan, there are no conscientious objectors. It's everyone's battle.

"If you have accepted Jesus Christ as your Savior, then you need to know that the enemy will stop at nothing to prevent you from knowing God and living for Jesus Christ," writes Charles Stanley in his book, *Landmines in the Path of the Believer*.[7]

"A disarmed, discouraged believer who has fallen into the dust of defeat, suffocated by guilt and shame, is no threat to him [Satan]," Stanley writes. "Be aware: he does not hesitate to use extreme tactics of warfare – ones that are specifically designed to separate you from God and His blessings, as well as the love and respect of friends and family."[8]

The apostle Peter gives a similar warning: "Be of sober spirit, be on the alert. Your adversary, the devil, prowls around like a roaring lion, seeking someone to devour. But resist him, firm in your faith, knowing that the same experiences of suffering are being accomplished by your brethren who are in the world." (I Peter 5:8-9) We are in this war together.

If you are a believer, the enemy has strategic "wiles" to destroy you and keep you from enjoying God and accomplishing His mission for you. Satan places just the right mix of sin in your path – and provokes just enough pressure to detonate the blast.

It is never pretty to watch.

As painful as it was to research military IED injuries and deaths, it has been more painful to watch explosions happen spiritually to people I know and love – and in the many people God has brought into my life through ministry. Families fractured from the explosions of infidelity, the heartache of homosexuality, and addictions like alcohol, drugs, pornography and gambling. I've seen homelessness, sexual abuse, rape, abortion, and the more respectable explosions from pride, ambition and various forms of idolatry.

Through all the tears and pain, the heart shredded by spiritual shrapnel never expected to be in their circumstances. So many situations started "innocently enough." The beginning stages of the explosion seemed right and justified somehow. They all stepped onto the sensitive pressure plate of sin with some level of ignorance.

Does it have to be this way?

The longer I study the Word of God, I am convinced that much of the spiritual devastation is avoidable.

The military uses armored vehicles, personal armor, detection devices, and surveillance to minimize explosive-related casualties. The Bible shows us much of the same protection, but we often don't make the connection. The military trains extensively how to recognize explosives and what to do if you see them. The Bible gives the same definition.

Military training doesn't eliminate casualties, but it greatly reduces them. Spiritual training, done effectively, could do the same thing.

In an interview with two Air Force Explosive Ordnance Disposal (EOD) technicians, I learned many important principles regarding explosives. (Some of their valuable information is included in the next few chapters.) At the end of the interview, I asked them to make parallels from their job to the battles of life. "What things have you seen explode in people's lives?" I asked. Without hesitation, they shared some painful situations within their own families and circle of friends. Even though they dismantle explosives in their military job, they had not fully connected their knowledge to the battles of life. The parallels are filled with practical wisdom.

Beating the odds

There is no way to completely avoid the landmines of life. We live in a fallen, broken world. Bad things happen to good people; fallen men make evil choices. That is the reality of life. The purpose of this section is to minimize the risk of life explosions – learn how to defuse them before they explode – and recover more effectively from explosions.

Soldiers like Travis Mills were trained and experienced. Their mission took them into dangerous territory. They were on a mission and accepted the risk to perform their assigned duty. This situation represents the usually unavoidable blast casualty. Mills did everything he could to avoid injury. He trained, he knew the risks, he wore the proper armor – his injury occurred within the line of duty. Contrast Mills to some hapless fellow who dressed for comfort in the heat, and wandered into the same mine field because it was a nice day for a walk. He is clueless of the dangers before him. This person walks in ignorance, has no protection, and foolishly exposes himself to harm. The latter example is the target of this section. Like the hapless fellow, we are too often foolishly in places and situations that can potentially explode – not in the line of duty – but in the pursuit of pleasure.

Minefield maps

When soldiers patrol in hostile lands like Afghanistan, the enemy unfortunately does not provide them with maps showing where landmines are planted. The enemy's greatest advantage is that soldiers have no idea where explosives are hidden. That ramps up the threat, and increases casualties. This is not true for the believer in Jesus Christ. Or, at least it shouldn't be.

For the Christian, God has provided a detailed minefield map. His Word brings clarity to the landscape of life. It details our mission. It shows precisely where the explosives are and what they look like. The Bible tells us what to do when we find them and also how to avoid them.

What people often see as an ancient, restrictive, irrelevant book is actually a detailed field manual filled with critical information for survival and instructions to accomplish our vital mission. When viewed along this military parallel, the Bible also becomes a vibrant, relevant resource. It is absolutely remarkable how detailed the Bible is regarding instructions for life.

I am amazed, particularly in Leviticus and Deuteronomy, by how precise God is in His guidance. The minefields are uncovered in every area of life – our church life, family life, community life, commerce, etc. So often, God even details the injuries that will happen when different types of "landmines" (or sin) are encountered. I always pay close attention to the "if-then" statements in the Bible. They usually expose a hidden fuse or two that I should be aware of.

Either/or

Since landmines and "IEDs" are a part of life, we are faced with a clear choice. It's a sort of "ready-or-not" scenario. We can be ready, or not. The encouraging factor in this whole topic is that, as a disciple of Jesus Christ, the odds are in our favor.

Charles Stanley offers the "either/or" choices – and also the encouragement of a 50-year, seasoned pastor:

> "I have watched people deal with the landmines of life, and their experience ends in one of two ways: either there is spiritual victory

and the person grows closer to the Lord, or he is tripped up by Satan's deception and begins a downward spiral that leads to feelings of regret, sorrow, anger, frustration, and – if left unchecked – depression. But you do not have to fall victim to Satan's ploys. Although physical landmines may be hard to spot, God will give you the ability to uncover and disarm the spiritual landmines the enemy has laid across your path. You may feel as though you are standing in a minefield and you do not know which way to turn. I want to assure you that God knows. He has a plan for your rescue. No matter how great the temptation, you can take back any spiritual ground you have given to the enemy and reclaim your rightful position as a child of God."[9]

The cross of Jesus Christ is the ultimate encouragement in the discussion of explosions and sin. Jesus not only "took a bullet" for us, but suffered the aggregate explosion of sin upon Himself. Jesus jumped on the global grenade of sin. By doing so, He removed the power of sin to rule over us. He disarmed it.

It is freedom from sin and its cruel authority over us that the Bible talks about in Galatians 5:1: "It was for freedom that Christ set us free: therefore keep standing firm and do not be subject again to a yoke of slavery." Loosely translated, don't step on sin because you don't have to. However, the flesh (our sinful desires) still lures us to the landmines of sin. Paul continues in verse 18: "You were called to freedom... do not turn your freedom into an opportunity for the flesh, but through love, serve one another."

We have a choice – but an empowered one. We have a map of the enemy's minefield. The truth of God's Word will expose landmines in your life, and God's power in you brings a supernatural resource to a fleshly fight.

Clearly, the devil is no match for the all-surpassing power of God, but like in Afghanistan, the devil can bring great devastation by cleverly-placed devices – especially when we are walking around in his territory.

If we're in the enemy's territory on a mission, we'd better be trained and protected. If we're there for pleasure, things will soon be "going boom."

CHAPTER 14: GOING BOOM

Most important "take-away" thought(s):

1. When you think of spiritual explosions, what is the first one that comes to mind? Did it happen to you, or someone else? What were the aftereffects?

2. Describe a situation that involves collateral damage. Did the damage bring in fear, limited movement, and a loss of the will to fight spiritual battles? Explain.

3. Who hasn't witnessed "explosives" tearing families apart? Give three examples of "camouflaged sin" that can rock a family in pieces? Why were the explosives so difficult to recognize?

4. What "explosives" are you currently playing with? (Please don't avoid this question. Give it prayerful consideration.)

5. The Bible is God's "mine field map." Find five landmines identified in Scripture. Use search words like: avoid, be careful to do, remember to…. Or look for imperative statements in Scripture.

*"He is on the path of life who heeds instruction,
but he who ignores reproof goes astray." Proverbs 10:17*

15
ORDINANCE OR ORDNANCE?

(Ordinance: an authoritative rule/Ordnance: weapons or artillery)

Bombs are their business – not making them – but making them not explode. It's not your average job – and these are not your average guys.

Technical Sergeant Rob Eisner enlisted in the Air Force right after the explosions of 9/11 because he wanted to make a difference. Master Sergeant Greg Pauli was a high school senior in New Salem, Mass., when he learned that a young soldier from nearby Ft. Devens had been killed by a bomb. Pauli also enlisted to try to make a difference.

Eisner and Pauli are EOD guys – Explosive Ordnance Disposal. Their job is to keep explosives from going boom.

Both men have each deployed three times to Iraq and Afghanistan and have encountered IEDs and UXOs (Unexploded Ordnance). But, before they could even hope to make a difference, they had to be trained.

After basic training, both attended EOD training at Eglin Air Force Base in Florida. It's a tough school with a 60 percent dropout rate. There is a huge volume of information to learn such as: ordnance types, protocol safety for each type, wait times, grounding, etc.

"Because every situation is different, you have to have true comprehension of the material, not just memorization," said Eisner.

"We train, train, train. You finally get to do what you train to do," Eisner said, referring to his first encounter with an IED on deployment.

Eisner takes EOD training seriously because failures in training could mean failures out on the field. Like the time a trainee was following Eisner as he cleared a safe path through a simulated mine field. "He was supposed to follow my path exactly as I cleared the way with a detector," Eisner explained. "I took a sharp turn, but the trainee carelessly rounded the corner – and stepped on a training mine."

Pauli shared an example from deployment. A young EOD sergeant took some risky moves while disarming an IED and nothing bad happened. "The next EOD person did the same thing – but this time, the device blew up and killed him," Pauli said.

These men are intelligent, dedicated, and dead serious, because if they aren't, people end up dead.

"When we train our guys, we don't worry about feelings. We are more worried about keeping them alive," said Eisner. "Fundamental mistakes could cost them their lives."

EOD personnel also study how the enemy builds explosives. "We study enemy TTPs (Tactics, Techniques and Procedures), and they study us," said Pauli. "The enemy is placing explosives more strategically – placing less – but in ways and areas more likely to cause damage," he said.

Pauli described a situation where they responded to the discovery of a large IED. They also discovered seven other devices around the larger one, placed to blow up as personnel approached to disarm the larger IED. "It was like the larger, more obvious IED was the lure to get us there, and the smaller ones were to take us out." He said EOD personnel are often prime enemy targets – for obvious reasons.

"As good as EOD teams are, they can't be on every patrol. It is vital that all troops are trained to recognize explosives," said Eisner. "Training is everyone's job."

And, training is what everyone gets.

How to recognize an IED

How do you recognize an IED? Unlike conventional bombs, they come in all different sizes and shapes. While it is impossible to cover every possible form of IED, the Army trains its people on the components of an EID and some of the ways they are usually camouflaged. One manual provides pages and pages of configurations, and photos showing all kinds of fuses, pressure plates, switches, trip wires, photo cells, ingredients, containers, etc.

Explosives can come packaged in containers, vehicles and people. Sadly, they can look like anything, and be anywhere.

Because that is true, how else can we detect them?

Mitigating threats

Nearly every military manual I checked contains ways to minimize the threat of IEDs by paying attention to peripherals. What is happening in your current environment? One Army IED awareness guide offered some of the following guidelines:

- Trust your instincts. If something does not seem right, it probably isn't.

- Watch the locals. Are familiar people not there? Are people moving away from you, or appearing nervous?
- Before EVERY patrol or convoy, brief personnel on latest IED threat intelligence
- Determine what types of IEDs are used in that area – techniques, patterns and likely locations
- What's the latest intelligence in the area of your mission?
- Maintain speed and movement whenever possible.
- Rehearse actions for a possible IED attack.
- Wear personal protective equipment!
- Be cautious of choke point, vehicle breakdowns, bridges, one-way roads, traffic jams, sharp turns, etc.
- If something stops movement, survey your immediate areas for IEDs.[1]

The threat of IEDs is ever-present, but vigilance, good intel, pre-planning, protective covering, and observation significantly reduce injuries.

A good soldier tries to do all those things, but what happens when they discover an IED before it explodes? They spot it on patrol. Do they just sidestep around it and move on? Fortunately there are rules for this, too.

UXO protocol

When an individual finds unexploded ordnance (UXO), there is a clear protocol to follow. The Air Force Manual breaks down the response procedure into five C's:

CONFIRM the presence of a UXO from a safe spotting distance. Identify size, shape, color and condition. Report the UXO to your UCC (Unit Control Center)

CLEAR personnel to a safe position and distance (these distances are listed in the manual). If evacuation is impossible, isolate or barricade the area to restrict access. Leave the same way you came in.

CORDON off the area. Prevent unauthorized personnel from entering the site. Place markers to mark the UXO. Ensure markers are visible in all directions and at night.

CHECK your immediate area for other UXOs

CONTROL the area. Only emergency services should be allowed to enter the cordon.[2]

Military protocol for UXO's not only seeks to protect the individual(s) near the explosive, but also to protect any others from approaching. Nothing is left to chance with such potential danger. There is even a quick reference chart at the back of the

Airman's Manual showing the various classifications of UXOs, although most of them are conventional explosives. You have to be able to recognize an explosive in order to avoid it. Once you find it, report it, protect the perimeter, and call in the professionals, then get the heck out of there.

Sin as an explosive

As we saw in the last chapter, sin does much the same damage as explosives. Part of the reason for the damage is a poor recognition of the threat and subsequent consequences. Sin is now seen as passé – and is even affirmed.

"The very word, 'sin,' which seems to have waned in usage was a proud word. It was once a strong word, an ominous and serious word. It described a central point in every civilized human being's life plan and lifestyle. But the word went away. It has almost disappeared – the word – along with the notion," writes Dr. Karl Menninger in his book, *Whatever Became of Sin?*[3] In his lengthy volume, he tracks the cultural shift from "sin" (God's laws through the church), to "crime" (man's laws through the State), to "symptoms" (minimizing law by lifting responsibility).

We live in a culture that blithely redefines sin according to its own proclivities. Basically, it is like calling an IED a knickknack and then not expecting it to blow up. Or, like deciding that cancer no longer exists, and then wondering why mortality rates keep rising. The culture removes the troubling diagnosis but then also blocks appropriate remedy to avoid the consequences that will come regardless. Why else would we be so perplexed at the rise of evil – with no explanation? Sin, like IEDs, ignores redefinition.

Ordinance versus ordnance

Sin is real, and it is exploding in lives all around us. As such, it demands definition.

Webster defines sin as "transgression of the law of God; disobedience of the divine will; moral failure."[4] In other words, sin is breaking God's law. We either follow the ordinance – or suffer the damage from ordnance.

Oswald Chambers gets more specific (and personal) in his book, *The Philosophy of Sin*. He writes: "Sin is a disposition of self-love that obeys every temptation to its own lordship. Sin is literally self-centered rule, a disposition that rules the life apart from God."[5]

Chambers writes that "the Bible is the only Book that gives us any indication of the true nature of sin, and where it came from."[6] Like the Army manual showing picture after picture of IED configuration, the Bible trains us to recognize sin by showing us commandments, statutes, precepts and ordinances.

I was stunned as I read through Psalm 119 in the context of explosive ordnance. The author, David, had suffered his fair share of sin blasts. Like a battle-bred gunnery sergeant, David has a reverent love for the Manual. God's laws – or ordinances – were now his delight. He truly appreciates God's Word as his "minefield map." In verse 116, he writes: "Sustain me according to your Word, that I may live."

Consider these verses:

> "I have chosen the faithful way; I have placed your ordinances before me." (v. 30)

> "Make me walk in the path of your commandments, for I delight in it." (v. 35)

> "And I will walk at liberty for I seek your precepts." (v. 45)

> "I considered my ways and turned my feet to your testimonies." (v. 59)

> "Your commandments make me wiser than my enemies, for they are ever mine." (v. 98)

> "I have restrained my feet from every evil way, that I may keep your word." (v. 101)

> "The wicked have laid a snare for me, yet I have not gone astray from your precepts." (v. 110)

> "Establish my footsteps in your Word, and do not let any iniquity have dominion over me." (v. 133)

> "Let my soul live that it may praise You, and let your ordinances help me." (v. 175)

Don't they just jump off the page in that context?

God's ordinances train us to avoid Satan's ordnance. God's Word is the detection device that alerts us to danger. David knew that when he paid attention to God's ordinances, he could confidently say, "Your word is a lamp to my feet and a light to my path" (v. 105).

Like the careless EOD soldier that lost his life, we too can be careless with the rules – particularly in a world that applauds breaking them.

God's laws are not restrictive – they are protective. All through Scripture, when God's laws are explained, it is so it will go well with God's people. God wants us to flourish and He gives us the blueprint to do so.

Minefield example

The first time I actually used military parallels to teach spiritual principles was at an educational co-op eight years ago. As I reviewed the theology learning goals, presenting the content with military principles made it easier for teenagers to understand.

As part of the teaching on the doctrine of sin, we used a minefield example. On a large dry-erase board we drew several circles, each representing different things that explode in people's lives. Searching Scripture helped us define them.

The apostle Paul is like the New Testament EOD guy in II Corinthians 12. He identifies the explosives of strife, jealousy, angry tempers, disputes, slander, gossip, arrogance, and "disturbances among them." (v. 20) Other verses add pride, insecurity, compromise, unforgiveness, fear, immorality, etc.

As we labeled the circles, we then brainstormed how these mines could be camouflaged. What are they covered with that make them seem harmless? Pride might be covered with confidence. Insecurity might be covered by false humility, fear with healthy caution, slothfulness with rest, gossip with concern, strife with problem-solving, etc. It's easy to rationalize our behavior and not see sin that can explode in life.

While the conversations with the teenage students were very enlightening, one aspect unfolded before us that I never planned, nor have I have ever forgotten. After we had discussed all the landmine circles, we drew a narrow path through them. Right before us was a striking illustration of Matthew 7:13-14: "Enter through the narrow gate; for the gate is wide and *the way is broad that leads to destruction*, and there are many that enter through it. For the gate is small and *the way is narrow that leads to life*, and there are few who find it."

God's ways are often labeled narrow, and the fallacy is that the broad way brings life. Looking at the minefield in front of us told us a different story. It illustrated that the broad way not only does not lead to life, but is deadly. However, the beautiful truth is that God's narrow way leads to life – but it also ultimately leads to a broad way. As we followed the narrow path through the minefield, the end of the path brought Psalm 18:19 to mind: "He brought me forth also into a broad place; He rescued me, because He delighted in me."

Moses saw life the same way. After God delivered His people from bondage in Egypt, God (through Moses) set before them elaborate ordinances for life. His commands were narrow – but He was preparing them to enjoy their land of promise – a broad land filled with milk and honey. God knew the explosives they experienced in Egypt, and the societal snares waiting for them in Canaan. God knew sin had left "corpses in the wilderness." (Numbers 14:29, 32) God knew sin would steal the Promised Land from them. Moses repeatedly told them to "be careful to observe all that God had commanded."

Sin explodes, but God's Word is the truth that provides a way around it.

Prone to wander

Sin originated with Satan. Satan set mines in Eden. Just like a buried mine, Chambers says: "Satan guards the main body of his purpose; neither Eve nor Adam had the slightest notion of who he was."[7] Sin exploded in Adam and Eve – and has ripped down through the generations.

But, God has always provided a way out. In the Old Testament, it was by precise practices of the priests through meticulous, repeated sacrifices. In the New Testament, it is through the once-and-for-all, perfect sacrifice of Jesus Christ – our eternal High Priest. The power of sin is broken by the cross but as Chambers notes: "It is gloriously possible not to sin, but never impossible to sin, because we are moral agents."[8]

It is not that we have to sin, it's that we are prone to wander – and that's never good in a minefield.

"Our Lord spoke about men as sheep: a sheep has no set conscious purpose to go wrong, it simply wanders; and our Lord used the illustration for men; the majority of men wander like sheep without any conscious bad intent at all," Chambers writes.[9]

We do wander like sheep, but intention makes little difference if you're in a minefield. Just as a soldier wandering "outside the wire" on his own is exponentially more likely to explode, so are God's disciples when they wander outside of the Word according to their own inclinations.

When Joshua gathered God's wayward people on the brink of the promised land of Canaan, God addressed their tendency to wander. "Only be strong and very courageous; be careful to do according to all the law which Moses My servant commanded you; do not turn from it to the right or to the left, so that you may have success wherever you go." (Joshua 1: 6-7,9)

God's Word is crucial to navigating through a life filled with danger. We can't rationalize it, adjust it, tweak or ignore it. Maybe that's why Paul emphasized sound doctrine throughout his epistles. He was always warning them of sin that explodes in individuals and churches – and how often it was linked to false teachers. That makes more sense now. If the Word of God is our minefield map – then any distortion of the map could lead to death and dismemberment.

Careless carnage

When Eisner and Pauli were asked to name the top things to never do with explosives, their instant answer was surprising. "Kick it," they said. Noting my look of unbelief, they said, "You'd be surprised how many people think it will be nothing."

I thought that was ridiculous until I thought of all the people who kick sin around thinking it will be nothing. Most of life's explosions have started with some "harmless" action. As people dabbled on the fringes of sin, they were sure it was innocent – and would stay that way. So many people broken by sin have said, "I never meant for this to happen."

This is exactly what the military is talking about concerning threat mitigation. Are we paying attention? Do we heed the warning signs? They are almost always there.

Let's look back at the military checklist and see some of the parallels to sin.

"If something does not seem right, it probably isn't."

In Malcolm Gladwell's book, *Blink*, he explores the ability people have to have "gut reactions" to situations – often backed up by the cues we unconsciously collect from our environment. If we are really paying attention to situations, we are more apt to respond to that sense that something is amiss. As a believer, we often have the advantage of the Holy Spirit in us, giving us needed discernment.

Because paying attention is so important, Satan does everything he can to get us distracted – which is not too difficult in our age of technology. It is not unusual to see people fixated on their smart phones, paying little or no attention to their environment. We are a multi-tasking society, and that can be a set-up for sin.

When the military gives explosive-avoidance tips, they don't have to convince soldiers that the threat is real. They know the IEDs are out there, and they see every patrol as a potentially dangerous process. The same is true about us and sin – except that we don't seem to be convinced the threat is real. If we did, we might follow Paul's advice to the Ephesians to "walk circumspectly...for the days are evil." (Eph. 5:15-16)

"Before every patrol or convoy, brief personnel on latest IED threat intelligence"

The operative word here is "every." The missions might be the same, but the threats may be different from day to day. Intelligence briefings combine all of the available data to give correct, timely information relevant to the mission and the area.

The same should be true as we live our daily lives. For us, our spiritual intelligence comes from the Holy Spirit as we pray regularly for His leading.

A threat briefing in our own lives may be as simple as researching a movie before attending the theater. It may be determining how much drinking might be at a party before you attend. It might be finding out ahead of time that a flirtatious co-worker is the only other one attending a business lunch. The point is that a little homework can be a big help in mitigating threats that might explode into sin.

"Maintain speed and movement whenever possible."

This maxim could be summed up: "Don't linger longer that you need to." To keep moving suggests that we stay the course of our mission. When we linger where we don't belong, trouble is more likely to happen.

"Rehearse actions for a possible IED attack."

We have seen that the military has a planned protocol for all types of situations that involve explosions or assaults. They don't just plan it, they practice it. In this context, we say, "Of course!" But, what about a sin context?

I've read many parenting books over the years. Many of them suggest rehearsing situations with your kids so they are better prepared if those situations happen. If you're at a party, and there is drinking, what should you do? If someone offers you drugs, what should you do? If responses are thought out ahead of time, the right response is more likely to happen.

If that's true in the military, and it's true with kids, why is it seldom true for believing adults? It may sound childish, but it's not such a bad idea. Even if you don't act out a proposed response, it's helpful to at least talk about it.

The main point is that, if you don't designate reactions to specific threats, you are not as prepared for them as you could be.

"Wear personal protective equipment"

Dressing for comfort and style is not a priority in the military. Full "battle rattle" dress includes at least 50 pounds of gear: a rucksack, flak vest, Kevlar helmet, ammunition, weapons, and other basic military equipment. The point is to be protected, at all times, on every mission. It's heavy, uncomfortable, and hot – but the alternative is far worse.

As disciples of Christ, what protection do we put on in our daily battle with sin? Do we put on the armor of God listed in Ephesians 6: the belt of truth, breastplate of righteousness, feet shod with gospel of peace, the shield of faith, and helmet of salvation. These pieces all represent the Word of God and they protect our heads (minds), hearts, feet, and body. Without the spiritual armor, we are basically fighting spiritual battles in our underwear – fully exposed to enemy attacks.

"Be cautious of choke points, vehicle breakdowns... traffic jams..."

On a military mission, any time your mobility is hindered, you are vulnerable to the enemy. Think stalled convoy, downed aircraft, or wounded infantry. There are many ways the enemy can clog our progress – and lure us into a vulnerable position. Spiritually, we can be slowed by opposition, sickness, discouragement, family issues, addictions, temptations, etc. Whenever our spiritual progress can be hindered, we are more open to explosive ambush.

Do we think this way? Do we see minor backsliding as a "choke point?" We haven't picked up the Word in a week. Do we see this as a vulnerability? Whatever slows us down ramps up the risk.

Unexploded sin

We saw how the military gave precise protocol with UXOs. Remember the five C's: confirm, clear, cordon, check and control? I am intrigued by how these steps might apply to unexploded sin. In a world that tells us all to mind our own business, what are we supposed to do when we see sin that might explode in someone else's life? How do we apply these protocol steps?

It may be as simple as finding a pornographic magazine under a couch cushion. Confirm it's there, restrict access (throw it away or burn it), check for other magazines, control the area, and bring in professionals (the parents).

It may be very complicated. The point is that we should not be passive when we discover sin that has the ability to destroy people's lives. We should report it, try to keep people from stepping on it, protect the area, and bring in professionals when needed.

What do we do when we see sin that could explode in the church? What do we do with gossip that can cause explosions in the life of the one gossiped about? What do we do with people undermining authority and not going through appropriate channels to problem solve? What do we do when we observe a friend exhibiting "dangerous" behavior? These are tough issues. The answers are not always as clear as a checklist, but they still demand action.

When I read I Corinthians 10:13, I am prodded to think about this unexploded sin thing. It says: "No temptation has overtaken you but such as is common to man; and God is faithful who will not allow you to be tempted beyond what you are able, but with the temptation will provide the way of escape also, so that you will be able to endure it."

I see temptation as unexploded sin. When the verse says that God will provide a way of escape so that we may be able to endure, or overcome it, I wonder if I could be a way God provides. In Matthew 18, Jesus tells us to go to a brother that has sinned, tell him his faults, and help to restore him. But, what about before we sin? If I am to be about my brother's restoration, what about his not sinning to begin with? This is what trench buddies do for each other. They pay attention. They watch for explosives. When they see something suspect, they initiate some form of the five C's – however they might apply. The first one might be sufficient – confirm the explosive exists.

A trench buddy did this for me. Years ago, I worked some evenings at the base with a male co-worker. Perfectly innocent. A few months later, I was having breakfast with my trench buddy, and she haltingly brought the subject up. She expressed her concern that I was mentioning this guy's name frequently. As a married woman who guards her marriage well, I thanked her for her concern, but pretty much shrugged it off. That evening, her words played over and over in my mind. Surely her concerns were unfounded. As I continued to search the matter through, I realized that I actually gave some thought about what I wore to work the nights he was there. Wow. A UXO was hiding under something so benign and unintentional. That one realization was enough for me. I purposely stopped working on any night he would be there, and shortly after that, he left for another position. I really don't think that anything would have ever happened in that situation, but, who knows? I have profound respect for my friend. She risked rejection by challenging me in love. She was a trench buddy.

I could not help but think how many other situations (UXOs) could be avoided by concerned warnings long before anything blows up. When trench buddies battle for the soul of another, they are willing to risk their own comfort for the sake of another. This is exactly the type of diligence it requires.

Not every warning will be heeded, but, at least the way of escape was provided. And, it certainly doesn't make us all everyone else's "sin police." It is a true heart of love that provides the right motive for these types of warnings. Just as a parent lovingly warns their kids, and a pastor lovingly warns his flock, so trench buddies lovingly exhort their friends when temptations are noticed.

Spiritual checklist

The military provides checklists as a quick-reference training guide. Gerry Bridges offers a similar spiritual checklist in his book, *Respectable Sins*. They don't fall into the five C's, but they do provide very helpful tips. Obviously, by the title of his book, Bridges highlights the sins that tend to stay hidden because of their general acceptability. Some of these include: anxiety, discontent, pride, selfishness, lack of self-control, impatience, irritability, judgmentalism, envy, jealousy, sins of the tongue, and worldliness.

To avoid the explosions of sin:

- Apply the gospel: face the reality of sin, but know the gospel makes us righteous and forgiven
- Depend on the Holy Spirit: it is not our will power, but the power of the Holy Spirit
- Recognize your responsibility: pursue practical steps in dealing with sin
- ID all respectable sins

- Memorize and apply appropriate Scripture: apply specific Scripture to specific sin
  - Cultivate a practice of prayer: both for sin committed and for temptation
  - Involve one or a few other believers: to give us accountability and more prayer[10]

Just as war is never easy, neither is our battle with sin. Our spiritual war is never over as long as we have breath, so our diligence and training is necessary until the end.

We are ever learning in this area, but the good news is that we can use our training – and even our explosions – to help others. That is what many of the wounded veterans are doing, and that is what we can do, too. Celebrate Recovery is one of many great examples of sin-wounded warriors helping others through the explosions of addictions.

The heart that risks

When you're an EOD guy, you tend to see life through a lens of life or death. It comes with the job. They know that unless they intervene, things can – and will – blow up. What is true on the battlefield can be true in life.

Because Eisner and Pauli see explosives up-close-and-personal, they are also more prone to intervene in the lives of those they love. They both related personal situations where they saw the potential for explosions and tried to warn the people in those situations. They were willing to take the flak for possibly offending people with their warning rather than feeling responsible for inaction. Their stories are too personal to share details, but these tough men were visibly upset because their warnings were ignored, and explosions occurred. They had tried to employ some form of confirm, clear, cordon, check and control – but they never got past the confirm stage.

The heart that cares is a heart that risks. It doesn't always work out. Just ask Eisner and Pauli. But, when lives are at stake, it's always the right thing to do.

CHAPTER 15: ORDINANCE OR ORDNANCE

Most important "take-away" thought(s):

1. Awareness is critical to avoiding explosions. In what ways are we distracted in our culture. Name at least five.

2. Write out the 5 C's protocol. Think of one example of something that spiritually explodes in a believer's life. Explain how these C's can be applied in that situation.

3. In what ways are you rationalizing (or camouflaging) the explosives in your life? Are the explosives hidden because of your ignorance of God's Word? (Hard question, but the stakes are high...)

4. What areas of your life are really familiar to you? Home? Work? Church? Have your stopped praying for "intel reports" in those areas through prayer? Have you ever considered these areas of your life as places where explosives could be planted? Explain.

5. What things does the enemy do to slow us down or isolate us to make us more vulnerable to attack? If you see it happening to someone else, how should you proceed as a good trench buddy? Be specific.

"My brethren, if any among you strays from the truth and one turns him back, let him know that he who turns a sinner from the error of his way will save his soul from death and will cover a multitude of sins." James 5:19-20

16
DEFUSING THE BOOM

The best advice about bombs: avoid them.

Good advice.

But, what if it's your job to defuse them like the EOD guys we met in the previous chapter? They are called to bombs the way firefighters are called to fires. It's not a job for amateurs – something sergeants Rob Eisner and Greg Pauli know all too well from their tours in Iraq and Afghanistan.

They live by the adage: "Distance and coverage are your best friends."

They also have careful protocols for every situation, because "sloppy" can get you killed.

In the parallel to life – and particularly spiritual warfare – EOD rules illustrate several biblical principles that are both practical and protective. These principles are especially important when we have to face explosive sin in the lives of others. Nearly everyone has seen explosive sins like infidelity, addictions, betrayal, dishonesty, etc. We've seen their shrapnel flying in every direction.

As we mature as Christians, we should become better trained to defuse these explosive situations because pastors can't be there for everyone. Like it or not, we will likely find ourselves faced with explosive situations. What will we do? EOD personnel have some gems to teach us here.

Know your bombs

This sounds basic, but EOD technicians exhaustively study the details of many, many types of bombs. They need specific definition if they are to understand the components well enough to disarm them – or even to determine the risk associated with any given bomb. Like Eisner said, "You have to have true comprehension of the material, not just memorization, because every situation is different."

Defusing bombs is obviously stressful, which is one more reason you really need to know your stuff. Uncertainty accentuates stress. The situation demands detailed knowledge, and the ability to use it in dynamic environments.

Do we have the same, studied, detailed knowledge of the types of sin that can explode in us, or the people around us? If the devil is in the details, then these details are of utmost importance because of the explosive nature of sin. Do we have a true comprehension of sin – especially in our media-saturated society with so many conflicting messages?

I had a conversation once with a woman who was brought up in a strong Christian home and said she was a believer. The topic of the 10 commandments came up, which is usually a generally-accepted basic understanding of the law and sin. She balked at the idea that the 10 commandments had any relevance to our lives as New Testament believers. "Jesus did away with the law," she said confidently. "We no longer have to obey that."

After I retrieved my jaw from the floor, I gently explained that Jesus did not do away with the law, but fulfilled it. (Matt. 5:17) I then asked, "Which one of the 10 commandments is it now okay to break?" She stared at me like I had stepped out of some medieval time machine. I spoke of the loving, covenantal nature of God's laws to protect us, much like a mother's admonition for her child not to touch a hot stove. She then glared at me, turned, and walked away. I was deeply saddened by the encounter because it reflected an ignorance of Scripture – especially when it came to the explosive nature of sin. It turned out to be a symptomatic ignorance because I learned later that she had already succumbed to an affair, and subsequently divorced, creating one more shattered home with children involved.

Without clear definition of sin, we are like the EOD guy that slacks off in class. Out in the field, he is a danger to himself and others.

We often ask the question, "Is it okay to do this or that?" We should be asking the more fundamental question, "Is this right or wrong based on God's truth."

God's Word can literally be a lifesaver from sin – which is why Satan distorted it with Eve. Once Eve veered from God's exact words, the slide into sin was set up. God's Word and God's character was presented as suspect instead of sure. Satan continues to do the same thing with us. All manner of sin is deemed "okay" today using a perversion of Scripture as justification.

Knowledge of the Bible – when practiced – shows us the difference between good and evil. "But solid food [of the Word] is for the mature, who because of practice have their senses trained to discern good from evil." (Hebrews 5:14) The writer of Hebrews chastises seasoned believers because they were still on the elemental principles of the Word, and they should have been teachers by that point. He also stresses that it is "by reason of use." If you're not studying the Book, you're not trained to recognize sin.

Defusing sin

During the Gulf War, SCUD missiles were a problem. If they reached their mark, and penetrated our defenses, they could cause great damage. The U.S. military had a solution: Patriot missiles. Patriot launchers were set up in strategic areas to launch counterstrikes. These heat-seeking missiles would home in on incoming explosives to disarm them harmlessly in the air. Patriot intercepts saved many lives during the Gulf War.

As we saw in the weapons section, the Word of God is a wonderful defense. Besides knowing the Word to recognize explosive sin, it is also a vital tool to defuse explosives before they penetrate – in this case, before sin penetrates into the heart and mind of a believer. Sin is like a SCUD missile hurling through the atmosphere, heading directly for our mind. It is the first sign of temptation. Do we have Patriot missiles ready to launch a counterstrike, or do we simply wait for the missile to hit? A careful study of God's Word arms us with an eternal supply of counterstrike missiles (as Jesus so brilliantly illustrated in Matthew 4). Do I know the Word well enough to launch a precision strike, or does my counterstrike fail to intercept the SCUD? For example, Satan attacks with a SCUD against my self-worth, and I counter with a missile on tithing. Oops.... Boom!

Instead, I counterstrike with Ephesians 2:10: "I am His workmanship created in Christ Jesus for good works that He before ordained that I should walk in them." Boom back! Launch Ephesians 2:4: "But God, being rich in mercy, because of His great love with which he loved us...." Direct hit! Another launch, I John 4:10: "In this is love, not that we loved God, but that He loved us and sent His Son to be the propitiation for our sins." Boom. Done. Defused. When we begin to battle like this, the Word is strong, strategic, and life-changing!

It's important to note that knowledge of sin is not to label people, but to protect them. There is not one ounce of self-righteousness in this process of training. If anything, it shows our own vulnerability. It should provoke trench buddy relationships – for our sakes and theirs – just like the EOD guys rely on each other.

The Word of God, properly applied, neutralizes the enemy's lies that bring so much destruction. It also can be skillfully applied in sin situations with other people, just as the EOD guys use their knowledge to save others.

EOD lessons

When we are drawn in to help with explosive sin situations, EOD protocol fits well. One of the things they stressed often was focus. "You can't focus on fear. It brings unnecessary stress that can divert concentration to the task at hand," Eisner said. Military EOD people focus on the bomb and saving lives.

Focus

In the spiritual parallel, we need focus as well. It is no casual event. As I write this, I think of several situations I've watched implode over the years. Explosions had already occurred in homes or workplaces. Emotions run extremely high. It hurts to see people hurt. There are usually many different dynamics going on in explosive situations. The trauma is draining on many levels – and can be confusing. It's easy to lose focus. Other explosions can happen in the confusion.

In these painful cases, the last thing a person needs is poor counsel. Prayer is crucial in these complex issues. Prayer brings focus. The Holy Spirit is able to bring needed wisdom to reduce collateral damage. God can reveal the hidden things through prayer. What secret fuses remain? Is the explosion a trap leading to a worse explosion? In the "he-said, she-said" craziness of explosions, clarity is key.

Work as a team

One of the non-negotiables for Eisner and Pauli is their three-person teams. "We've been asked to go into situations with less than three, and the answer is always 'no'," said Pauli. "We need many eyes on the scene for the best results."

According to Pauli, one member of the team disarms, and the other two provide peripheral safety in case other threats show up. The two observers provide constant communication to the one disarming, and they can also see the explosive up close via a robotic camera at the scene. That makes a total of six eyes for every defusing job.

That's the idea behind Proverbs 11:14: "Where there is no guidance the people fall, but in abundance of counselors there is victory." The King James Version says: "the multitude of wise men brings safety."

When explosives threatened the early church through disagreements about circumcision for the Gentiles, Paul and Barnabas appealed to the apostles and elders in Jerusalem. A team approach brought wisdom and consensus to defuse a volatile situation.

Working as a team not only brings greater wisdom to explosive situations, but it also protects the team members themselves. "They have your back no matter what," Eisner declares, referring to his EOD team.

How many pastors have attempted to rescue troubled marriages on their own – and get caught up in affairs with the couple's wife as a result? A team approach brings in accountability and safety to all parties. Matthew 18 advises us to approach a sinning brother alone the first time, but if no repentance occurs, bring two or three others. It is the stubbornly rebellious that cause the bigger explosions, so it takes a team.

It also brings God preeminently to the mix in Matthew 18:20: "For where two or three have gathered in My name, I am there in their midst."

Distance and cover

No EOD technician ever approaches an explosive unless absolutely necessary. The initial approach to the explosive is accomplished by robotics so they can get reliable, up-close information. Good thinking. If something is going to possibly explode, I would want to know as much as I could before trying to defuse it.

Depending on the nature of the explosive, often the robot can disarm or safely detonate the device, and EOD personnel never have to get near the danger. Other times, they must physically approach the device, which is called manual entry to the site. To manually disarm the device, "hand jamming" is usually the last resort. Obviously, the risk rises exponentially the closer you get to the device. The same is true when we get close to sin situations.

It is foolish to run into explosive sin situations without prior knowledge about the details. If we don't have reliable information, our protocol may be faulty. Getting prior information may be through prayer, through speaking with someone close to the situation, etc. To be safe and effective, we need to know what we are dealing with. This can be much harder in spiritual situations because of the presence of demonic activity. The Holy Spirit can provide critical guidance in these areas – and some people are more gifted in these areas than others.

Often prayer can defuse the situation all by itself. We often don't pray before rushing in to rescue others. The Holy Spirit convicts people of sin much better than we could ever hope to. Prayer also brings spiritual resources to a spiritual explosive. We should only approach an explosive situation when we are qualified to do so.

I remember an article about a team of three pastors called to intervene in an explosive, demonic situation. Just prior to entering the room with a man obviously possessed by a demon, one of the pastors hung back. When the other pastors questioned his reticence, the pastor confessed that he had unconfessed sin in his life and therefore lacked the true spiritual authority needed to defuse the situation. This soiled pastor was wise.

Maybe that's why Paul tells the Galatians that only the spiritual should be helping those caught in sin. "Brethren, even if anyone is caught in any trespass, *you who are spiritual*, restore such a one in a spirit of gentleness; each one looking to yourself, so that you too will not be tempted." (Gal. 6:1)

Bible teacher John MacArthur sees the Matthew 18-principle as pivotal for keeping explosions out of the church. MacArthur says the principle, if followed, has a multiplying effect. If I have to be right with God to be qualified to approach someone else in sin, then, according to MacArthur, two people are purified for every one person approached. Clearing my own sin before approaching the explosive sin in another also helps me to think clearly, and be a more fruitful vessel of the Holy Spirit.

The Galatians verse talks about our risk of temptation as we help others. Because risk is a reality in any potentially explosive situation, distance and cover are extremely important. We should never get any closer to sin than we absolutely need to in order to help another. We should also be covered by protection and accountability from our own trench buddy team. I unashamedly ask for prayer when I know that I am heading into volatile situations. I need the added spiritual cover, and fare much better with the protection. It is like the two EOD team members providing cover while the one member approached the explosive device.

When EOD personnel perform manual entry to an explosive, they hide beneath the cover of an 85-pound bomb protection suit that covers every part of their body but their hands – which they need exposed for dexterity. It's cumbersome, bulky and hot – "but you don't approach an explosive without protection no matter how trained you are," said the experienced Eisner.

Don't risk your life for nothing

No two EOD missions are the same. Some devices are disarmed, and others are destroyed by controlled explosion. "It depends on the location," explained Eisner. He said the simplest way to remove the threat is a BIP, or a blow-in-place. Many questions have to be considered: Are there people nearby? Is it on a main supply route? Can the area withstand a high-order detonation? Is it a trap?

For every situation they consider personnel, property, and the presence of possible evidence. All extenuating circumstances determine how an explosive is neutralized. There are no rubber stamp answers, but one thing is clear: "We don't want to risk our lives for nothing," Pauli said.

That is good advice for the believer in Jesus Christ. Spiritual situations provide an equally plentiful plethora of possible solutions.

Sometimes the easiest solution (although not emotionally) is to allow a "BIP." There are some situations where God clearly wants us to stay out of the way, and let the situation blow up. It's one of the toughest things to watch (I've had my share of them), but God may be using the explosion to bring a person to the end of themselves, and to the beginning of a deeper walk with God. There are situations, particularly the ones when people have been warned repeatedly, where sin has to run its course to teach needed lessons. In other situations people are just not listening at all and still really love playing with explosives. There is a right time to risk, but some of these situations present a wrong time.

Like the EOD considerations, we have to consider other people in proximity, and remove them from the area before the blast occurs. We may need to protect the people around the one exploding. In still other situations, our role may mean being there to restore the person after the blast.

In some situations, it's not our role, but God has called someone else to intervene.

When we have prayed and weighed our options, there are times that we are called to do a "manual entry" and approach the person. This may involve a longer investment of time after the initial approach, as we may need to provide an extended discipleship period to further disarm explosive sin issues. This may include providing temporary housing, financial assistance, and always prayer and encouragement. No two situations are the same.

It's not easy to discern our role at times in explosive situations. Whatever it is, we must stay trained, and steer clear of explosives ourselves. Like the EOD heroes, we should not let fear or our own safety dictate our mission, but we should also never, ever take unnecessary risks.

What if it's you?

We've discussed a variety of situations involving other people. But, what if it's you? What if no one is around to help? It's not the best-case scenario, but it happens. How do you defuse explosives in your own life? We've already talked about the importance of distance and cover. Keep your distance from the common things that explode in people's lives. Provide cover in the areas of accountability, prayer, the armor of God, and godly fellowship. Fight temptation in the form of lies with the truth of Scripture. These are familiar concepts to most believers. But, despite our best efforts, things can still explode. What then?

How do you quell residual blasts associated with the initial explosion? These questions make me think of a badly-scarred Vietnam veteran I heard speak during Desert Storm. His name is Dave Roever.

Eight months into his Vietnam tour, the Texas native was a river boat gunner with the elite Brown Water Black Berets. On July 26, 1969, Roever had just released a white phosphorous canister grenade which was hit by a sniper bullet. The explosion melted most of the skin on his head, destroying one eye, an ear, and several body parts. Much of his body was burned as he fell into the water and the phosphorus continued to burn. The left side of his head was exposed to the skull and the rest of his head was charred. His rescue helicopter caught fire, but he eventually made it to a MASH unit and then to a fixed overseas hospital.

He spent 14 months in the hospital enduring skin grafts, prosthetic preparation, and multiple major operations. He is still married to his childhood sweetheart, Brenda, and they have two grown children and four grandchildren. Roever speaks all over the world, encouraging military and civilians alike as they face explosions of their own.

It was Roever's unwavering faith in Jesus Christ that brought him through the explosion – defused it – and brought great ministry through it. He offers hope to the hurting, and models a pattern that fits many situations.

Everyone gets hurt

Roever doesn't see his situation as special.

"Everybody gets hurt," Roever says. "Sometimes the scars on the inside are worse than the scars on the outside."

He's right. And spiritual injuries can be some of the worst.

When spiritual explosions occur, we too can face a long road to recovery. When Roever was hit, at some point someone had to determine the extent of his injuries and figure out a rehabilitation plan. Whether our spiritual explosions are large or small, spiritual triage always precedes treatment. Where have you been hit? What has sin damaged? What's no longer working as it should? What's missing that should be there? Where are we bleeding dry?

Sin damages relationships with God, with others, and with ourselves. Our praise, prayers and priorities are missing or damaged. Just as the blood of life ebbs from gaping physical wounds, so our spiritual life wanes when sin cuts into our souls. The problem is that physical injuries, especially like Roever's are painfully apparent. There is no hiding them. But often, when a soul bleeds, no one notices. This is especially true when sin is involved because we tend to keep that hidden.

After triage, then what?

So, after the triage, what are some of the things we can do spiritually to help someone survive a blast and blunt its effects? I realize that cases vary and situations are complex, but a few of Roever's steps can be ours.

First, get them out of the burning explosion. Get them to a safer place to see the extent of the injury. Move the spiritual casualty away from the explosion site.

Stop the bleeding. Apply a tourniquet to keep other vital organs from dying. In a spiritual sense, stem the loss of spiritual life.

Treat for shock. Most people in violent spiritual explosions go numb. They don't know what they need – it's up to others to provide essential care.

Stop infection. The initial wounds are bad enough without adding infection to the mix. The wounds need additional protection from bacteria. A spiritually wounded person needs a cleaner-than-normal environment because their spiritual health is compromised and open to infection. Nothing cleans a spiritual wound like repentance. The well-known verse says: "If we confess our sin, He is faithful and just to forgive our sin, and cleanse us from all unrighteousness." (I John 1:9) This may be applied to a fresh spiritual wound, but also to any other open sin wounds present.

Hopefully a medic arrives on the scene at some point in this process, or the injured person is taken to some kind of medical facility for more professional care with better medical equipment. Often, in the case of spiritual explosions, our initial care should be followed quickly by the help of those more qualified.

Prepare for airlift. Our base had three medical squadrons that provided medical care at different distances from the battlefield. One prepared patients for airlift to medical facilities, another cared for them during the flight, and the third worked in a clinic/hospital setting. The treatment process for war wounded took many skill sets at different levels of care. The same thing is true with spiritual wounds. God has gifted people in the church with diverse gifts – and they all work together well (or should) to provide consistent care for the best possible outcome. Do we take advantage of these gifts?

This last point is an important one. I have been in many spiritually-explosive situations, and greatly appreciate the care provided by blended gifts. Often, my take on a situation is limited, and complementary gifts offer greatly needed perspectives that improve the quality of spiritual care. It has been a joy to watch this happen, and a greater joy to see the spiritual results.

Healing and redemption

Pursue healing. Those that fare the best after explosions are those determined to heal – to do the hard work of recovery. Like Roever, those that allow God to redeem explosions, do it one day at a time, with determination. Roever admits that he battled suicidal thoughts for 20 years after his explosions, but he even has a positive spin on that. "I won that battle every day for 20 years," he said. "At some point, the victory is fully won." Depending on who else may have been involved in a spiritual explosion, forgiveness may be necessary for healing. Roever has been involved in ministry in Vietnam for years.

Defusing the full effect of explosions, physical or spiritual, is no flash-in-the-pan experience. Outside of miraculous healings, redeeming explosions take time. It takes patient endurance. It takes a resolute spirit that believes that if your life has been spared, then you still have a grand purpose. Roever sees his explosive injuries as a vehicle to greater ministry than he could have had otherwise.

On the battlefield of life, of course we want to avoid explosions of sin. But in a fallen world, there will always be the inevitable blast from situations we could never have anticipated. When we are felled on the spiritual battlefield, our Great Physician is the best Combat Medic ever. He has absorbed the majority of the explosion in Himself on the cross. Now he fights for us, treats us, forgives us, cleanses us, heals us, and prepares us for ministry that fully redeems our explosions.

Jesus risked His life for us. May we wisely do the same for others.

DIGGING
DEEPER

CHAPTER 16: DEFUSING THE BOOM

Most important "take-away" thought(s):

1. On a scale of 1-10, how well do you know Scripture to clearly identify sin in your path? Based on your assessment, explain how your rating affects your vulnerability to spiritual explosion.

2. Incoming explosives can create chaos and fear. How can you practically stay focused in these situations to best protect yourself? How do you provide distance and cover?

3. EOD teams work together in groups of three. Give a practical situation that utilizes the three-person team approach for a spiritual/life situation.

4. Have you ever rushed into an explosive situation and found you were not trained to intervene? What are some practical things we should have in place before we enter into explosive situations? When should you leave an explosive situation alone? Be specific and provide a practical example – either fictional, or one you have seen or experienced.

5. What if you've been hit? What then? Explain redemption from personal experience, if possible. If not, describe a situation where you've seen full redemption after an explosion has taken place.

He stores up sound wisdom for the upright; He is a shield to those who walk in integrity, Guarding the paths of justice, and He preserves the way of His godly ones. Then you will discern righteousness and justice and equity and every good course.
Proverbs 2: 7-9

17

DIRTY BOMBS

There is one last category of bombs that are perhaps the scariest of all – dirty bombs. The presence of harmful chemical agents is very difficult to detect, and the damage can be devastating.

Syria has recently been in the headlines for allegedly killing approximately 1,400 people with deadly sarin gas in August 2013, and injuring scores more.

According to *National Geographic News*, one of the earliest known uses of chemical weapons also occurred in Syria in 256 AD, when the area was controlled by the Romans. According to the article, Syrians (Sasanians) mixed burnt bitumen and sulfur, added it to fire, and pumped choking clouds down tunnels when Roman soldiers were advancing through them.[1]

Another nation in the news appears as the next recorded chemical warfare event in 1346. The Crimean city of Caffa, in what was part of Ukraine, was fighting against a Tartar force when a mysterious plague overtook the Tartars and swiftly cut down their numbers. Dead Tartars became chemical weapons as they catapulted their dead corpses into the city. In the article, University of California, Davis professor Mark Wheelis believes the catapulted corpses likely spread Black Death to Caffa.[2]

In the 1700's, it was reported that British troops may have used smallpox-infected blankets to reduce the Indian population during the French and Indian War.[3]

But, it was not until World War I that chemical weapons became more sophisticated. It became known as "the chemists' war" when the Germans released thousands of cylinders of yellow-green chlorine gas across the battlefield (even though small amounts of tear gas has been used earlier by French and Germans alike). The chlorine gas was a choking agent causing fluid to build up in the lungs, which killed hundreds of French soldiers. They also used mustard gas, which was harder to escape and caused painful blisters.[4]

The estimated 100,000 casualties from gas attacks in WWI prompted the League of Nations to ban chemical and biological warfare in 1925. Thirty nations signed on then and 100 nations have signed since.[5]

Napalm (a sticky, gasoline-like substance that melts the skin off its victims) was used in WWII and also in Vietnam. The 1960's added Agent Orange and the toxic ingredient of dioxin – now linked to many residual diseases, and the 1980's ushered in deadly nerve agents, and sarin gas – able to kill a person in minutes. Iraq was accused of chemical warfare against the Iranians in the 80's, and also used mustard gas and nerve agents against the Kurdish residents of Halabja, in Northern Iraq, in 1988.[6]

Biological warfare in the form of smallpox came on the scene in the 1990's, and sarin gas incidents occurred in Japan in both 1994 and 1995 – these attached to individuals or terrorist groups – like the anthrax spores used in 2001. Who knows what else the new millennium will bring? We are already seeing its continued use.

What do we do with the threat?

How do we protect ourselves against such insidious, diverse threats? We are spending billions of dollars each year to find answers to those questions.

Meanwhile, the military trains according to what they do know. It's called CBRNE training. It stands for Chemical, Biological, Radiological, and Nuclear Environment. Training focuses on threat levels, and corresponding protection. Because the agents listed above are fast-acting agents, a rapid response is critical to survival. You can't be fumbling with your gas mask – or find out that you have the wrong fit. Response times are measured in seconds, because a minute or two may prove deadly.

MOPP

The average person sees "mop" as something that cleans up a mess. The military person sees "MOPP" as something that prevents a mess. The military acronym stands for Mission Oriented Protective Posture, and it basically determines how much chemical protection you need based on the threat.

- **MOPP 0-2:** Alarm conditions green to yellow, meaning no threat of attack, or an attack may be probable in less than 30 minutes. These levels require no gear, or just the chemical warfare gear without the gas mask.

- **MOPP 3-4:** Alarm conditions red to black requiring full ensemble because an attack is imminent or has already occurred.

It's critical that there are no gaps anywhere in your chemical ensemble. Usually, military members don their chemical warfare gear with a buddy to check for any gaps they cannot see. While encumbered with this bulky ensemble, breathing through a carbon filter, military members are expected to perform their mission while sheltered in place. In this hot, stuffy, protective suit, minutes feel like hours. But, it's what it takes to survive and perform the mission in a toxic environment.

Detect and protect

The military spends billions of dollars on equipment and training against something they can't even see. Why? They know it exists because they have seen the horrific effects. From past experience, continual intelligence gathering, and research and development, the military develops ways to better detect the presence of harmful agents, and then to neutralize them. It's an ongoing process.

Chemical weapons have claimed the lives of hundreds of thousands through the history of their use. Spiritual warfare, another unseen agent, has claimed exponentially more – yet hardly any effort goes into ways to detect and protect ourselves from this widespread, more common, devastating threat. Generally speaking, chemical warfare happens to pockets of people, but spiritual warfare is universal and happens to everyone.

Like so many other topics in this book, it is impossible to offer a detailed, theological treatment of this one. The aim of this chapter is to get us to examine our spiritual warfare threat levels, and then offer some practical protective measures illustrated through military examples.

Detect

In a military exercise, participants prepare for a possible chemical attack on the base using M8 and M9 detection paper. These specially treated paper strips are designed to detect the presence of nerve and blister agents. Prior to a possible attack, M8 strips are placed at strategic points throughout the installation. For larger items like vehicles, M9 paper is used.

Once an attack has taken place, each unit sends out Post-Attack-Reconnaissance (PAR) teams to check the detection papers to determine if a chemical attack has occurred and the exact locations. (Different color dots appearing on the detection paper indicate if a chemical has been dispersed in the area, and what type it is.) Obviously, PAR teams are in full MOPP-4 gear to do these assessments. All units report back to their Unit Command Control (UCC) person who communicates unit information up to the Central Command and Control (CCC) to map out an overall post-attack picture. What sectors of the base have been hit, and which sectors are still clean?

When all the reports are in, the CCC is able to determine a "chemical footprint." They pinpoint exactly what sector of the base is contaminated, and then seek to quarantine that sector from the rest of the base. They protect the rest of the base from contamination by creating entry control points (ECPs) between installation sectors. People can only travel from sector to sector through these ECPs to minimize the threat of contamination. Anyone coming out of a contaminated sector must go through a prescribed decontamination (or washing) protocol before entering a clean sector.

Stop the bleed

This process stops the "bleed" from dirty sectors to clean sectors – and helps the rest of the installation to keep performing their mission. The goal is always to stay operational. The military recognized this years ago, and developed the "split MOPP" approach to designate the chemical footprint, then to decontaminate the affected area while keeping the rest of the base running. The affected area may stay in MOPP 4, but the clean areas may go back down to MOPP 1 without the hindrances of all the extra protection – and stress.

This is a vital concept for every believer. Are we able to contain an attack in one area of our life, or does it bleed into every other area – rendering us inoperable? Prior to my exposure to these training concepts, I don't think any of those questions ever really occurred to me. Yet, their importance is huge. When I had no awareness of these principles, the enemy regularly disabled all life sectors with a single strike. Thinking and acting by these principles encourages us to be more proactive – and not a victim.

Consider the following from Tim Keller's book, *Walking with God through Pain and Suffering*:

> The loss of loved ones, debilitating and fatal illnesses, personal betrayals, financial reversals, and moral failures – all of these will eventually come upon you if you live out a normal life span. No one is immune.
>
> Therefore, no matter what precautions we take, no matter how well we have put together a good life, no matter how hard we have worked to be healthy, wealthy, comfortable with friends and family, and successful with our career – something will inevitably ruin it. No amount of money, power, and planning can prevent bereavement, dire illness, relationship betrayal, financial disaster, or a host of other troubles from entering your life. Human life is fatally fragile and subject to forces beyond our power to manage. Life is tragic.

We all know this intuitively, and those who face the challenge of suffering and pain learn this all too well that it is impossible to do so using only our own resources. We all need support if we are not to succumb to despair. In this book, we will argue that inevitably this support must be spiritual.[7]

According to Keller, one of the Bible's main themes is pain and suffering, with Christ, a "man of sorrows" as our most heroic Figure. Keller uses a furnace metaphor, because a furnace can destroy, but it can also refine. He says all suffering presents a choice between the two, and shows how the gospel message presents suffering as a path to God rather than away from Him.

So what happens when the inevitable sorrows occur?

What if a spiritual attack hits one sector of our life?

If each of our lives represents an installation with an important mission, what would some of our sectors be? What are the components of our life? Most people have several: family, extended family, church, work, entertainment, ministry, school, shopping, gym, etc. On any given day, we move back and forth through these sectors that make up our life.

On any given day, a spiritual explosion happens. A close relative struggling with drug abuse is homeless and living on the streets. A nasty church split occurs at your church. A family member is injured and recovery is long and painful. A co-worker makes life a living hell. A relative dies suddenly. The military calls for active duty mobilization. A baby is born 12 weeks early and spends three and a half months in the hospital, often critical. Marriage problems prompt counseling. Medical biopsies yield uncertain results.

Hard things explode in life – and all of the above have been mine, plus others too personal to mention.

So, then what?

The enemy loves to use these events to disable us completely. The invisible droplets of worry, grief, exhaustion, anger, and fear seep into every crevice of life, choking the life out of us. While some major life events legitimately shut down our "installation" for a given time, many other events should not. They often do anyway because we have no plan for containment. We have no spiritual "split-MOPP" process.

A bad day at work

It's like the guy who has a bad day at work and then comes home and takes it out on his family. Instead of recognizing that he is "contaminated" from work and decontaminating before he enters his "home sector," he lets work bleed into home.

He still has to deal with a bad day at work, so what should he do? It might be as simple as decontaminating in the car.

When a military person goes from a dirty sector to a clean one, he passes through a Contamination Control Area (CCA) where he sheds his dirty outer-garment and passes through a series of cleansing points. Actually, if he was exposed on the battlefield, he would have administered an antidote shot to himself (or a buddy would if he was already losing consciousness). If skin was exposed to a chemical agent, the area would be cleaned by rubbing a M291 decon pad on the area affected.

For a spiritual analogy on the original battle front, let's go back to the guy having a bad day at work. When his work day started to tank, he could have self-administered an antidote as soon as he recognized symptoms. Let's say he got passed over for promotion, and a lesser-qualified person got the position. Jealousy, anger, offense, discouragement are released into the atmosphere and begin to settle on this unprotected employee. As soon as he detects it as a harmful agent, he can immediately inject prayer into the situation. While he waits for it to take effect, he begins to rub off the toxic agent with the M291 paper of the Word. He confesses his jealousy, anger and lack of trust, and begins to quote verses from the Word about God providing, God's faithfulness, and His sovereign plan that is always for his good. This would be an example of decontamination as soon as the harmful agent is detected. This would probably defuse the agent's toxicity, and the guy would be back on duty with his mission in mind.

Now, let's say, he's clueless about the toxic environment of work and detects nothing amiss except his missed promotion. He finishes his work day in grim silence, brooding over the news. On the ride home, he's at a low simmer, rehearsing the hurt, and breathing harmful spiritual vapors deep into his soul. No way would he even think of calling a friend to pray him out of his unbelieving funk. (That's what Trench Buddies are for.) He's good and angry – and he feels justified. He encounters a few bad drivers on the way home, and it only fuels the fire.

But, theoretically, he still has time to decontaminate before he enters his house. He could pray in the driveway, and bring his emotions and concerns to God. He could confess his grumbling and sense of entitlement, and renew his commitment to trust God to provide for him and his family. He might not be able to change the situation at work, but he certainly can keep his family safe from his spiritual contamination.

This is a simple example of preventing a "bleed" from one life sector to another. It doesn't mean we don't process spiritual explosions. It just means we keep them in perspective – and don't poison clean sectors. It also doesn't mean that he doesn't talk to his wife about a hard day at work; it's just that he first washes off damaging anger and resentment that can harm his family.

I've heard heartbreaking stories as I have presented the Trench Buddies conferences. In private conversations, or during prayer sessions, I have heard stories where one contaminated sector of life has bled into every area. Most prevalent are abuse situations and parents dealing with wayward, adult children. One woman shared the story of her drug-addicted son, and poured out her deep pain. So great was her anguish over her son, she mentioned her bout with breast cancer like she had just had a tooth pulled. These situations bleed into our marriages, our friendships, our churches, and our ministry – if we have any energy to even pursue one. We are drained dry.

When explosions hit one sector of our lives, they can also become our identity – an identity that is contrary to how God defines us.

Like the chemical agents that destroy people, spiritual agents attack our nervous system, give us blisters on our heart, and make us choke on our circumstances. There is protection available, and antidotes we can take, but we are not trained.

It's not easy – but it's possible

This process is not easy. It is such a foreign concept to most of us, that when we begin to think in these terms, we think it can't happen. It can. It takes much prayer, time in the Word, and trench buddies.

I have had a few situations over the past few years that threatened to consume me. Issues with loved ones were heartbreaking. Fear and sorrow crept in like a silent fog, obscuring love, joy, peace, patience, self-control – every aspect of the fruit of the Sprit that is mine as a believer.

I fought for containment. When I processed the raw emotions attached to this life explosion, I purposed to discipline my mind to fight for the other areas of my life. I am a wife, mother, daughter, friend, teacher, etc. All the other areas don't deserve the fallout from one sector of my life. When one of the sectors gets hit, I need to keep the other areas clean. As hard as it was, I decontaminated repeatedly and quarantined this situation over the holiday season. A wise friend counseled me: "Don't let (blank) steal the joy of the holidays." Good trench buddy advice. (That holiday season was surprisingly joyful.)

Every time particular situations threaten to consume me, I commit them to prayer and declare the Word as it applies to the situation. God is God, and I am not. He is in control, and I can trust Him for the outcome – no matter what. God has consistently shown me what to do with the contaminated areas. What should love look like in that sector at that period of time? How extensive was my role? The answers came – and continue to.

All of these are practical considerations when one area of life is hit. This is not a "stuff-it" approach to hard things in life. We have to process hard things to be healthy physically, emotionally and spiritually. We don't ignore the area – we allow God to show us what wisdom looks like in that area. The split-MOPP concept brings in a balanced perspective when we need it the most.

In some of these situations – actually in all of them – I can only achieve containment if God is the highest priority in my life. When He is at the center, then my core is always strong and stable. Whenever I place any other relationship at the core, and that relationship suffers an attack, all my relationships suffer. I become dysfunctional, wrongly enmeshed in contaminated areas.

I may not be able to change my circumstances, but I can always change how I think about the situation. Additionally, the more I contain a sector to its appropriate priority, I am ultimately a stronger resource for whatever the contaminated sector may require.

Those that deal with addicts echo this advice. Many addicts survive, but those that love them die of worry and heartache. Loved ones get dragged into the addict's cycle instead of pursuing healthy boundaries for their own lives.

By pursuing the split-MOPP approach in life, we don't allow any one sector to control the rest – rather we acknowledge that God controls all the sectors, and we submit to His control.

Trench buddies

My trench buddies have played a key role to keep my perspective balanced. More than once I was ramped up from a situation. In one situation, I prayed, I recited Scripture, but wasn't able to get my emotions under control – or stop my mind from rehearsing self-defending dialogues. I finally called a trench buddy and explained my struggle. Her objectivity allowed her to recognize the spiritual warfare aspect that I could not see in my emotional reaction. She brought badly-needed balance and perspective. She defused the situation by reminding me of all that God had done in that area and told me not to take it personally. Whew! I got off the phone victorious. The enemy did not hook me as he had so many times before.

I can say from experience that this is hard – but very possible. Two dear women I know are currently struggling with breast cancer. One just recently received the diagnosis, but the other woman, Maria, is now post-surgery and undergoing chemotherapy. Maria is "Exhibit A" for the living the split-MOPP principle spiritually. Her life has been a series of "explosions" including her husband's debilitating stroke ten years ago, her mom's bout with lung cancer last year, and periods of unemployment over the past two years. Maria has squarely faced every challenge with courage and wisdom. She contains the contamination with buoyancy not feigned. I've seen her tears over the years, yet have also seen a remarkable joy in the midst of deep pain. Her mission in life has never waned. She would be the first one to be there for a fellow sufferer. She has never succumbed to bitterness, and has loved with an unconditional love when circumstanced made it very hard to do so. She prays hard, and has a consistent group of trench buddies for counsel, encouragement, care, and perspective. I've been on the receiving end of her care in a few of my own trials.

The apostle Paul understood this concept, taught it well – and modeled it even better. His life was filled with exploded sectors. He lists some of them in II Corinthians 6: prisons, shipwrecks, lashings, beatings, attacks from the Jews, problems in the churches he planted, hunger, danger from robbers, sleeplessness, etc. Most of us would have succumbed to despair with this list of painful sufferings. Not Paul.

It wasn't that he didn't hurt, but he contained it. Paul said: "we are afflicted in every way, but not crushed; perplexed but not despairing; persecuted, but not forsaken; struck down, but not destroyed..." (II Cor. 4:8-9). His pain had boundaries because Paul had perspective. He knew his power came from God (v. 7) and knew why in verses 10-11: "always carrying about in the body the dying of Jesus, so that the life of Jesus may also be manifested in our mortal flesh. So death works in us, but life in you." No bleed for Paul – at least not spiritually. He was operational in his ministry until the very end.

This is a powerful perspective! If we understand this key principle, we will still hurt when painful explosions happen like Paul and Maria, but we will stay operational. We will quarantine the toxic sectors so we can continue to perform the mission God has given us. Then, the devil will not get even one inch of extra ground through his insidious attacks – or by piggybacking on our normal life trials.

Staying pure in a toxic environment

How do we stay pure in a toxic environment? That is the goal in military chemical warfare – and the goal behind the protective ensemble. Wearing the "J-list chemical warfare training ensemble" may be uncomfortable; may limit movement, and cause us to feel restricted. It may not be stylish. But it is necessary to be safe.

Looking at someone in a J-list suit, you'd say they were safe. But say the gas mask was missing its filter. Even with all the protective garb, the person would still be dead because of this small detail.

The Word of God is like the filter. We can protect ourselves from activities, people, etc., but it's not enough. Those are externals – and we cannot even make reliable decisions without filtering out decisions through the Word of God. In fact, some people insulate themselves in legalism without a clear knowledge of what should be guarded most.

The Word of God protects the heart, just as the mask filter protects the lungs. If the core is not protected, then the externals are secondary. King David understood this principle as he penned the Psalms. As he looked back on a life of many mistakes, he said: "How can a young man keep his way pure? By keeping it according to Your word. With all my heart I have sought You; do not let me wander from Your commandments. Your word have I treasured in my heart, that I may not sin against You" (Psalm 119-9-11).

David was a seasoned war veteran. He had seen his share of battlefield victories yet didn't fare as well in his personal battles. In the end, he realized that God's Word was the filter he needed all along. Armor wasn't enough to protect the heart.

The EOD guys have 85-pound protection suits, but their book knowledge of explosives keeps them safest of all. Rather than sustaining blast after blast, hoping the suit keeps them alive, how much better to know the Book and prevent explosions from occurring in the first place?

As Keller says in his book on suffering, we cannot face the struggles with human resources only. We need spiritual help – and it is through the truths found in the practical outworking of the gospel message. The Word helps us detect the presence of the invisible (both good and evil), helps us decontaminate when we've suffered an attack, and keeps us pure in a toxic world as we embrace and walk in the righteousness of Christ through the blood He shed on the cross.

DIGGING DEEPER

CHAPTER 17: DIRTY BOMBS

Most important "take-away" thought(s):

1. Explain the MOPP levels and what they have to do with threats and corresponding protection. To make it more practical, apply them to a personal situation.

2. Detection paper (M-8 and M-9) indicate if a chemical attack has taken place. What detection measures indicate whether or not a spiritual attack has taken place? Do you have any in place in your own life? Why or why not?

3. Describe a situation where something "exploded" in your life and you felt unable to function in all areas of your life. What are some situation that legitimately shut down life? What are other situations that should be "sectored off" to prevent contamination or "bleed" into other areas of our lives?

4. What role should trench buddies play in detecting possible explosions? How about if an explosion has already taken place? What can a trench buddy do to stop "contamination" from spreading? Do trench buddies function well in these situations? Why or why not?

5. How do we stay pure and holy in a toxic world? What lessons do you learn from the chemical warfare example? Why was the full suit and mask not enough? What strategy do you have personally to stay pure?

THIS PAGE INTENTIONALLY LEFT BLANK

Section
4
Security

SECURITY: A Personal Profile

The more Jane learned, the more she realized that she was never properly trained for spiritual warfare.

Her lack of training had cost her dearly.

She discovered that she not only had let down her guard, but that she didn't really have significant protection to begin with. She was largely ignorant of the threats around her, some due to lack of training, but also due to her preoccupation with her own pleasure.

Growing up in church, Jane often heard about the importance of guarding her heart. She thought the pastor was a bit paranoid – always warning them about the things of the world. "What's so scary about the world?" she often thought.

The clarity of hindsight taught Jane that the world can be very scary. Flirting with sin is dangerous. Her unfiltered thoughts took her places she never expected to be.

Looking back, Jane saw that her thought life had been unchecked by any clearly defined parameters. No improper and untruthful thoughts were rejected. What she had embraced as tolerant and modern was destroying her.

It didn't help that she had no filter on her entertainment either. Jane realized that all the TV, movies and songs had more influence than she thought. All the sensual exposure took its toll on her self-image, her marriage, and her behavior. The fiction of media made her real life seem boring by comparison. All the wrong behaviors depicted in media never seemed to have negative consequences.

Jane had never really pulled Scripture apart to discover what the Bible actually said about current issues. She had a false sense of confidence.

Finally, Jane could now see that the godly friends that she had pushed out of her life had really loved her. They were part of the provisions God had given for her security. Like a foolish soldier, she had ventured out without her unit – and became a casualty as a result.

No more. Jane learned to pay attention to her surroundings and identify high risk areas – and avoid them. When temptation reared, she asked friends to pray and make her accountable. She began to regulate her entertainment choices based on what the Bible taught. Jane also learned to pay attention to her thought life, and found that her mental victories changed her emotions and her behavior.

The enemy stepped up his game, but Jane was hard to fool with all the added protection.

Life was changing – for the good.

"Watch over your heart with all diligence for from it flow the springs of life."
Proverbs 4:23

18
SECURITY: CAN I SEE AN ID?

The black sedan turned off the main road, taking the road that led to the military base. As the sedan approached the base gate, jersey barriers prevented straight entry, and floodlights illuminated the whole area. The gate was guarded, and barbed-wire fencing stretched around the perimeter.

The car was new and shiny, and the driver highly educated, well-dressed, and influential. If appearances mattered, he should be able to drive right in, but he couldn't.

The military guard stepped out as the car approached and asked, "Can I see an ID?"

Flustered at the detention, the driver fumbled in his wallet. He pulled out his bank statement and handed it to the guard.

"Sorry, sir; I need to see an ID," the guard said.

Growing impatient, the man pulled out his phone and showed the guard how many Facebook friends he had. Unimpressed, the guard once again asked for an ID.

The driver handed him his charge card.

"No," said the guard.

How about my license?

"Negative," said the guard.

Here is a picture of me with my kids.

"No," said the guard.

But, they all show that it's me.

"I need a military ID, sir," said the guard.

Not having a military ID, the driver pulled out some cash and winked at the guard.

The guard stood firm. "I can't grant you access. I'm sorry, but you'll have to turn around," he said as he radioed for backup in case there was trouble.

The driver eyed the guard's weapon, the surveillance cameras, fences, and listened to the approaching sirens. Disgusted, he backed out and slowly drove away cursing the guard's paranoia.

Paranoia or protection?

Was the guard paranoid? No, he was doing his job.

This story is made-up, but the need for security is not.

Each military installation has an important mission – and has to protect the assets needed to accomplish the mission. Those resources include people, aircraft, buildings, vehicles, weapons systems, runways, etc. Anyone entering the base has to show appropriate credentials to gain access. Security personnel are always vigilant. They can show no mercy, nor partiality. When they do their job, they protect everyone.

Where the resources are most valuable, there is constant surveillance and greater security. On an Air Force base, this is usually the flightline because multi-million-dollar aircraft are located there. The flightline is patrolled by security police and also by cameras from every angle. The perimeter of this protected area is called the "red line."

One of my co-workers experienced the consequences of crossing the red line. He was a well-known, professional, respected sergeant who knew flightline security protocol. He was shooting a flightline photo assignment on a snowy day when police cruisers raced to his location. He was handcuffed and thrown in the back of a cruiser. It didn't matter that the red line had been recently moved, and snow obscured the red boundary marker. It didn't matter that they knew who he was. He had breached a boundary meant to protect the aircraft. They apprehended, and asked questions later. He was "taken captive" until someone could prove he had a legitimate right to be there.

As his supervisor, I was called to vouch for him and saw his embarrassment as he sat like a criminal in the back of a police cruiser. It was a security lesson well learned. It didn't matter whether his infraction was intentional or unintentional. Boundaries are there for a reason, and they are not to be breached.

Protecting you

In the spiritual parallel, you are the installation. Your body is the perimeter and the most protected interior location should be your soul. How well are you protected? Are there fences in place with no broken places? What type of surveillance is set up? When information or thoughts approach your mind, what credentials are required for access? Is the gate unguarded, or does everything flow in without examination? On a scale of one-to-ten, how would you rate your security protocol on a spiritual level?

We provide security in a lot of other areas of our lives. We cover ourselves to block out the cold in the winter and excessive sun in the summer. The health-conscious reject junk food, carefully examining nutrition labels on the products they buy. We ingest medicines to kill bacterial intruders that have snuck past our defenses. We do all that we can to secure our investments. We put passwords on our computers, lock our doors, install alarm systems, and protect our air and water. Ironically, we protect most what is temporal and fleeting, and least with what is eternal and vital – our soul.

Most of us understand the importance of guarding a military installation and its resources, but many of us fail to see that we have an important mission and resources to protect as well. God has created each of us with purpose, with a calling of good works. (Ephesians 2:10) As believers, we serve the Kingdom of God. We should protect spiritual assets, especially the high-risk areas of the heart and mind.

Guard your heart

Two verses have become brilliantly clear to me through this parallel. The first is Proverbs 4:23: "Watch over your heart with all diligence, for from it flows the springs of life." The King James Version uses the term "guard" and says that all the issues of life flow from our hearts. If all the issues of life flow from my heart, then how am I guarding it?

In Kris Lungaard's book, *The Enemy Within*, he defines the heart as the source of what our mind believes, what our will decides, or what our affections feel. It is the source of what determines our sense of right and wrong – what approves or condemns our mind, will and emotions.[1] Even though we have a new heart through salvation, the work in our renewed heart is not finished, so it is open to the relentless pull of the flesh. It must be guarded.

I've heard the proverb about guarding my heart hundreds of times, but it was the military gate parallel that made me consider it in a very practical way. If you need authentic military credentials to gain access to a military base, what credentials are needed for something to enter into my heart? That question brought another verse into sharp focus.

Take every thought captive

Paul instructs the Corinthians: "We are destroying speculations and every lofty thing raised (or exalted) up against the knowledge of God, *and bringing into captivity every thought* into the obedience of Christ." (II Cor. 10:5)

To take every thought captive means that I need criteria to evaluate each thought. The criterion is the Word of God. It's like the red line around the flightline. Whatever crosses the red line of the Word gets apprehended like my co-worker on the flightline. What do I allow in, and what is denied access? What is a vain imagination? What exalts itself above the knowledge of God? Intruder thoughts should be pinned down with the weapon of the Word.

If the knowledge of God is found in the Word – but I don't know the Word well – then my security is immediately compromised. My filter is flawed. My red line has gaps. My boundaries are blurred. My heart is at risk because my mind is un-protected.

The apostle Peter addresses this vulnerability in I Peter 1:13-16: "Therefore, prepare your minds for action, keep sober in spirit, fix your hope completely on the grace to be brought to you at the revelation of Jesus Christ. As obedient children, do not be conformed to the former lusts which were yours in your ignorance, but like the Holy One who called you, be holy also in all your behavior; because it is written, 'You shall be holy for I am holy.'"

Chuck Swindoll describes very succinctly the dangerous condition of an unguarded mind: "Adultery occurs in the head long before it occurs in the bed."[2]

I envision an armed guard set at my eyes and ears on the perimeter of my "installation," and another armed guard posted in the command post of my mind with surveillance cameras watching every area of my life. Other armed guards patrol my heart searching for intruders that somehow have made it through security defenses. Once apprehended, they are escorted out, or killed if they resist.

Credible criteria

Boundaries abound in the Bible – put there by a loving God Who wants us to be secure in Him. What God means for protection, the enemy distorts as restriction. The enemy's deception is that boundaries restrict freedom, despite the fact that broken boundaries usually lead to bondage and pain. God's boundaries actually bring great freedom and security, providing the ideal climate to do what is right – for God and us. The Ten Commandments are great "red-line" boundaries because they provide security in our relationship with God (vertical) and our relationship with others (horizontal). Breaching those boundaries not only breaks the boundary but also breaks our relationships.

The prophet Hosea warns of a life without boundaries provided by the knowledge of God:

> "Listen to the word of the Lord, O sons of Israel, for the Lord has a case against the inhabitants of the land, because there is not faithfulness or kindness or *knowledge of God* in the land. There is swearing, deception, murder, stealing, and adultery. They employ violence, so that bloodshed follows bloodshed. Therefore the land mourns, and everyone who lives in it languishes along with the beasts of the field and the birds of the sky...." (Hosea 4:1-3)

Hosea shows what happens to a nation when they lose the knowledge of God as their boundary lines. What happens to a nation also happens to individual believers. Hosea sums up the problem in verse 6: "My people are destroyed for lack of knowledge." Our information age provides an accumulation of knowledge never previously available, but an overabundance of general knowledge cannot provide the security the knowledge of God brings. Rather than help us, general knowledge has obscured the spiritual boundaries that provide for the safe use of all other knowledge.

Long before the present computer age, wise Solomon addressed the effects of accumulated random knowledge: "But beyond this, my son, be warned: the writing of many books is endless, and excessive devotion to books (or blogs, Twitter, Facebook or RSS feeds) is wearying to the body." Solomon concludes with the priority: "fear God and keep His commandments." (Ecclesiastes 12:12-13) Solomon lived a life most of us could only imagine, but by the end of his life he saw that a life without God's boundaries was only vanity.

So, how do we begin to build a reliable list of credentials to post at the gate of our heart and mind?

Short list

There is a short list of credentials provided in Paul's letter to the Philippians: "Finally, my brothers, whatever things are *true*, whatever things are *honest*, whatever things are *right*, whatever things are *pure*, whatever things are *lovely*, whatever things are of *good report*; if there is any *virtue* and if there is any *praise*, think on these things." (Philippians 4:8)

If I am guarding the gate of my heart, and something attempts to enter through my sensory modes, does it meet these credentials? Is it true? No? Wrestle it to the ground. No access. So many things we watch or hear with no filter are not even true. This is especially relevant because the devil is the father of all lies, and lies are his primary weapon. He twisted truth with Eve in the garden and he continues to do the same today.

When you begin to arrest each incoming thought or media offering by these criteria, you may discover that you have intruders everywhere. Is it honest? Is it right? How about pure or lovely, with virtue or praise? Think about what you have heard or watched in the past 24 hours. How much of it satisfies these criteria? Most television and music don't. Many conversations don't.

Paul instructs Timothy to "keep (or guard) that which is committed to his trust, avoiding profane and vain babblings, and oppositions of science falsely so called." (1Timothy 6:20)

It may also explain why the Bible tells us not only to guard our hearts – but our lips also.

Here are a few verses:

> Psalm 34:13: "keep your tongue from evil and your lips from speaking deceit."
> Proverbs 6:2: "You are snared with the words of your lips; you are caught by the speech of your mouth."
> Proverbs 13:3: "He who guards his mouth keeps his life, but he who opens wide his lips comes to ruin."
> Proverbs 21:23: "he who guards his mouth and his tongue keeps himself from troubles."

If we have trouble with what comes from our lips, then it is probable that others do as well, which is a good reason to carefully evaluate conversations. What gets to come in and what is turned around and denied access?

With our daily bombardment of stimuli, data coming at us from every electronic venue, a global array of data, is untested and unfiltered. Our entertainment is filled with violence and every immoral act imaginable – the world's filth flowing into our hearts. Are guards on duty 24/7?

Some of the hardest things to filter out come from within us in the form of the lies we believe about us. Think of the many things we tend to believe about us that stands in stark contrast to what the Bible says about us. "I am a failure." "I am hopeless." "Nothing will ever change." "God could never use me." The list goes on – and our thinking often goes on without a spiritual confrontation with truth. Are these thoughts apprehended and checked for credentials? Spiritual scrutiny must be applied to all that comes at us from without, but also from within.

A mind with no guard is easily infiltrated by enemy forces that steal and defile resources needed for our mission – to serve Christ and bring Him glory.

New gate guards

You may have to train mental "gate guards" with godly criteria, and send other guards inward to evict wrong messages that have already crept through lax security.

Think of the average person you meet at supermarkets, airports, family gatherings and church. People are increasingly fearful, depressed, and hopeless. "What is this world coming to?" they say. They medicate with Prozac, Valium, illegal drugs, sex, food and entertainment – often never considering the problem to be one of an unguarded heart. Our mental maladies may stem from spiritual contamination. Because we don't take every thought captive, we often seek to solve our mental dilemmas without an accurate diagnosis.

The reward of filtering according to the credentials listed in Philippians 4 is security and peace. If we practice these filters, verse 9 says the "God of peace will be with us."

Guard and capture

The two main themes of this chapter are "guard your heart," and "take every thought captive." The reason they are so important regarding spiritual security is that there is a continuous threat. If we are believers in Jesus Christ, we are eternally secure in Christ, but we need our daily spiritual security measures because our hearts and minds are always under assault.

"Never think for a moment that the war against sin is over in this life," writes Kris Lungaard in his book *The Enemy Within*.[3] He explains the role of the imagination that entangles us in lust. It all starts in the mind. "The flesh ambushes you with sudden, overpowering temptation so that you have no time to think about consequences. It pleads extenuating circumstances," writes Lungaard, who adds that the flesh often tries to balance good deeds with the bad.[4]

God tells Cain that sin crouches at the door and its desire is for him. (Genesis 4:7) Jesus tells Peter that Satan desires to sift him as wheat. (Luke 22:31) Peter (having been assaulted) warns believers to "be of sober spirit, be on the alert. Your adversary, the devil, prowls around like a roaring lion, seeking someone to devour." (I Peter 5:8)

God repeatedly addresses this weakness and our need to be vigilant and diligent. All through the Old Testament, God warns his people to be careful – be careful to remember, to do, to obey. In Deuteronomy alone, I counted 72 warnings. Despite God's faithfulness, His people failed to heed the warnings. Only twenty years after inheriting the Promised Land, God's people are already going against God's commands. The rest of the Old Testament chronicles cycles of obedience and disobedience until all 12 tribes are brought into captivity because they failed to take their thoughts captive.

What to guard

Not only are there many warnings to be careful, but the Bible also gives us specific things to guard. Here is a sampling:

Guard against other gods (Ex. 23:13) Many warnings against idols (I John 5:21)
Guard against making covenants with pagan nations (Exodus 34:12)
Guard your soul (Psalm 25:20)
Guard your ways (Psalm 39:1, Psalm 91:11, Proverbs 4:26))
Guard your going in and coming out (Psalm 121:8)
Guard instruction (Proverbs 4:13)

Guard your steps as you go to the house of God (Eccl. 5:1)
Guard against your neighbor, brother... (Jeremiah 9:4)
Guard against greed (Luke 12:15)
Guard against dissipation, drunkenness and worries of life (Luke 21:34)
Pastors should guard their flocks (Acts 20:28)
Guard against false teachers (II Timothy 4:15)
Guard your faith (Jude 1:20)

Consider all that we should be guarding – and how little most of us even think about these areas. Life is busy and demanding. A lot of us are in survival mode – just trying to make it through the day. The Bible contains warnings that deal with every part of life. Are we intentional in our spiritual life?

The good news is that God is always available to help us. We are partakers of His divine nature. (II Peter 1:4) At the end of the book of Deuteronomy, God promises to be with them to give them victory over their enemies. In Deuteronomy 33, He comes down from heaven to go before them, and underneath are His everlasting arms. (v.26-27) In Isaiah 58:8, God is our rear guard. In Psalm 3:3, God is a shield about us. God wants to surround us in our battles, but we forfeit His assistance when we turn our backs on Him.

Mind/Body connection

As I was studying the topic of taking every thought captive – and trying to live out what I was learning – I came across some fascinating teaching. Dr. Caroline Leaf has been studying the brain for 25 years and she shares some of her teaching in a series called *Your Body, God's Temple*. In her fast-paced, clipped Australian accent, she explains the physiological makeup of the brain and then shows how thoughts are processed in the brain. The teaching brought new appreciation to the fact that we are indeed "fearfully and wonderfully made," but it also showed physiological evidence to back up Scriptural teaching about our thinking. Dr. Leaf showed how the brain processes healthy thoughts versus toxic thoughts, showing the connection between electrical impulses and chemical reactions, and the emotional and physical results.

It was amazing to see how harmful toxic thinking is to our emotional, physical and spiritual state. When all the pathologies of wrong thinking were presented, it provided great motivation to take every thought captive as the Bible teaches.

The Bible gives numerous verses regarding our mind, our imaginations, speculations and our thinking. Dr. Leaf categorized all those areas down to two types of thoughts: faith-based or fear-based. She explained that faith-based thinking was actually healthy for the brain and body, and produced chemicals stronger than the toxic fear-based chemicals (Showing proof that we can actually renew our mind as it stated in Romans 12:2).

In the weeks following the teaching, I began to capture every thought according to the criteria of faith or fear. It was amazing how clarifying it was. I was shocked to see how many of my thoughts were fear-based. I began to reject many thoughts I had previously allowed.

In Dr. Leaf's teaching called, "13 Steps to Detox Your Thought Life," she tops her list with, "Take Every Thought Captive."[5] She says that God will help us to control our thought life. "Don't let your thoughts go unchecked," she said.[6] Dr. Leaf cautioned against negativity (which lowers serotonin), guilt statements, replaying conversations in our head, things that lack congruence, and "owning our physical maladies." She encouraged listeners not to call it "my arthritis" and attach it to our identity, but to say "I have arthritis symptoms."

Dr. Leaf said that thoughts create attitudes which result in behaviors, so we should quickly apprehend every thought and be very selective about what we let in. The structures in our brain give us the ability to bring logic, reason, and truth to our emotions. Regarding emotional strongholds already in place in our brains, she instructed listeners to consistently feed statements of truth to long-standing toxicity. For toxic bitterness and hurt, we might say, "I choose to forgive. I choose to love. I release the hurt, etc."

According to Leaf, as long as we embrace toxic thoughts, our hope wanes. "You are the product of your thoughts," she said, and encouraged people to enlist the help of others in their "security sweep."[7] It takes a great deal of discipline to pursue healthy thinking, but Leaf said that it brings a cascade of benefits, including more endorphins and greater intelligence.

Paul's teaching to Timothy stresses the same points as Dr. Leaf in II Timothy 1:7: "For God has not given us the spirit of fear, but of power and of love and of a sound mind." (MKJV) Thoughts rooted in fear diminish power, love and a sound mind. Interestingly, the NASB renders sound mind, "discipline." It takes great discipline to take every thought captive – and to reject thoughts rooted in fear.

Dr. Leaf said it is much easier to capture a toxic thought at the beginning stages rather than trying to undo the toxic process once wrong thoughts have taken root.

Peace, power and freedom

It is amazing how liberating it is to capture thoughts and reject them. Like the guard at the gate, we can send unauthorized thoughts in the other direction. We can guard access to our mind because we have precious resources to protect. Paul said that we have this treasure in earthen vessels (II Corinthians 4:7) – and that treasure is the Holy Spirit. Since He is the source of truth, comfort, guidance, and power, it is well worth the effort to guard that treasure so wrong thinking doesn't diminish His role in our lives.

It may mean shutting off the television or radio. It may be selecting a different movie or choosing a different activity. It may be interrupting a toxic conversation, or silencing the self-talk we used to think was truth. It may mean forgiving others, and putting away long-standing hurts. It means that we have to spend more time in the Word to sharpen our discernment to capture "sneaky" thoughts that pose as acceptable. The more I spend time in the Word, I can not only banish wrong thoughts, but I can declare truth to the intruder to shut the gate firmly.

Spiritual security can be exhausting at times, but it is empowering.

The guard at the start of the chapter may not have been as rich, good looking, or as educated as the man in the black, shiny sedan, but the guard had authority. With the authority vested in him by the military, he had the authority – and responsibility – to guard the installation.

In Christ, we have the same authority and power to guard our hearts and minds from toxic intrusion. Like the guard at the gate, we need to stay at our post – and call for back up if an intruder refuses to leave.

DIGGING DEEPER

CHAPTER 18: SECURITY: CAN I SEE AN ID?

Most important "take-away" thought(s):

1. What is your mission as a believer in Jesus Christ? What assets need protection if you are to successfully execute your mission?

2. Give one clear example of an "intruder" to your heart – and the Scripture reference that denies it access because it lacks the right credentials.

3. What are some credentials listed in Philippians 4? Name at least three things we typically allow into our hearts that violate these credentials.

4. Review the list of what we are to guard. Which ones do you do well? Which ones do you neglect? How can you make positive changes to spiritual security in your life?

5. What do you think of Dr. Caroline Leaf's findings on the physiology of the brain? Review your thought life over the past several days. Do your thoughts gravitate to fear or faith? What is the most encouraging part of her teaching?

"He heard the sound of the trumpet but did not take warning; his blood will be on himself. But had he taken warning, he would have delivered his life."
Ezekiel 33:5

19
THREAT LEVELS

What does Severe Red, FPCON Delta, Alarm Red, and a wavering siren tone have in common?

If you don't know, you may be in trouble.

All four threat indicators mean an attack is either underway, or extremely likely. The first is issued on a national level by Homeland Security, the second is force protection conditions issued by the Department of Defense for military installations, and the last two are threat warnings related to a chemical attack of some kind.

Threat level warnings are crucial to security and protection. To ignore warnings is foolish. Not having them at all is even worse. Ask me, I know.

Just this week as I was writing this security section, I experienced a security breach – on my computer. How ironic.

I have security programs on my computer, but no pop-up warnings occurred. I diligently typed away with a false sense of security as spyware, malware, and vicious viruses were creeping into my computer system allowing enemy access to my system. Within a short time, the damage became evident as my computer slowed to a broken crawl and eventually stopped responding. Only deep scans with several programs located the intruders which resisted arrest. It took almost a week of my time and energy to clean up the mess. The intruding viruses were labeled "high risk" and "severe risk." If only I had gotten the warning before they infiltrated my computer. If only....

My irritating computer infiltration reminded me that a lack of threat level warnings is dangerous.

We can apply this to almost every area of life. Ignore warnings in your car and you could end up replacing an engine instead of your oil. Who hasn't jarred their car in a cavernous pothole because no warning cones were placed on the street? High blood pressure, and excessive blood sugar or cholesterol levels are silent killers unless medical tests provide early warnings of trouble.

What is true of computers, cars, and medicine is also true for us – in our nation, our state, our town, our home, and our heart.

Security measures

The military (and our nation) employs a variety of threat level indicators – especially since 9/11. Unfortunately, before a major attack, we tend to be somewhat complacent in our security measures. We live in a false sense of security like I did with my computer. We might have some programs, but we never get around to running them. It's not until something bites us that we get serious about security protection.

For more than half of my military career stateside, warnings were infrequent and low. Our typical force protection condition (FPCON) was normal – meaning there was no real threat. While there was still a fence around the base and guards at the gate, base access was somewhat lenient.

Desert Storm provided an example of this in the early 90's. Our commander made a commitment to welcome home any soldier(s) returning home through our base no matter what time of day or night. The base hangar was transformed into a welcome hall with a red carpet, patriotic bunting, and flags from the 50 states. Hundreds of community civilians were on base daily to participate in the moving homecoming ceremonies. Lee Greenwood's "Proud to be an American" boomed off the hangar walls as tanned, desert camo-clad soldiers walked the red carpet to applause from their military counterparts, their families and the community. It never got old to see families tearfully reunited, and our troops honored for their service. It is one of my fondest military memories. But, it would be an unthinkable risk today. During Desert Storm, the battle was "over there." On 9/11, the battle came home. It changed everything – and brought threat levels into our everyday lives.

September 11, 2001, was our wake-up call. On a grand scale, it was like my computer experience. We were living our lives with no warning indicators flashing, but terrorists had infiltrated our country planting "viruses" to damage the way we live and function. Because they were undetected, they achieved their harmful purposes.

On 9/11, our base went to FPCON Charlie – meaning an attack was in progress. Since 9/11, I don't think the base has ever been at Normal again. They have seesawed between Alpha (general threat of terrorist activity, the nature and extent of which are unpredictable) and Bravo (an increased and more predictable threat activity exists).

Military bases have had threat level indicators for a long time because defense is their business, but after 9/11 the nation developed one as well. Borrowing from the forest-fire colors, Homeland security developed a color code to address national threat levels. Severe RED indicates a severe risk, while high ORANGE indicates a high risk. Elevated YELLOW indicates a significant risk, guarded BLUE a general risk, and low GREEN indicates a low risk.

Risk response

The whole point of threat levels is the corresponding response to them. What good is a threat assessment if there is no planned response against it? What security measures kick in at each level? In the military, all of that is planned and set as protocol.

For each of the FPCON letters, there is a corresponding action. At FPCON Alpha, expect full ID checks at the gate, random vehicle checks and increased crime prevention efforts. At FPCON Bravo, expect stricter inspection of vehicles, deliveries, and ID checks, as well as a greater presence of guards on the installation. At FPCON Charlie, things ramp up. At this threat level, intelligence reports indicate that some form of terrorist action is imminent and strong protective measures are required – but the installation must continue its regular mission activities. Rigorous inspection of all personnel, vehicles and facilities happens. Traffic routes are restricted and buildings are locked with one access entry with guard and full ID check in each building.

There are also corresponding threat level/countermeasure protocols in place at a national level, sometimes for the whole nation, and sometimes for a region. When Homeland Security issues an elevated threat level, it is everyone's responsibility to increase vigilance. The most dangerous thing is to get too familiar with threat levels – particularly when nothing bad has happened in a while.

The bridge to faith

We live in scary times. We are a target as a nation. We are threatened from without by other nations and terrorist groups. We are threatened from within by "home-grown" terrorists, crime, etc. It doesn't look like the threat is going to end any time soon. In fact, world events appear to be escalating as more and more countries are destabilized by revolution, and hateful rhetoric rises.

Interestingly, the Bible predicted these scary times. In his last letter before he dies, Paul warns Timothy what the last days will be like. Like a good mentor, he offers a sober warning:

> "But realize this, that in the last days difficult times will come. For men will be lovers of self, lovers of money, boastful, arrogant, revilers, disobedient to parents, ungrateful, unholy, unloving, irreconcilable, malicious gossips, without self-control, brutal, haters

of good, treacherous, reckless, conceited, lovers of pleasure rather than lovers of God." (II Timothy 3:1-4)

Paul tells it like it is. A quick look around our culture tells us Paul was right.

Jesus gives His disciples an even harsher warning when they ask Him what it will be like when He comes back at the end of the age. Jesus says to them:

> "See to it that no one misleads you. For many will come in My name saying, 'I am the Christ,' and will mislead many. You will be hearing of wars and rumors of wars. See that you are not frightened, for those things must take place, and that is not yet the end. For nation will rise against nation, and kingdom against kingdom, and in various places there will be famines and earthquakes. But all these things are merely the beginning of birth pangs. Then they will deliver you to tribulation, and will kill you, and you will be hated by all nations because of My name. At that time many will fall away and will betray one another and hate one another. Many false prophets will arise and will mislead many. Because lawlessness is increased, most people's love will grow cold. But the one who endures to the end will be saved. This gospel of the kingdom shall be preached in the whole world as a testimony to all the nations, and then the end will come." (Matthew 24: 3-14)

These warnings, while difficult to address, should make us realistic and responsible. It should give us a truthful assessment of our world and make us more appreciative of threat levels and the corresponding protective measures.

They also remind us that we are fighting for our faith. Jesus poses a question at the end of one of His parallels in Luke 8: "...When the Son of Man comes, will He find faith on the earth?"

Paul warns Timothy that people will turn from the faith to a "consumer faith,"— an eclectic faith of their own choosing: "For the time will come when they will not endure sound doctrine; but after their own lust shall they heap to themselves teachers, having itching ears and will turn away their ears from the truth and will turn aside to myths." (II Timothy 4: 3-4 KJV)

Every aspect of spiritual security measures is to protect our faith – because it is under constant attack – from without and within.

During the Trench Buddies conferences, we explore spiritual vulnerabilities using the 9/11 parallel. This is the question: "What made us vulnerable as a nation to the 9/11 attack?" Participants come up with great observations. Here are a few from a recent conference: Apathy, denial, open borders, pride, ignoring warnings, false sense of security, distractions, selfishness, agencies not communicating with each other, lack of preparedness, ignorance, and lack of knowledge of the enemy.

The next question is: "How many of these characteristics make us vulnerable to a personal 9/11 on a spiritual level?" All types of mental light bulbs flash on as they review the list.

Listed are many of the same factors that raise our threat levels spiritually. Some people simply don't care very much about their spiritual health. Others deny a threat or an enemy. They think everything can be handled by human effort alone. Many people have no clear boundaries, or if they do, they don't guard them well. Most of the things in the list are self-explanatory and have already been covered previously, but there are a few other things that specifically affect our spiritual threat levels. Here is a short list:

> **Fatigue:** We are more vulnerable when we are tired – from lack of sleep, a season of great demands, having a new baby, etc.
> **Illness:** Various sicknesses wear down our defenses and can bring added stress.
> **Stress:** So many things can bring seasons of stress which lower our defenses.
> **Change:** Things like moving, starting a new job, empty nest, etc. can raise our threat levels.
> **Prosperity:** When things are going well, we can become complacent, or anxious about maintaining our current level of comfort.
> **Travel:** New places can raise our threat levels – especially business travel.

How often do we consider these factors as threatening to us spiritually? They make us vulnerable because they tax our resources or get us distracted physically, emotionally or spiritually. When we don't assess our spiritual threat levels correctly, we subsequently don't employ safeguards against increased threats. Just as the buildings fell in New York City, lives fall apart in full-scale spiritual attacks.

Trench buddy involvement

Trench buddies can play a huge role in threat mitigation. They bring needed perspective to us. When our threat level rises due to life events, it can skew our thinking. Since Satan majors in deception, a trench buddy can sort through our swirling thoughts and emotions and break the grip of confusion. Countless times, trench buddies have done that for me. In my fatigue, anger, confusion, fear, hurt, etc., I develop tunnel vision. A wise trench buddy listens prayerfully and gently brings in a godly perspective. Many times I have received godly counsel and my reaction has been, "I never saw it that way." A clear, calm perspective brings my threat level down.

Another thing that happens with a good trench buddy is that issues are brought into the light. Rather than stew over a situation (which tends to exacerbate the problem), I should first pray. Prayer is the best first protocol because it prepares my heart to see a situation as God sees it. God may then use a trench buddy to give me clarity, encouragement and love. Often, just hearing myself explain the situation helps me to see my own error and what needs to change in me. Sharing a situation (wisely) also makes me accountable for my behavior, now and in the future. It is no longer something hidden in my mind, but out in the open for examination. A good trench buddy will follow up with me. Has bitterness crept in? Am I getting victory?

The last illustration is one of prevention. Since travel is listed as vulnerability, particularly business travel, I used a trench buddy before the trip. I was attending an Air Force training course for five days. The only other person attending from our base was a male officer – and we were only authorized one rental car. Since my husband and I practice a marriage safeguard prohibiting us from being alone with a member of the opposite sex, this presented a potential threat. So, besides telling my husband, I notified a trench buddy before I left. This step gave me extra prayer coverage and accountability. I knew she would bring it up when I returned. She did – and there was nothing to report.

Many would call this overkill or paranoia, but I've seen too many marriages crumble in similar situations not to see the threat for what it is. I was appropriately protected on the trip.

The benefit of spiritual security measures is not just for my own victory, but also for the corporate impact it potentially has on my family, my church, work, etc. My life is lived in all these areas so I need security measures for each of them.

Layers of security

The military is probably the best example of hierarchy – a clear delineation of rank, purpose and function. A general is no more valuable than a private, but their functions are vastly different, as is their level of authority. In the military, good security is accomplished with a multi-level approach. If any level is left out of the security loop, security suffers.

After 9/11, it became apparent that good security was everyone's business – not just the military. State and local agencies were included in overall security, and greater emphasis was placed on security agencies (FBI, CIA, NSA) working seamlessly. This comprehensive approach to security should be applied spiritually as well. God has set up a hierarchy as well, and it is for our protection.

Charles Kraft brought this principle to my attention in his book, *I Give You Authority*. He wrote about the importance of layers in spiritual warfare. He explained that both spirit worlds (good and evil) operate in hierarchy, and there is a delegated power within each hierarchy. Good security protocols tap into these layers of delegated power.

According to Kraft, there is greater protection when the prayers of delegated authority positions are brought into play. This could mean a pastor's prayer, or someone in church authority. It could mean a husband's prayer as he has been given a position of leadership by God. It could be a father or mother who also hold authority positions. As I have worked on this book, I have enlisted the prayers of both my pastor and my husband for spiritual protection. Spiritual protection is meant to be a corporate process within the home and the church. Because this runs contrary to our individualistic society, we need to purpose to pursue this protection.

My greatest experience of layered spiritual protection was when I got hit in the face with a line-drive while pitching in a co-ed softball league. I needed surgery to repair several broken bones in my face, and to have my eye socket plated back together. It was a painful season that could have raised my threat levels significantly had it not been for the prayers of so many people. For a period of about two months I felt the most tangible corporate prayer coverage in my life. I literally felt lifted above my circumstances during the painful healing process. After the crisis of the accident passed and I was well into healing, I remember feeling "uncovered." I could sense the waning of prayers on my behalf, and I missed them.

During the four years of writing this book, I have experienced various levels of spiritual warfare – at times, intense. I have sought out layered protection, from delegated authority and other intercessors, and it has been a great help. It has also deepened my burden to come alongside others to strengthen their spiritual walk. I no longer read the church prayer requests and think, "I'll get to it later." If others have fought on my behalf in prayer, how can I not fight for them?

Watch

As we wait for Christ's return, we've already seen in Matthew 24 that things will get ugly. Mark echoes Matthew's warnings and encourages diligent caution. Mark says: "What I say to you I say to all, 'Be on the alert!'" (Mark 13:37)

To be alert means to watch, be diligent, to not be surprised or entangled by temptations. In the vernacular of this chapter, it means knowing what raises your threat levels and guarding accordingly.

"You know that you've fallen into spiritual laziness when you aren't stirred by warnings against sin, when you can't be motivated to spiritual duty, and when you are easily discouraged and give up at the sight of difficulties," says Kris Lundgaard.

"A lazy soul realizes he'll never be perfect, so he says, 'Why bother?' and is content with spiritual deadness and apathy."[1]

Be on the alert. A lack of security invites ruin.

DIGGING DEEPER

CHAPTER 19: THREAT LEVELS

Most important "take-away" thought(s):

1. Could you rate an experience in your life as red, orange, yellow, blue, or green? Why was the threat level so high or low? What happened?

2. Name three things in your life that currently make you vulnerable to spiritual attack? Which vulnerability is the most dangerous? Why?

3. On a daily basis, do you assess your current threat levels? Do you have a plan to address the vulnerabilities you assess? Why or why not?

4. Describe a time when you saw a threat a friend did not. Describe a situation where someone else brought badly-needed perspective to a hard situation in your life.

5. What threatens your faith the most? How can you respond to that threat? How might authority figures help of hurt that threat?

"Like a city that is broken into and without walls is a man who has no control over his spirit."
Proverbs 25:28

20
OUTSIDE THE WIRE

Another pastor down.

In the midst of studying and writing about guarding hearts, taking every thought captive, and threat levels, I learned that a prominent pastor has resigned because of a moral failure. He founded and served as head pastor in one of the fastest growing churches in the country—rich in ministry and making a great impact in their community. I've been to his church and heard him speak at pastors' conferences.

My heart was broken as I read the news on the church web site because I have been in a church wracked by the moral failure of a head pastor. It is gut-wrenching to see the fallout in the fallen pastor's family, the church members (particularly the youth) and the reputation of the church in general. I am praying for this pastor's cleansing and restoration, for his family to survive this explosion, and for the church to be warned that it could just as easily have been one of them.

But, in the light of security, I wonder what happened. Where did his guard drop? How did the enemy get in? What was going on in his life that raised his threat levels? At his level of leadership, he must have had some spiritual men as trench buddies. Did he block them out? What precaution was overlooked, or not in place to begin with? If God provides a way of escape for every sin, what warning was ignored?

I can't imagine what level of attacks pastors endure, and I will never know what really happened, but this situation has heightened my passion for the principles presented in this book. None of us are immune – and all of us need to pursue greater security in our spiritual walk.

What I do know, is that at some point, this pastor stepped "outside the wire."

The safety of obedience

In the explosives section we learned that "outside the wire" is the area beyond the perimeter of a military installation, a term mostly used for installations in hostile

areas such as Afghanistan. "Inside the wire" is the relatively safe area on the base –
surrounded by a guarded perimeter and patrolled within. It is the safest place for a
military member to be while in that country. When the mission takes military
members "outside the wire," their security is up for grabs. It's when the most deaths
occur.

On a spiritual level, when we live within God's commandments or moral
boundaries, we are the safest we can ever be. Bad things may still happen to us, but
we have not caused them by our carelessness. By contrast, when we stray "outside
the wire" of God's commands we put ourselves at great risk. Every person that has
ever fallen into sin, at some point, has stepped outside the wire of biblical principles.
Some of us dabble just outside the wire and nothing happens at first. Emboldened,
we stray further from the wire until something finally blows up.

The main point is: threat levels soar outside the wire – the wire of God's
protective barrier by obedience to his Word.

Out of exile

In the Bible, Nehemiah was a man of God in exile. He understood the
importance of "inside and outside the wire," both for himself and for his people in
Jerusalem.

His people (the Southern Kingdom of Judah) had stepped outside the wire of
God's ways for far too long, and were thus defeated and captured by the Babylonians
in 586 B.C. Despite the prophets' security warnings, the people persisted in their
defiance and paid a heavy price. Many of them were displaced 600-800 miles from
home. Jerusalem, their once-vibrant center of worship, lay in ruin – the city deva-
stated, and the walls broken down. Only a remnant of God's people remained in the
deserted city.

In 538 BC, an odd twist of events occurred. God prompted a Persian king to let
the people in exile return to Jerusalem to rebuild the temple. King Cyrus gave the
Jews provisions and protection on the way. The amazing part of the story is that 150
years before King Cyrus made his generous offer, the prophet Isaiah had foretold
the event naming the king by name. (Isaiah. 44:26-28) Nearly 50,000 Jews returned
to their home city of Jerusalem – which was only about 2% of those exiled.

Some years after their arrival home, under the leadership of Zerubbabel, they
began to work on the house of God – the core of their city and life. They first built
an altar, then the temple foundation. They celebrated the completion of the
foundation, but as with any redemptive building process, enemy opposition was
relentless. The people lost heart and stopped building. With only a temple
foundation built, they focused on the safer details of life and languished for two
years before the prophets Haggai and Zechariah motivated them to get back to work.
The temple was finally complete and dedicated in 515 B.C.

In 458 B.C., Persian King (Artexerxes) paved the way for another wave of Jews to return to Jerusalem under the leadership of Ezra, a priest and scribe. Ezra was told to appoint new leaders and lead the people of Jerusalem in the laws of God. Apparently, the people had a temple, but it had no impact on their daily lives. Ezra "cleaned house," charging the people to repent and to re-establish God's laws as their perimeter rather than getting their cues from the pagan culture around them. Now Jerusalem had people and a temple, but the walls were broken, so they had no protection.

What does this have to do with me?

Let's make a few applications before we get back to Nehemiah.

In our spiritual battles, we are often like Jerusalem. We are warned about the enemy over and over, but we ignore the warnings. At some point, the enemy comes in like a flood, defeats us, and carries us off into the exile of sin. We live there for varying periods of time and God uses whatever is required to draw us back to our true home. (Or, like the exiles in Persia, many never return.)

When we do make the journey home, it's a tough season because our soul is in ruins. (It was a 5-month journey to return to Jerusalem.) Our soul is what houses God (as New Testament temples of the Holy Spirit), and it needs rebuilding. Like the Hebrews, we need an altar first because "unless the Lord builds the house, they that labor, labor in vain." (Psalm 127:1) We often try to renovate the shambles ourselves instead of giving the process to God.

Then, we need to rebuild the foundation – patterned after the grandeur of the vibrant walk we had before our exile – or at least according to how God says to build it. When our soul is in ruins we often want a quick, patch-up restoration. We want to build on old, faulty foundations – the very ones that got us into trouble in the first place. God wants a foundation built according to His exact specifications. As He was so particular with the tabernacle details, God is just as picky with the details of our foundation and the rest of the building process.

When we return home, like them, the pain of our exile is fresh in our minds. It motivates us to build the altar. We're still motivated when it comes to building the foundation. Things are starting to change. We get a glimpse of hope.

Here is where the enemy gets worried – and gets busy. He opposes the redemptive rebuilding process. Recovery gets hard. Things happen. We get discouraged. We want to get better more quickly. Why does it have to take so long? The memory of our exile dims and our sin starts to look easier. We can quit here – with only a foundation of faith. We can languish with only a foundation for a lifetime – or some "trench buddy" prophets can motivate us to get building again.

People are vital to our building processes. I love how God so often lists families by name, the ones that return from exile, the ones that work, etc. Spiritual building is never a solitary work – and there are no shortcuts. A foundation is not enough. We need full redemption if we expect to walk in the full purpose of God and in greater security. We need to stay engaged in the process – together.

Once the temple was built, Ezra had to re-establish the priesthood and purify the people. Our restoration requires continual repentance to our eternal High Priest, Jesus Christ, so that we can walk in purity, power, and protection. Anything God has built in us needs to be maintained. It is a relationship – and all relationships need nourishment if they are to remain meaningful.

In Ezra's time, like in ours, temples need protection. The temple in Jerusalem was complete, but there was no wall around the city to protect the temple. Their temple was vulnerable and so is ours. It needs a wall. Back to Nehemiah.

Walls

In 445 B.C., Nehemiah is serving as a cupbearer for the king in Susa (Persia, the land of exile) when he hears reports that the people in Jerusalem "are in great distress and reproach, and the wall of Jerusalem is broken down and its gates are burned with fire." (1:3) He says to God: "We have acted very corruptly against You and have not kept the commandments, nor the statutes, nor the ordinances which You commanded Your servant Moses." (1:7)

Nehemiah knew their captivity came from living outside the wire.

Nehemiah begins to pray about Jerusalem. His heart is heavy. The king notices his sadness. Nehemiah explains his burden and is granted permission to return to Jerusalem for a set time.

When Nehemiah gets to Jerusalem, he does a "post reconnaissance" survey. He takes a few men out at night to inspect the entire perimeter before revealing his plan to rebuild the wall. His assessment is bleak: "You see the bad situation we are in, that Jerusalem is desolate and its gates burned by fire. Come, let us rebuild the wall of Jerusalem so that we will no longer be a reproach." (2:17)

The men respond to Nehemiah's plan: "Let us arise and build." (v.18)

The mocking and opposition begin in the very next verse with Sanballat, Tobiah and Geshem. The enemy hates sturdy walls of protection. He hates strength. Broken walls allow his domination.

But, Nehemiah is undeterred by the enemy: "The God of heaven will give us success; therefore we His servants will arise and build...." (2:20)

Work commences on the wall and Scripture notes which families worked where, and even how hard they worked. For example, Shallum made repairs and worked with his daughters (3:12), and Baruch zealously repaired his section (3:20). As the work progressed, opposition increased in the form of more mocking, anger, and a conspiracy to riot. Nehemiah responded with prayer and kept on working.

The enemy then played the trump cards of negativity, fatigue, fear, and discouragement. Nehemiah posted guards in all the vulnerable places and stationed people in families with their swords, spears and bows. Then he spoke to them: "Do not be afraid of them; remember the Lord who is great and awesome, and fight for your brothers, your sons, your daughters, your wives and your houses." (4:14) From that day on, Nehemiah divided his servants – half to work – half to provide protection. The workers worked with a tool in one hand and weapon in the other. They set up a trumpet system so if an attack occurred in one part of the wall, other workers would run to their defense. "Our God will fight for us," Nehemiah repeated. (4:20) The Jews guarded the work in Jerusalem day and night, and they were on guard continually, even taking their weapon to the water. Even though God would fight for them, Nehemiah still set up prudent protection.

When the wall was done except the gates, the enemy proposed a meeting with Nehemiah. His response speaks volumes to the importance of wall building: "I am doing a great work and I cannot come down" (6:3). Enemy opposition continued in the form of harassment, accusations, lies, false prophets, and politics. It never stopped once during the entire building process. But, the wall got done. The city was now protected.

Ezra returns to teach them the Word of God to bring protection *in* them as well as around them. They celebrated with worship and praise to the God that restored their home.

I love the imagery presented in Nehemiah. He wisely led the people to build the wall and protect themselves at the same time. He provided watchmen on the wall as the corporate work progressed, and he developed a plan where they could help each other even though they were on separate parts of the wall. Most of all, he prayed through the opposition and kept the people working – reminding them of the Source of their victory.

Back to us

In a parallel way, our broken lives need good boundaries for protection if we are to rebuild anything else. Broken boundaries are often the reason for ruin, so restoring a stable perimeter is vital to full inward renewal.

It's interesting to note that when Jerusalem had a temple without a wall, the city was still uninhabitable. The same can be said of us. We are the temple of the Holy Spirit, but without a clear perimeter of protection, our lives become uninhabitable. Our lives without walls are like an overseas military installation without a perimeter fence or guards. In a hostile country, there would be no way to tell whether you are inside the wire or out. There would be no boundaries, or sense of protection anywhere. That is a picture of our lives spiritually when we fail to build wall of protection, or rebuild broken walls.

I have a friend that works with female inmates, most of whom are addicts. Statistically, once they are released, they are back on drugs within 24 hours. Part of her job is to build walls for these women before their release. In addition to providing recovery help in prison, she helps those close to release find support groups in their city or town. They are allowed to visit these support groups before their release to provide a type of wall of protection for when they get out. Good idea.

Have you ever tried to build good, protective walls around your soul – built according to blueprints from God's Word? (Not self-protective walls that promote isolation rather than protection.) What wall protects your from ungodly influence? What wall protects you from relationship attacks? What wall keeps out lusts issues? What wall protects your relationship with God?

I can guarantee that the attacks will come as you begin to build. As I have built certain walls in my own life, I have met ridicule and judgment – even within the church. People can find your walls threatening. "You are paranoid," some said. "You're being legalistic," others said. As I wrestle through the Word looking for answers, I often find verses that I would prefer to ignore. It seems too radical, too uncomfortable. Sometimes I find lots of biblical guidance on a topic but don't know exactly how to apply it in my everyday life. But, I continually ask God, "What does this look like in my life, in my family, at my job?"

I read an article the other day about how many young Christians today live in "sexual atheism." The article talked about young people whose faith is not reflected in their sexual choices. If they have a wall at all, there is a huge breach in the area of sexual activity. They live "outside the wire" of God's Word in this area, and they are in great distress and reproach, to borrow Nehemiah's words.

The paradox of hardening

When it comes to walls, the military presents a paradox of terms for the Christian.

Facing battle, soldiers create a barrier against barrage – a protective structure against enemy weapons. When the threat of battle looms, soldiers "harden" their facilities. If no permanent structure is available in battle, the Airman's Manual instructs soldiers to build sandbag barriers between them and the enemy. In the absence of a fixed wall, this is called "expedient hardening."

By contrast, the believer's strongest spiritual protection comes through brokenness and a submissive heart – a softening that brings paradoxal strength. Strong spiritual walls require softening. In humility comes true spiritual strength.

David understood this principle as he led armies into battle, and evaded Saul's plot to kill him. In Psalm 18, David recounts God's faithfulness in battle: "You have also given me the shield of your salvation, and Your right hand upholds me; and Your gentleness makes me great." (v.35)

In the New Testament, Paul warns Timothy about those that "power up" over others, and those that seek strength in riches. (See Proverbs 18:11 regarding the false wall of wealth.) Paul tells Timothy to flee those false types of "hardening," and instead pursue "righteousness, godliness, faith, love, perseverance, and gentleness." (I Timothy 6:11)

The word gentleness pops up again in I Peter in the context of defense. As we defend our faith, we are to do so with "gentleness and reverence." (I Peter 3:15)

In the weapons section we saw that our weapons are vastly different from conventional weapons, and our walls follow the same pattern. All warfare for the Christian finds strength in God alone, so our subjection to Him is vital for true strength. We can never "power up" in spiritual warfare. We "go low" in submission to His authority to be able to fight in His authority. In our "Rambo world" this is counterintuitive, so we always need the reminder that humility, love, and gentleness give us true spiritual strength.

Wall building 101

In building, materials matter, but foundations matter even more. This is true as well for building spiritual walls.

The apostle Paul borrows building terms in his epistle to the Corinthian church. Paul says that each man must be careful how he builds, but "no man can lay a foundation other than the one which is laid, which is Jesus Christ." (I Corinthians 3:9-10) The prophet Isaiah also speaks of a costly cornerstone in the foundation (Isaiah 28:16), and Paul tells the Ephesians that the Cornerstone is Christ Himself. (Ephesians 2:20)

Any spiritual wall built on any other foundation but Christ will crumble in the first series of attacks.

If Christ is the foundation, what are the bricks? We already saw a few of the bricks in I Timothy 6:11: "righteousness, godliness, faith, love, perseverance and gentleness..." The Bible is full of verses that give us great ideas for bricks, but there is a particular order of building in II Peter.

Peter speaks to "those who have received a faith of the same kind as ours, by the righteousness of our God and Savior, Jesus Christ." (II Peter 1:1) Peter lists out the amazing provisions God has given us as partakers of His divine power. He has "granted to us everything pertaining to life and godliness, through the true knowledge of Him who called us by His own glory and excellence. And He has granted to us His precious and magnificent promises..." (1:3-4) What more could we possibly need? Good question. Peter then lists a progression of building that provides a good plan to build a spiritual wall.

Peter says that we should diligently add moral excellence. In my spiritual wall, I slather mortar on my foundation of faith, and add the building blocks of moral excellence. The next layer is knowledge. More mortar, add self-control, and then a layer of perseverance. These are heavy topics and I'm sure building times vary per individual. For quality assurance, frequent inspections are helpful. If the early stages are crooked or flawed, the higher levels will not fit well. The building so far is worth it, because the next layer is godliness. After godliness is brotherly kindness, and then the wall is capped with love.

Peter gives great reasons to build with these materials: "For if these qualities are yours and are increasing, they render you neither useless nor unfruitful in the true knowledge of our Lord Jesus Christ. For he who lacks these qualities is blind or short-sighted, having forgotten his purification from his former sins." (v.8-9) Peter tells us to be certain about our calling and says, "for as long as you practice these things, you will never stumble; for in this way the entrance into the eternal kingdom of our Lord and Savior Jesus Christ will be abundantly supplied to you." (v.10-11)

Wow. These qualities are not only building blocks for our spiritual walls, but also character building in us. The two go hand-in-hand. Strong spiritual walls protect our character, and keep us from stumbling. These are just a few verses that identify good "wall materials." The Bible provides plenty more. In fact, God's Word is filled with hundreds of imperatives – commands concerning how we are to live. Each imperative is like another brick for the wall.

Here are a few imperatives from the book of Colossians for some "brick" ideas:

Set your mind on things above (3:2)
Put to death (3:5) (immorality and other self-autonomous sins)
Put aside (put off) anger (other venting sins- towards others) (3:8)
Do not lie (3:9)
Put on a heart of compassion (3:12)
Put on love (3:14)
Be thankful (3:15)
Let the word of Christ richly dwell in you (3:16)
Wives be subject, as is fitting in the Lord (3:18)
Husbands love, do not be harsh (3:19)
Children obey, in everything (3:20)
Whatever you do–work hard (3:23)
Continue steadfast in prayer (watchful with thanksgiving) (4:2)
Be wise in your conduct toward outsiders (use time well) (4:5)
Speak graciously and appropriately (4:6)

When we look at these verses, we realize that we know them. But, they are often like random bricks on the ground instead of bricks brought together to build a spiritual wall of protection. For instance, I know the Bible says that I am to be subject to my husband, but do I consider that part of my wall and behave accordingly to be safe? I have learned that my subjection to earthly authority is a reliable indicator of my subjection to God. For strength and protection, that part of my wall is important. When I am willful and autonomous, the "subjection brick" breaks off my wall and I am vulnerable. We know many of these principles, but fail to use them strategically.

Watchmen on the wall

Once walls are built, they are manned. Imagine the foolishness of posting random guards around a military post that had no perimeter to guard. I can't have watchmen on my wall if I've never created a wall to begin with.

Remember Nehemiah's trumpet system to call for back-up? That reminds me that guarding is a group process. Our walls provide individual protection, but they also connect for a corporate wall – or they should.

Military guards now use radios to call for back-up, but what do I use? What if there is an ambush on my part of the wall? Do I have a strategy in place to call for assistance – to rally the troops to my area?

I have encountered countless cases where attacks never prompted alarms for help. One example is very subtle. This person was attacked in her thought life for months and never sounded an alarm for back-up. She fantasized about a former boyfriend while her discontent with her current husband grew each day. Her discontent morphed into private plans to divorce, as she rehearsed ungodly justifications for her actions. All the while, her wall was torn down brick-by-brick. The enemy eventually won as the marriage crumbled and she implemented her own agenda. What would have happened if she had recognized the attack and called for back-up? Hers was an example of having no wall, no watchman, and no group process.

Just yesterday I spoke with a young mom with children. For years, she endured a domineering husband controlling her every move, using violence to retain his neurotic control. This sweet woman suffered in silence as the situation worsened and they are now separated. This husband was called to be the watchman for his family and instead became the very threat he was supposed to repel. In this particular case, other watchmen intervened and are now involved in the rebuilding process – at least for the woman and her children.

Our role as trench buddies is first to set a guard our own lives. If we fall, we are of no use to anyone else. As we build our spiritual walls of protection, we also provide security for others. If our area is properly fortified, we can risk running to another breach elsewhere on the corporate wall.

Trench buddy security actions are not always easy to discern. It takes prayer, wisdom, right timing, etc.

"The finest compliment I was ever paid was by a man who brought me up short and told me to straighten out my life, and named several areas where it needed attention," said Bible teacher Chuck Swindoll. "He loved me as few men have loved me."[1]

As a former Marine, Swindoll exhorts believers as a pastor and a trench buddy: "When is the last time a loving brother or sister confronted you with wrong in your life, caring enough to put you back on track – which is a biblical exercise? Probably never. Maybe once."[2]

In his message on purity (and the need for strong walls), Swindolls gets his cue from the apostle Paul in I Thessalonians 4:

> "Finally then, brethren, we request and exhort you in the Lord Jesus, that as you received from us instruction as to how you ought to walk and please God (just as you actually do walk), that you excel still more.... For this is the will of God, your sanctification; that is, that you abstain from sexual immorality; that each of you know how to possess his own vessel in sanctification and honor, not in lustful passion, like the Gentiles who do now know God.... For God has not called us for the purpose of impurity, but in sanctification. So He who rejects this is not rejecting man but God who gives His Holy Spirit to you." (4:1,3-5,7-8)

The point is that we are called to live holy lives. God's will is for us to be sanctified – to be increasingly purified – to excel still more. It is a process God builds in us until the day we die. The process of sanctification is hindered if there is not an ongoing wall-building process utilizing the bricks of God's truth. How can we know how to possess our vessel in sanctification and honor if we have no protection against everything that seeks to ambush and defile us? God is the One that sanctifies us, but a lack of protective walls can sabotage the process.

This topic rarely comes up in Christian conversation yet it is a vital aspect of the Christian walk. In the absence of walls and watchmen it is completely logical to see so much ambush among believers. The prophet Jeremiah saw the same spiritual climate in his day: "And I set watchmen over you saying, 'Listen to the sound of the trumpet!' But they said, 'We will not listen.'" (Jeremiah 6:17) They didn't listen and suffered defeat and capture as a result.

"When the watchman fails, not only is he lost, but the whole city is laid waste," writes Kris Lungaard. "When the mind surrenders its watch after the soul... the affections and will are sure to follow."[3]

DIGGING DEEPER

CHAPTER 20: OUTSIDE THE WIRE

Most important "take-away" thought(s):

1. Give a clear example from your own life concerning what would be considered "inside the wire" versus "outside the wire." (It can be a real situation or hypothetical.)

2. Has God brought you out of captivity in an area of your life? Explain. What walls have you built to keep you from being captured again?

3. Explain the difference between walls that keep everyone out versus wise walls that allow wise influence in your life.

4. Soldiers build sandbag structures to "harden" their area against hostile attack. What "hardening" can you provide in potentially-dangerous situations? Be specific. What "bricks" can you use for strong spiritual protection?

5. How have you functioned as a "watchman on the wall" guarding someone else? Describe possible problems you might encounter as a watchman for someone else. Should you still do it? Why or why not?

Section

5

SABC

SABC: A Personal Profile
(Self-Aid-and-Buddy-Care)

Jane now understands the value of a true friend.

In the struggle to rebuild her life, Jane feels most badly about all the people she hurt – people that cared for her soul.

Her independence told her she didn't need them.

Her pride told her that she could call the shots, and make it on her own.

Deception told her she was fine.

Once things began to explode in her life, her insecurity kept her from the vulnerability she needed to reach out for help.

Shame told her she didn't deserve help.

"What I needed most, I avoided," Jane lamented. "I desperately needed accountability, but I didn't want it."

Looking back, Jane realized that she had defined friendship incorrectly. God had not given her friends to provide a shallow, superficial love. God had given her godly friends to love deeply – to inspire, encourage, exhort, and battle for strong faith – together.

She had not known how to welcome help, but most of her friends also lacked the training to know how to help.

The more Jane studied the Word, the more she recognized the best trench buddy model is found in Jesus Christ. He didn't just die for His friends – but for His enemies! Jane is learning that she shouldn't just care for people she likes, but needs to battle for the "unlovely" people in her life as well.

Finally, Jane learned that she couldn't stop people from battling for her in prayer. The more she heals and grows in her faith, the more she appreciates the tenacious prayers offered on her behalf. Praying friends petitioned heaven for her. They never gave up. They believed God for her when she no longer could. Now Jane wants to do the same for others.

The enemy is not happy with what Jane is learning. He is losing his hold on her. Jane is breaking free.

We know love by this, that He laid down His life for us;
and we ought to lay down our lives for the brethren.
I John 3:16

21
SABC: SELF-AID-AND-BUDDY-CARE

Pinned down and taking heavy fire on the Khost-Gardez Pass in Afganistan.

The young combat medic we met in Chapter 13 watched as grenades exploded around his armored vehicle and all the way down the convoy line. Enemy fire rained down from the mountain ridge. Army Sergeant Michael Azevedo said the firefight lasted about 45 minutes until the Apache helicopter's strafing runs silenced the enemy.

Not knowing what to expect, Azevedo said, "It's time to dismount and do our thing." In addition to his full combat gear with body armor, Azevedo hoisted his 40-pound MOLLE (Modular Lightweight Load-carrying Equipment) medical pack and headed down the convoy to help with casualties.

To his great relief, there were no fatalities. No medic call came. Those injured were already being treated – by their buddies – and that's exactly how it's supposed to work.

What Azevedo witnessed on the K-G Pass in Afghanistan is called Self-Aid-and-Buddy-Care, or SABC. Simply put, can you provide life-saving care to yourself or your combat buddy when no medics are around? Every casualty thins the ranks and jeopardizes the mission, so survival is everyone's business.

SABC is a high-priority training required every year – and more intensively prior to a deployment. Individual soldiers carry IFAKs, or Individual First Aid Kits that carry essential supplies like combat application tourniquets, tape, gloves, bandages, etc. All military personnel receive training in the medical ABC's (Airway, Breathing, and Circulation) and have to recertify each year. Since you have no control over your battle environment, you have to be prepared to treat yourself, or provide care to someone else. The military inherently includes risk and danger so you have to be prepared. Combat buddies have each other's backs. Trust and training are critical because your life may depend on it.

SABC is what Trench Buddies is all about. It's about keeping you alive, keeping you in the battle, and getting the mission done. It's about trusting each other, and being trained to care for each other. On the battlefield, all the other details of life are stripped away. That June day on the K-G Pass, the focus narrowed to fighting the enemy and fighting for each other. Petty differences fell away. The mission at hand demanded full focus and unity.

Fighting a deeper battle

The essence of Trench Buddies is how to battle for each other on a soul level.

We can care for each other on an emotional level. (How can I make you feel better?) We can care for each other on a physical level. (How can I help your physical health, or meet your physical needs for food, clothing and shelter?) These two areas are important, but they are also temporal. Caring on a soul level is eternal and it will have the most impact as you live out God's plan for your life, so it is also a high-level target of the enemy.

How can I battle for your soul? This is the hardest question, and the one least asked and answered. We cannot be an effective trench buddy without addressing the spiritual questions.

Enlightening illustrations

A simple activity provides great insight into SABC at a soul level, and it has been used effectively in the Trench buddies conferences. Each table picks a "victim" for the activity, and that person holds a card listing their physical symptoms. Each group is charged to triage and treat their victim using information found in their military Airman's Manual. Once they successfully diagnose and treat their victim, they have to give the Airman's Manual page reference where they found the information.

People usually do really well with this exercise – often with comical simulation of treatment. Every group gets the right answer. While their confidence is still soaring, they are given a new challenge.

New symptom cards are given to each "victim"—only this time it shifts from physical symptoms to spiritual – and the Manual is the Bible. Same assignment: triage and treat the victim, and give the Manual page reference where you found the information. This is not so easy. Gone are the obvious outward physical clues to the problem. Vital signs are harder to measure. Minutes tick by... Gone is the quick confidence from the previous exercise... Conversations buzz at each table...

How does the Bible counsel me to counsel others (or myself)? In any given struggle, do I know what the Bible says about it? Can I counsel in nourishing truth, or do I give shallow spiritual platitudes? Am I prepared for the messy ministry of a Trench Buddy, or do I slap a band-aid on an oozing spiritual wound and then walk away?

In every trench buddy situation, I am completely dependent on God because only God can see the heart of a hurting person. I am dependent on the Holy Spirit to help me to see the invisible spiritual issues going on beneath the surface. But, I also need to know the Word to navigate through the nuanced situations that may include physical, emotional, and intellectual factors beside the spiritual. In short, I need deep wisdom that only comes from God.

It is often excruciating to come alongside someone else's deep pain. Just yesterday during a women's Bible study in my home, a couple showed up at our door. The woman was in deep spiritual pain and they came to pray with us. In the midst of writing about SABC, I saw it happen around my kitchen table as we prayed with and for this couple as the woman openly wept. This was battle up close and personal. Like on the K-G Pass, all superficiality fell aside. All that mattered was the battle – and fighting well. We all silently begged God for wisdom in this unexpected situation. We cried out to God in prayer, and each sought God's Word to bring the stability of truth into a situation filled with confusion and painful lies. Our "classroom" Bible study setting became a "lab" of prayer to apply our training.

In situations like these, people are hurting – and the last thing they need is poor counsel. I have agonized over many of these situations, praying that my counsel was sound and helpful. Typically I would read something in the Word or hear a message shortly after such encounters to confirm the counsel in some way – and I would feel relieved. Each situation would also drive me to the Word more deeply because the need to be prepared is so great. Just like Azevedo's MOLLE pack contains medical supplies for any type of injury, I must have a broad knowledge of the Word for multiple types of spiritual injuries. The medic never knows what he/she will encounter, and the same is true of me.

Hurting people need healthy advice. Trench Buddies need to be willing to come alongside someone else's pain and bring healing truth with gentleness – even if it hurts at the moment.

Pursuing the hurting

Remember the conversation from Chapter 11 about the injured soldier in the trench? Here's a refresher:

"Do you leave the safety of the trench to save him?"

"Yes!" is the typical answer. "Of course you do."

"What if I break his arm dragging him to the safety of the trench?" I ask.

"Yes! Get him! He could die if you don't," they counter.

"So, it's okay if I hurt him a little to save his life?" I ask.

"Yes! It's a matter of life and death!"

I posed these same questions to a group of 9th grade students, and then asked: "Ok, so what if it's your friend and he's sneaking out at night to hang out with friends that drink?" Glimmers of insight reflected in their eyes as they saw how the military analogy could relate to them and their friends. I asked them to raise their hands if they knew someone who was making destructive decisions and falling into sin. Every hand went up. Wow. What followed was a thought-provoking conversation about the challenges of pursuing the hurting. Why would we be so willing to risk our lives to save a fallen soldier, yet not even risk our reputation by reaching out to someone hurting spiritually?

Tradition tells the story of two friends in the military. They fought side-by-side. One day one of them was hit while the other made it to the safety of the trench. The friend requested permission to help his fallen friend, but his officer denied the request as too risky. Defying orders, the friend ran to his fallen comrade. As the life ebbed out of his friend, he cradled his head. His dying words were, "I knew you would come." Whether the story is tradition or truth, it captures the essence of Trench Buddies – a loyal, selfless devotion that pursues the hurting at personal risk.

Who is your Wingman?

The Air Force promotes the Trench Buddies idea but uses the term "wingman."

"The term Wingman stems from a time-honored tradition within our Air Force flying community that essentially says a lead pilot will never lose his/her Wingman. It's a promise, a pledge, a commitment between Airmen who fly."[1]

The official Wingman program was initially started to reduce the number of suicides in the military, but it expanded to a broader application. According to the Air Force fact sheet, all airmen are encouraged to "be alert, get involved, and take action."[2]

> "Airmen at all levels of command have a role as Wingmen. Commanders bear responsibility for the total welfare of their assigned personnel, including the physical, emotional, social and spiritual dimensions. They recognize when their people need help and know where to send them to get it. Supervisors are the first line of defense for the well being of the people they supervise. Often they are in a position to spot the first signs of trouble and are in the best position to listen and engage. All Airmen are encouraged to lead by example -- to be good Wingmen, by taking care of themselves and those around them -- and taking action when signs of stress are observed."[3]

As an Air Force supervisor, it was my duty to be a "wingman." Sometimes it was mundane issues, but one time it was a potential suicide. A subordinate had hit hard times. She was alone, lost her civilian job, and had health and emotional issues. It was nearing the end of our military weekend and she lived in another state. The wingman concept played heavily in my head as I worried this woman might be suicidal heading home to her problems. As her supervisor, she was my responsibility. I spent the afternoon making support phone calls to find out what services were available and then had a frank conversation with her. She agreed to meet with a chaplain that afternoon. The intervention was successful and the combined efforts gave her a different perspective on her problems, identified some physical issues that aggravated her emotional state, and provided practical help. What might have happened had I not initiated as her wingman? Thankfully, I will never know.

The dangers of isolation

Remember the couple that came to the Bible study for prayer? One thing really stood out to me as the wife tearfully shared her heart after the prayer. A group of women she didn't know had prayed for her and each one was grabbing for tissues when the prayer was done. These women did not know her, but they had cared for her deeply in prayer. The wife dabbed her own eyes as she thanked the group. As she looked around the table at these loving ladies, she said, "I've been so isolated, that's a big part of my problem."

Isolation is a big part of many of our spiritual problems. For this dear woman, the enemy's lies and confusion flourished because she had no trench buddies to speak truth to counter her lies and cover her in prayer. The truth that flowed from each woman's prayer that day was like salve to her soul. The truth of God's love broke through the enemy's lies of damnation and self-loathing.

Pastor Tim Dilena addressed the dangers of isolation in his message recently at the Brooklyn Tabernacle entitled, "I Can't Do This Without You."[4] He taught from Psalm 142. The author, David, was hiding in a cave, probably with 400 men. Verses 3-4 set the stage as David writes: "When my spirit was overwhelmed within me, You knew my path. In the way where I walk they have hidden a trap for me. Look to the right and see; for there is no one who regards me; there is no escape for me; no one cares for my soul." David was in the midst of many people but felt no connection in his adversity. No one cared for his soul. Dilena said that we often feel the same way as believers: "The body of Christ is so valuable to our lives, and for us to sit here and not feel connected or feel there are people that are part of us, and caring for us, is a tragedy that not only can happen, but is probably happening."[5]

He made a strong appeal to the church: "I cannot be a strong Christian without the body of Christ. I can't be a growing Christian without the people of God around me. We need each other... We are in this together. We may have problems but we are still the people of God and we have got to look out for each other."[6] He cited Romans 12 to stress that each person's role is important to the collective mission of the church and to each other. Proverbs 18:1 makes a strong statement against isolation: "He who separates himself seeks his own desire, he quarrels against all sound wisdom." The proverb shows that isolation is a form of selfishness – we seek our own desires.

According to Dilena, Satan loves to isolate us. It was how he got to Eve – and it is how he has greater access to us. Dilena gives three spiritual consequences of isolation[7]:

1. To be isolated is to be alienated from wisdom. The wisest man (outside of Jesus Christ), Solomon says there is wisdom in the multitude of counselors (11:14). In isolation, you counsel yourself. Dilena challenges this: "Who can tell you the truth without you becoming offended? When you alienate yourself, there is no one to argue with because you are the best... and you are in trouble."

2. To be isolated is to lose strength in fighting your battles. There is strength in numbers. One is not only a lonely number, it is a dangerous one. Ecclesiastes counsels against it in chapter 4: "Two are better than one because they have a good return for their labor. For if either of them falls, the one will lift up his companion. But woe to the one who falls when there is not another to lift him up." (v. 9-10)

3. Isolation will make you vulnerable to the enemy's attack. Dilena said we need encouragement and also need to be with people totally unlike us. "The differences sanctify us," he said. "The people that annoy us the most may be the people we need the most."

Unity in diversity

Pastor Dilena makes accurate observations about isolation. The military acknowledges the same vulnerabilities and strategically promotes a buddy system and team building. The military is about building dignity, honor, earning respect. They shred your superficial self-esteem and build hard-earned value. Everything about military training is designed to fail lone ranger types. They know you will need each other on the battlefield, so they design training the same way. They take diverse people and build unity.

I remember reading a story about a Marine drill sergeant who had a white southern racist and a black former gang member in his training platoon. He wisely assigned them to the same tent on a difficult field training exercise. Faced with challenges bigger than either of them could handle alone, they forged a friendship. The battles brought unity. If your life depends on the guy next to you, differences must be overcome.

The Bible is full of diversity and unity. Look at the disciples Jesus called for His first "platoon." He called fishermen, a doctor, tax collector, a zealot... His followers were prostitutes, lepers, Jews and Gentiles, men and women, soldiers, sailors, and tent makers, just to name a few. The cross is the great leveler that breaks down societal divisions. We are all sinners in need of a Savior. We are all in a battle bigger than any of us can handle alone. We need each other – especially people different from us.

What stops us?

With all these reasons to need a trench buddy –and to be one – what stops us? Why do so many people shy away from relationships that battle at a soul level? Pastor Dilena offered a few common excuses such as: "I'm just not relational," or "I'm too shy," or "I don't make friends easily."

One of the biggest reasons is the issue of trust – often because people have been hurt in previous attempts. They have had bad experiences so pride and fear keep them from the vulnerability needed for true Trench Buddy relationships. I ran into one of these people just last month.

I was speaking with a single mom who had faced many challenges. I probed to learn what kind of support system she had so she would not battle alone. I explained the concept of a trench buddy and asked if she had one. She said, "Not really," and then mentioned a man she interacts with as part of a business venture. The man is married, in another country, and they interact only occasionally. This situation hardly constitutes a trench buddy – and is not even wise. In further conversation I learned that she had experienced negative "drama" with other women before, and while she had female friends, none of them functioned in a trench buddy role in her life. She is not planted in a local church and has no close, accountability person. She has no balance, no counter-perspective, even though she describes her life as very spiritual. "It's me and Jesus, and that's enough," she said.

Jesus is the ultimate Trench Buddy to all of us, but He also teaches us that we are to battle for each other in many ways. While this woman has spiritual disciplines such as prayer and fasting, she has neglected a pivotal provision mandated in the body of Christ – His church. I saw several areas where this woman needed balance and support, but she was not open to it. She had been hurt before and she wasn't going to let that happen again. I understood, but it made me sad.

I know about the kind of hurt she speaks of. Having led women's ministry for a season, I experienced the malicious gossip of other women, the maligning, and misunderstood motives. It was hurtful, but it did not eclipse the joy of serving women, nor did it diminish my need to trust godly women to be trench buddies in my life. It made me wiser in relationships, but did not make me afraid. Fear is never a good place to battle from. Trench buddies provide too many advantages. Like Dilena, I know that I can't do this Christian life by myself. Besides God and my husband, I need other women in my life to encourage, correct, and love me. I have lost many battles on my own – and won many victories "with a little help from my friends." Trench buddies are a gift to us and apparently God wired us that way.

Wired to care

In a Reader's Digest article titled, "The Brave Among Us," author Jeff Wise recounts an incident in Afghanistan on November 21, 2010. Marine Lance Cpl. Kyle Carpenter was defending a village from a Taliban attack when a grenade landed near him. Carpenter reportedly shielded a nearby comrade from the blast. Military psychologists say the instinct to protect those we love is "one of the most powerful forces motivating bravery in combat," overcoming even concern for their own well-being. According to the article, bravery on the battlefield or elsewhere may come from the release of oxytocin, a bonding hormone that purportedly reduces fear.[8]

Health psychologist Kelly McGonigal also touts the advantages of oxytocin in our battles. McGonigal says oxytocin is a stress hormone formed in the pituitary gland where adrenalin is also released. It is a neuro-hormone that fine-tunes your social instincts and primes you to do things that strengthen your social relationships. "It enhances empathy and makes you more willing to help and support the people you care about," she explained in her popular TED talk.[9]

Oxytocin motivates us to seek support – and also to notice when someone else is struggling. "When life is difficult, your stress response makes you want to be around people who care about you," McGonigal explained.[10] Oxytocin acts as a natural anti-inflammatory agent to protect our cardiovascular system from the effects of stress, and helps the blood vessels to stay relaxed. According to McGonigal, the heart has receptors for this hormone and oxytocin even helps heart cells regenerate and heal from any stress-induced damage. "When you reach out to others under stress, either to support, or to help someone else, you release more oxytocin and your stress response becomes healthier and you recover faster from stress."[11]

McGonigal doesn't appear to have a Christian perspective, yet she offers exciting evidence proving what the Bible has said for thousands of years. We are wired to care for each other deeply, and we are greatly benefited when we do so. She cited a study of 1,000 adults, age 34-93, which gauged participants' responses to high-stress events. Those that cared for others during stressful events fared better than those who did not during the same stressful events. "Caring produced resilience," McGonigal said. "It creates a biology of courage. When you choose to connect with others under stress, you can create resilience."[12]

We can all come up with excuses to isolate, to live superficially with others, or to live selfishly, but we will pay a price for our choices. We are created for community and we are commanded to love and care for each other. Living as a trench buddy and with trench buddies is loving and living as Jesus commanded and modeled for us.

CHAPTER 21: SELF-AID-AND-BUDDY-CARE

Most important "take-away" thought(s):

1. If you saw someone in physical peril, would you try to rescue them? What about spiritual peril? Why is there often a difference in our approach to others in these two areas?

2. Do you have someone that battles for your soul? If so, how? If not, why do you think you don't?

3. Think of a situation where you tried to battle for someone in a spiritual struggle. Did you feel equipped? Why or why not? How would you have liked to be more proficient? What could you pursue in the next three months to improve your spiritual counsel?

4. Describe a situation in which someone was ambushed spiritually because they were isolated. What do you think caused the isolation? How was the enemy able to exploit the isolation?

5. Do you try to battle for others spiritually? Do you let others battle for you? Which one happens more often? Why? Discuss. Have you been "battle tested?"

*"Greater love has no one than this, that one lay down his life
for his friends."*
John 15:13

22
TRENCH BUDDIES

Through the centuries, combat connections have run deep. More recently, Sebastian Junger provides a rare glimpse into combat camaraderie in his award-winning documentary, *Restrepo: One Platoon, One Valley, One Year*. He and fellow journalist Tim Hetherington spent a year with a platoon of U.S. Army soldiers deployed to Death Valley – the most dangerous mountain corridor in Afghanistan – the Korengal Valley.

The remote military outpost carved in the craggy, six-mile mountain pass was named Restrepo after the well-liked combat medic who was killed while serving there. They lived in makeshift shelters behind sandbag walls – no bathrooms, running water, food services, or laundry – in fact, they wore their uniforms 24/7 for a month straight. Fierce firefights contrasted days of watching boredom. These men had bullet holes in their uniforms. They conquered fear daily. They mourned the death of friends and hoped they would see another day.

Junger and Hetherington spent a year with these men and both were wounded while documenting combat. In Junger's sequel to *Restrepo*, called *Korengal*, he explores a fascinating question: "Why do soldiers miss war?" His answer stuns me.

I'll share Junger's answer later in the chapter, but today is actually Memorial Day as I write, which provides a perfect build-up to his discovery.

Memorial Day

The holiday began as "Decoration Day" in 1871 to honor the lives lost during the Civil War. It was a day to remember those who paid the ultimate sacrifice, and to decorate their tombstones as a tribute to their service.[1] In the years and wars that followed, it morphed into Memorial Day.

I think of my uncle who died during the Vietnam War. I remember the interviews I've done with families who lost loved ones in more recent wars. My husband and I watched the annual Memorial Day concert aired from Washington

D.C. and heard stories from courageous soldiers who survived catastrophic injuries, and from grieving mothers who lost dearly-loved sons and daughters.

It's fitting that we should honor those that gave their lives in service to our country. But every year, Memorial Day brings a deeper brokenness as I reflect on Almighty God Who gave His only Son for an eternal freedom no mortal man can achieve on his own. I've read heartbreaking stories of the excruciating physical and mental suffering endured by soldiers, but I cannot even imagine what it was like for Jesus to not only endure the agonizing physical suffering of the cross, but also to take on the sins of the world. I know how painful my personal sin has been – what could His pain have been like? I shudder to imagine.

Jesus is the Ultimate Trench Buddy. I mean no irreverence in using the term, but I can think of no greater example as we seek to wage battle for each other's souls. Jesus sweat great drops of blood in the Garden of Gethsemane as He faced His agonizing task ahead – all for love – all for the mess of mankind –most of which would never even appreciate His sacrifice.

When it comes to pain and suffering, God has gone before us, not only as a Savior, but also as an example. Tim Keller offers this insight:

> "For God has purposed to defeat evil so exhaustively on the cross that all the ravages of evil will someday be undone and we, despite participating in it so deeply, will be saved. God is accomplishing this not in spite of suffering, agony, and loss but *through* it – it is through the suffering of God that the suffering of mankind will eventually be overcome and undone. While it is impossible not to wonder whether God could have done all this some other way – without allowing all the misery and grief – the cross assures us that, whatever the unfathomable counsels and purposes behind the course of history, they are motivated by love for us and absolute commitment to our joy and glory..."[2]

The gospel message is that "God so loved the world that He gave His only begotten Son..."(John 3:16) It is the ultimate rescue mission – a selfless sacrifice for others – a cosmic liberation of global proportions. To even begin to tease out all the implications of Jesus Christ as a Trench Buddy is overwhelming, but this chapter requires some definition if we are to imitate Him as trench buddies for one another.

The Model of Jesus

Scripture is teeming with examples of how Jesus Christ is the Ultimate Trench Buddy. Let's start with how Jesus identified Himself throughout the gospel of John:

John 6:35: He is the bread of life.

John 8:12: He is the light of the world

John 10:7: He is the gate for the sheep

John 10:11: He is the Good Shepherd who lays down His life for the sheep

John 11:25: He is the resurrection and the life

John 14:6: He is the way, the truth, and the life

John 15:1-4: He is the true vine and His Father is the Gardener

A quick review of these metaphors reveals that Jesus nourishes, sheds light, protects sacrificially, guides, renews, lights a stable path to new life, and brings fruit to those attached to Him. These characteristics are important as we minister Christ to each other in the battles of life and in spiritual warfare.

Jesus also highlights something else throughout the gospel of John. Over and over, Jesus emphasizes that, while He is God, He listens to the Father and does and says what the Father tells Him to. John 5:19 says: "Therefore Jesus answered and was saying to them, 'Truly, truly, I say to you, the Son can do nothing of Himself, unless it is something He sees the Father doing; for whatever the Father does, these things the Son also does in like manner.'" Jesus Incarnate models submission to the Father to reveal His nature. Basically, Jesus is saying to follow His example because He follows the Father's example.

The apostle Paul follows Jesus' example. Throughout Paul's epistles he follows Christ's example, and then tells believers to follow his example. As we seek to be better trench buddies to other believers, what do we model? Are we dependent on God for every situation? Do we reflect His characteristics? If we aren't, then we are not modeling Jesus – and probably not fighting as we should.

As we look through Scripture, we see that Jesus is overwhelmingly loving and always relational. He is in tight relationship with the Father and reaches out in relationship to people across all races and economic levels. Jesus is merciful, forgiving, gracious, and giving. He is patient and slow to anger. He is discerning. He is not swayed by man, but pleases the Father. He reflects the glory of the Father, but seeks no glory from men. He treats people differently depending on their situations and needs. He doesn't give shallow answers but prompts deep reflection. He is tender with the broken, and strong with the proud. He weeps and He heals. He challenges and He soothes. He mentors and He mourns.

To learn to be a better trench buddy is to study Jesus.

I can already anticipate your objections. "But, I am not Jesus," you might say, and of course you would be absolutely correct. God must have anticipated that concern because the Bible is filled with many other verses that give us specific direction in our human relationships with each other.

The "one another" verses

A cursory Bible word search on "one another" provides some interesting instruction on the dynamics of trench-buddy relationships. It is amazing to see how specific the Bible is on topics when we take the time to search the Scriptures.

Think of your own relationships and your role in each of them. Think of situations that involve hurting people you feel burdened to help. Look at some of the "one anothers" below and see how these verses guide all relationships – but are particularly important in trench-buddy situations. Here are a few just from the book of Romans:

> "Be devoted to one another in brotherly love; give preference to one another in honor." Romans 12:10

> "Be of the same mind toward one another; do not be haughty in mind, but associate with the lowly. Do not be wise in your own estimation." Romans 12:16

> "Therefore let us not judge one another anymore, but rather determine this--not to put an obstacle or a stumbling block in a brother's way." Romans 14:13

> "So then we pursue the things which make for peace and the building up of one another." Romans 14:19

> "Therefore, accept one another, just as Christ also accepted us to the glory of God." Romans 15:7

> "And concerning you, my brethren, I myself also am convinced that you yourselves are full of goodness, filled with all knowledge and able also to admonish one another." Romans 15:14

These verses address what is in our own hearts, and how right attitudes should flow into right behavior. They address our thinking – love, honor, humility, acceptance, and preference. These right attitudes come easily when we keep in mind that God has done all those things for us first. How can I freely receive these things from God and then withhold them from others?

When we come alongside a hurting person who needs a trench buddy, they seem to intuitively know when we are genuine or not. In their pain, they can sense any attitude of superiority or condemning spirit. They sense whether we are "safe" and can be trusted with their pain. The best trench buddies have been through enough battles to connect with the pain of others. They have either been where you are, or they know they could be there in a heartbeat. There is no pretense.

Job's friends did okay when they just sat in the ashes with him and held their tongue. It was when they began to speak that their proud hearts were revealed. After the fourth friend spoke his mind to Job, God intervenes and says: "Who is this that darkens counsel by words without knowledge?" (Job 38:2) Job's friends may have meant well (it's often very hard to know what to do with people in extreme pain), but they missed the essence of the "one another" verses.

Here are a few more "one another" verses for some added definition:

"... so that there may be no division in the body, but *that* the members may have the same care for one another." I Corinthians 12:25

"Let us not become boastful, challenging one another, envying one another." Galatians 5:26

"Bear one another's burdens, and thereby fulfill the law of Christ." Galatians 6:2

"Be kind to one another, tender-hearted, forgiving each other, just as God in Christ also has forgiven you." Ephesians 4:32

"Do nothing from selfishness or empty conceit, but with humility of mind regard one another as more important than yourselves..." Philippians 2:3

"Therefore, confess your sins to one another, and pray for one another so that you may be healed. The effective prayer of a righteous man can accomplish much." James 5:16

This list gives both things to do and things not to do. We are to bear each other's burdens in humility, unity, gentleness – in prayer and truth according to the Word of God. Go back over the two lists of "one another" verses. Which ones do you find the most challenging? Which ones would be most important to you if a trench buddy were ministering to you? These verses can also serve as a diagnostic tool. If I scored myself on each verse (10 if I'm consistently showing that behavior – to 1 if I rarely, if ever, display that characteristic) it might reveal some weak areas that need improvement.

Behavior and faith

How we live these "one anothers" can also reveal our faith. Ray Ortlund writes: "The kind of God we really believe in is revealed in how we treat one another. The lovely gospel of Jesus positions us to treat one another like royalty... But we will follow through horizontally on whatever we believe vertically."[3]

Ortlund listed a few of our "one anothers" behaviors that are completely contrary to Scripture: "humble one another, pressure one another, embarrass one another, interrupt one another, defeat one another, shame one another, judge one another, run one another's lives, confess one another's sins, intensify one another's sufferings, and point out one another's failings..."[4] Ouch. I can recall at least one personal behavior from this list I unfortunately modeled during a conversation with my husband just this afternoon. The contrast between these lists is very convicting. And, that's a good thing.

According to Ortlund, if the gospel grips us with real conviction, we will obey its implications whatever the cost. "Therefore," writes Ortlund, "if we are not treating one another well, then what we're facing is not a lack of niceness but a lack of gospel... What we need is not only better manners but, far more, true faith."[5]

Wisdom with friends

Beth Moore offers some wise counsel about godly friendship (and trench buddies) in her series called "Wising Up." She cautions believers to choose friends carefully. "We will be influenced one way or the other by the people we allow close access to us," Moore warns.[6] She offers four characteristics of wise friendships:

Distinctiveness: Friends are heart-to-heart relationships. We have many co-workers, acquaintances, relatives, mentors, but usually only have a few relationships that constitute deep friendships.

Closeness: Proximity is important if a person is to have regular, positive impact.

Influence: Friends should make us better, wiser, more holy – but not dull. They should make us better spouses, parents, workers, etc.

Endurance: Deep friends go the distance. Deep relationships overcome conflict and love at all times. (Proverbs 17:17)

"A true friend is one we fight to keep," said Moore. "They battle at a soul level – they take needs seriously."[7] The popular Bible teacher said we should take the time to store up biblical truth so we can provide counsel that is sound.

One of the most important parts of her "A Wise Friend" teaching involved the wounds spoken of in Proverbs 27:6: "Faithful are the wounds of a friend." Often a trench buddy has to communicate hard truths to a hurting friend. If not done right, it can cause even more damage. Moore said the word "friend" in that verse indicates that there has been "a tremendous emotional investment of love" in the relationship so that "love always precedes the wound."[8] She said we are never self-appointed wounders, but the faithful wounds of a true friend are always meant for healing.

A trench buddy should be trustworthy. They should care for others more than they care for themselves. They should love sacrificially – to lay down their lives for their friends.

Back to Junger's answer

We are desperate for trench buddies whether we admit it or not. Often crisis highlights our need. Life becomes overwhelming and we feel the desperate ache of loneliness in our trial. We are not enough.

Physical war presents crisis, so soldiers are trained to rely on each other. Beginning with basic training, continual crises are planned to force recruits to trade independence for interdependence because combat demands teamwork.

What Junger discovered at a remote outpost in the Korengal valley was deeper than simple teamwork. What he discovered was brotherhood – trench buddies.

According to Junger, almost every guy that served at Restrepo was almost killed at some point during their duty, at least once, if not many times. Many came back traumatized by combat – reliving the nightmares – day and night. One of these men is Brendan O'Byrne, who remains Junger's friend. At a dinner at Junger's house, a dinner guest asked O'Byrne if he missed anything about Afghanistan or the war. "Ma'am, I miss almost all of it," he replied.

Junger has explored O'Byrne's answer in interviews and in his TED talk, "Why Veterans Miss War".

"What is he [O'Byrne] talking about? He's not a psychopath. He doesn't miss killing people. He's not crazy," said Junger. "He doesn't miss getting shot at and seeing his friends get killed. What is it he misses?"

"I think what he missed is brotherhood. He missed, in some ways, the opposite of killing. What he missed was connection to other men he was with," Junger explained.[9]

Junger said brotherhood is different than friendship. In friendship, the more you like someone, the more you are willing to do for them. "Brotherhood has nothing to do with how you feel about the other person," he said. "It's a mutual agreement in a group that you will put the welfare of the group – you will put the safety of everyone in the group – above your own. In effect, you're saying, 'I love these other people more than I love myself.'"[10]

This brotherhood became paramount during combat. During one firefight, one of O'Byrne's men (Kyle Steiner) was hit in the helmet with a bullet and was knocked out. During the chaos of the firefight no one could attend to him and they feared he was dead. Steiner came to shortly after getting hit, but O'Byrne was shaken. "Brendan realized after that that he could not protect his men, and that was the only time he cried in Afghanistan, was realizing that," Junger said. "That's brotherhood."[11]

Junger spoke about the bond that soldiers experience:

> "So you think about Brendan, you think about all these soldiers
> having an experience like that, a bond like that, where they loved 20

other people in some ways more than they loved themselves, you think about how good that would feel, imagine it, and they are blessed with that experience for a year, and then they come home, and they are just back in society like the rest of us are, not knowing who they can count on, not knowing who loves them, who they can love, not knowing exactly what anyone they know would do for them if it came down to it. That is terrifying. Compared to that, war, psychologically in some ways, is easy, compared to that kind of alienation."[12]

That is a startling statement! Preferring war to the alienation in society? It sounds crazy, but I actually hear evidence of that somewhat regularly. Young moms feel isolated at home. Men work long hours and have families to care for, which doesn't leave much time to connect with other men. It's tough for the average man to be vulnerable with his battles. Women compare themselves with other women and let their perceptions keep them from connections. Most kids lead stressed lives running from school to sports to music lessons, or they are latchkey kids with working parents. And the elderly can languish at home pining for visits, lacking the health or finances to actively seek connection – keeping virtual company with Pat Zajak or Alex Trebek.

Whether it's in school, work, church, or their neighborhoods, people feel increasingly disconnected from each other. The reasons are many and complex – but they never erase the deep-seated need for the brotherhood described by Junger.

During our high school staff meetings one year, we read Jeff Myers' book, *Cultivate: Forming the Emerging Generation Through Life-on-Life Mentoring.* Myers gives 12 characteristics of the younger generation. It was interesting to see the contrast between a few of the characteristics. While that generation is the most connected through many virtual venues, they were also reported to be the loneliest. They reportedly valued relationships, yet seemed frustrated in their ability to connect in nourishing ways. Myer's assessment of younger generations seems accurate for society in general. The emerging generations need deep connection and so do we.

So what do we do?

At the risk of sounding simplistic, if we desire the brotherhood of combat then maybe we need to start fighting for each other.

All the previous chapters have made the reality of our battles clear. We don't need physical firefights to acknowledge the battles we fight daily. Battles abound.

I've even battled through the logistics of Trench Buddies. When I present this material at conferences, it is easy for people to realize they need a trench buddy. "How can I get one?" is the common response. After hearing it numerous times, I'm convinced it's the wrong question. The more powerful question is: "How can I be one?"

I can't force a trench buddy relationship – I can only choose to be a trench buddy to others. In doing so, I am most like Christ – the Ultimate Trench Buddy. Jesus saw the mess we were in and demanded nothing from us. He initiated. He loved us first. He loved us while we were His enemies. His investment creates capacity.

To choose to be a trench buddy is to choose to be vulnerable with another. It is taking the first step, risking "real" and refusing superficiality in order to pursue authenticity. It is loving another more than you love yourself. It is protecting the welfare of the group more than your individual interests. It is about making the mission more important than your personal comfort. It is about following orders – God's imperatives – His "one anothers."

All that God does in my life is to conform me into His image. Fundamentally, a trench buddy is like Christ. Jesus came down to earth to bring us to the Father.

The longer I walk through the battles of life with others, I am convinced that the essence of being a good trench buddy is simply to take someone's hand – walk with them through their battle – and then transfer their hand into Jesus' hand. Our goal is never to make someone dependent on us, but to faithfully support them and shift their dependence to the only One who can bring true, enduring victory. That is what discipleship and training is about. That is what trench buddies are about.

Note: After Tim Hetherington and Sebastian Junger completed their "Restrepo" documentary, both went on to cover other war stories. While documenting the conflict in Libya, Hetherington was killed by a mortar in 2011. His death shook Junger so much that he removed himself from combat coverage a month later. But, the military lessons were not lost on Junger. He founded RISC (Reporters Instructed in Saving Colleagues) because he saw the value of SABC in saving lives. His organization now provides a free three-day instruction course (and free combat medical kit) in three major cities to any freelance journalists willing to attend.

DIGGING
DEEPER

CHAPTER 22: TRENCH BUDDIES

Most important "take-away" thought(s):

---

1. Which top 5 "one another" verses are most important to you relating to how you want to be treated if you are in a battle? Why did you pick those top 5?

2. Now pick 3 "one another" verses that you think need improvement in your life. (Try scoring yourself on them all to reveal the 3.) How might those weaknesses affect your effectiveness as a trench buddy?

3. What is the most hurting truth you have ever been given? Did it strengthen your friendship with this friend? Explain how your faith is tied to being an effective trench buddy. Why is it so important?

4. According to Junger, what did men miss most about war? Compare their combat experience to their readjustment to civilian society. Is that how you feel in your spiritual battles? Explain.

5. On a scale of 1-10, how "connected" do you feel in your closest relationships? (1=not connected at all, 10=deeply connected)

"Reproach has broken my heart and I am so sick. And I looked for sympathy, but there was none, and for comforters, but I found none."
Psalm 69:20

23
BATTLE BREAKDOWNS

Sebastian Junger was leaning back on the makeshift sandbag wall when flecks of sand stung his cheek. Because bullets fly faster than sound, it took a second or so before he heard the rat-a-tat gun fire. A bullet missed him by inches... again.

During Junger's year documenting combat in Afghanistan, the soldiers manning outpost Restrepo faced death over and over. Over time, it takes its toll. Nerves fray. Coping mechanisms break down. Performance suffers. The soul languishes.

Where is the breaking point in battle?

A good soldier knows there is one. They must respect their limits, and protect their ability to fight. Leaders are trained to watch for cracks in a soldier's courage.

The platoon assigned to that section of the Korengal Valley in Afghanistan attempted to minimize battle stress by rotating 20-men units to the dangerous outpost for only a month at a time. After serving a month with constant threat and austere living facilities, they rotated back to their headquarters post further down the valley. Despite their best efforts, some men succumbed to battle fatigue, and still struggle to recover years after their tour.

Part of self-aid-and-buddy-care is recognizing the symptoms of battle stress – in yourself – and in those around you in battle. Unlike a physical wound, battle stress is harder to detect because there is no visible bleed. It may manifest through simple fatigue, anxiety, depression, difficulty concentrating, sleeplessness, nightmares, flashbacks, sensitivity to loud noises, or pervasive negativity. In the stress of battle, fear nibbles away at your courage. Battle fatigue is also linked to misconduct stress behaviors.

All through this book, we've looked at the parallel between physical war and spiritual war. Of all the concepts presented, this is one that I didn't see coming. I've walked with military friends through the challenges of PTSD (Post Traumatic Stress Disorder), but I have honestly never considered the implications on a spiritual level with any clarity. How we minister to each other in ongoing battles is greatly affected by this topic. Believers in Jesus Christ experience spiritual battles on a regular basis

– some big, some small – but there is no rotation to a safer place until heaven. This is incredibly relevant.

Battle fatigue affects people's capacity for battle, and reveals how vital the role of a trench buddy is to properly recognize and treat the symptoms – before great damage is done. Tragically, battle fatigue is often not diagnosed in believers until they completely lose their ability to ever return to the battlefield, so they end up casualties in spiritual warfare.

Battle fatigue

According to Army Field Manual 22-51 (chapter 5), battle fatigue is a broad group of physical, mental and emotional signs that naturally result from the heavy mental and emotional work of facing danger under difficult conditions. It feels unpleasant, may interfere with mission performance, and usually improves with reassurance, rest, replenishment of physical needs, and activities which restore confidence.[1]

"Battle fatigue is a term used in World War II to describe a psychological disorder that developed in some individuals who had major traumatic experiences. Although a person was initially numb from the experience, symptoms like depression, excessive irritability, and survivor guilt often happened sometime after the event. Battle fatigue was renamed post-traumatic stress in the 1970s as Vietnam veterans struggled to adjust after the war."[2]

According to the Army Field Manual, there are four major causes to battle fatigue:

- **Sudden exposure** – This is common with initial combat experiences and often involves intense fear, shocking stimuli, and the life-and-death consequences of battle.
- **Cumulative exposure** – This can be an on-going battle trauma, repeated grief and guilt over the loss of fellow soldiers, or the impending sense of one's own death.
- **Physical stressors and stress symptoms** – Sleep loss and dehydration are the most common physical stressors, but it can also include physical overwork, extreme heat or cold, noise, vibration, chronic discomfort, poor hygiene, disrupted nutrition, low-grade fevers, infections and other environmental illnesses.
- **Home front and other existing problems** – Negative home-front problems such as a "Dear John" letter, a sick parent or child, or financial issues add to normal battle stress. It may be positive home events like a recent marriage or a birth of a child

that distracts soldiers from their combat focus and using their psychological resources for the battles.[3]

Interesting observations

There are many fascinating fatigue factors that are relevant to the spiritual parallels that follow.

First of all, it's important to recognize that battle fatigue is normal. It is common, and in most cases, very treatable. It is not something that disqualifies a soldier from continued service – in fact, soldiers recover best when they are able to rejoin their units and return to battle. It is not avoiding future battles that heal battle fatigue, but getting appropriate treatment and returning to battle.

The field manual (instruction appendix E) says: "History shows that most battle-fatigued soldiers can be restored to duty quickly if they rest close to their units and are treated positively as soldiers, not as weaklings, cowards, or sick patients. This restoration requires planning and coordination. If they are evacuated too far to the rear, many may never recover."[4]

Battle fatigue can occur before an event due to excessive anticipation, during an event, or after an event. Both new soldiers and veterans can experience battle fatigue, although it is more common in new soldiers. It is more likely to occur when soldiers lack confidence in the purpose of war, or have a lack of confidence in their leaders, fellow soldiers, supporting units, or equipment. When fatigue occurs, soldiers lose confidence in themselves.

The field manual also cautions against prejudging whether a battle fatigue soldier will recover quickly or slowly based on initial appearance because the symptoms are very changeable. There is no "rubber stamp" approach to battle fatigue due to the complexity of contributing components. One soldier's experience doesn't always match another's.

Research shows that the incidence of battle fatigue is linked to a soldier's expectations of battle – and the intensity of preparatory training. Interestingly, Army Rangers and other special forces experience a drastically lower incidence of battle fatigue despite the fact that their special operations demand more from them than the average soldier. Special Forces expect their missions to be harrowing and challenging. Much of their work is behind enemy lines. They expect a higher risk, but they also complete the toughest training in the military. These soldiers risk the most, but also tend to be the tightest units, which leads to the next observation.

The most cohesive units experience the least amount of battle fatigue. Units with strong, caring, competent leadership fare better than those with weaker leaders with poor communication skills. Strong leaders build strong teams. They raise soldier confidence and help soldiers resolve conflicts that affect their ability to perform their duty.

So battle fatigue is common, treatable, happens to new and experienced soldiers, and a return to the battlefield is vital to full restoration. Lack of confidence promotes battle fatigue, and expectations of war matter. Unit cohesion, intense training, and strong leadership are key to minimizing battle fatigue. All of these factors are important to consider, but one factor is fascinating to me.

Perception of stress

One of the most important factors in combat fatigue is not the battle stressors, but our perception of the stressor. For example, two soldiers experience an intense firefight. Both are wounded and both lose a friend in battle. One experiences battle fatigue a week after the event and the other is fine. What is the difference? Background and personality aside, one soldier perceives the event as overwhelming while the other sees it as something normal in war. The second soldier expects these things to happen so his perception of the event is much different than the first soldier who holds out hope that these things will not happen to him during his tour of duty.

Health psychologist Kelly McGonigal cites studies that show that our perception of stress determines the impact of stress. "The harmful effects of stress on health are not inevitable," McGonigal says. "How you think and how you act can transform your experience of stress. When you choose to view your stress response as helpful, you create the biology of courage. And when you choose to connect with others under stress, you can create resilience."[5]

What McGonigal observes about social stress is shown to be true in combat stress. If viewed as helpful to performance, it keeps the soldier alert and energized, without maximizing the harmful effects. According to McGonigal, our stress prompts social bonds that run deep.

Avoiding battle fatigue

The field manual includes an appendix to teach signs and symptoms of battle fatigue, as well as treatment options. It lists the following key principles for reducing stress of combat and preventing battle fatigue casualties: (Read each one and think of a specific spiritual application.)

> a. Encourage unit cohesion by integrating new replacements quickly, assigning buddies, and using other team-building techniques. Unit cohesion is the personal trust and loyalty of soldiers who have worked together to overcome hardship and danger to achieve a common objective.

b. Stabilize the home front by helping soldiers resolve their home front problems. An Israeli study found that having uncertainties at home was the strongest factor which distinguished soldiers who became stress casualties from those who were decorated for valor. Unit cohesion is the second strongest.

c. Instill unit pride by honoring historical examples of initiative, endurance and resilience, of overcoming heavy odds, and of self-sacrifice leading to triumph. This is needed to give direction and hope to the cohesive unit so that it does not become preoccupied solely with the survival and comfort of its members.

d. Assure physical fitness. This must enhance muscle strength and agility as well as endurance through a regular training program. Not being physically fit almost guarantees battle fatigue when the going gets rough.

e. Conduct tough, realistic training that is as much like the combat mission and environment as possible (sights, sounds, pace, confusion, fatigue, discomfort and feedback). Soldiers' first exposure to combat, to enemy weapons and tactics, and to strange, hostile climates produces battle fatigue.

f. Practice casualty care and evacuation routinely. Everyone must know lifesaving techniques for self and buddy. Talk about the possible loss of leaders and comrades. Prepare junior leaders (and yourself) to take over. This way soldiers know that they can receive immediate care and the chain of command will not break.

g. Plan and practice sleep discipline. Plan ahead to make sure all soldiers get enough sleep, especially leaders and those with critical tasks. Sleep discipline means reviewing sleep as a resource to allocate to soldiers just like water, food, ammunition and fuel.[6]

These are amazingly practical concepts, both on the battlefield and in our lives.

Taking it into our battles

The four major causes of battle fatigue are events that are common to us at some point in our lives. I met with a woman just this morning who could sadly serve as "Exhibit A" for the factors contributing to battle fatigue. Deb lost her father three years ago after caring for him through a prolonged, extremely painful battle with mesothelioma, a lung cancer caused by asbestos exposure. Since her father's death, Deb has been caring for her mother who has battled a series of significant health issues. Just this month, Deb learned that her mom has lung cancer, and possibly breast cancer as well. Deb told me she was struggling with high anxiety, was having trouble sleeping, and was experiencing flashbacks from her father's excruciating death. So, Deb has the sudden exposure to the shock of the cancer diagnosis of her mom, the fear that her mom will die in the same manner as her dad, and the life-and-death consequences of the battle.

Secondly, Deb has cumulative exposure – from her father's recent death, her brother-in-law's death to Leukemia just eight months ago, and now new trauma.

Thirdly, Deb has physical stressors due to her own health issues which include chronic pain from psoriatic arthritis which is deteriorating her spine. Her condition often affects her sleep patterns as the pain keeps her up at night.

Finally, there have been challenges on the home front as the constant care of an aging, ailing parent taxes the time needed to nourish her marriage. Even good events can contribute to home-front trauma as Deb and her husband married off their only daughter last year, and the new couple moved to a nearby state.

As Deb shared her anxiety problems, we reviewed the battle fatigue factors affecting her life. It helped reduce her stress to see that, in light of the situation factors, her symptoms were normal. As simple as it sounds, she already found some relief just by sharing her burden.

How else could I help? I could show her love and concern – and listen well. I could encourage her by reminding her that God gave her the grace to go through her father's decline and death – and He would be faithful again. I could minimize the enemy's taunting fears by comparing the two situations and reminding her that her mom's diagnosis was far different then her father's, and likely less painful. I could protect Deb by suggesting she take lesser priorities off her plate as she coped with the bigger issues she was facing. I could build her confidence by reminding her of her true identity in Christ – and how strong she has been in her previous crises. I could affirm how brave she is – and minimize her self-assessment of weakness. I could affirm my love for her and tell her how much she has helped me in my battles. As her trench buddy, I can place no timetable on her process, or her recovery from grief. Since Deb is a part of our bi-weekly inductive Bible study, I can rally our cohesive group around Deb so we can collectively minister and pray. We are in this together as we all experience the ebb and flow of life's challenging events.

Cohesive community

All of the military literature on battle fatigue and PTSD state that the most cohesive units have the least amount of battle fatigue. This is obviously true on a spiritual level as well, which is probably why Satan expends so much energy causing division. I candidly admit that our Bible study has experienced its bumps and bruises along the way. What group of flawed individuals doesn't? It has been challenging at times to live out the "one another" imperatives in Scripture, but it is equally rewarding to reap the benefits of a cohesive support network when we do. The enemy throws divisive explosives into churches to promote battle fatigue in the very groups that should be working to defuse it.

The typical lack of "trench buddies" connection was illustrated by a new woman who recently joined our Bible study. "When I walked in the door I wanted to cry," she said. "I could feel the sense of deep community as soon as I arrived, and it's so hard to find that today." This woman represents a population that is very common today – and often without a trench buddy. She and her husband live miles away from family because his job requires him to move frequently. She is from a broken home, and is a mom with three small children. She needs deep connection and finds it elusive at best.

Young moms of multiple children seem especially vulnerable to battle fatigue – emotionally and spiritually. Many experience social isolation, and little support. Daily life rarely resembles the expectations formed while expecting. The routine is relentless and "R&R" is rare. Most of us are thrown into parenting with little formal training for the task, so we struggle with confidence. Am I doing a good job? Will they turn out right? Will our marriage survive?

When I think back to the 16 years I led a community homeschool support group, I can see now that one of the main goals was to alleviate battle fatigue for moms. We met once a month, shared encouragement from the Word of God, and offered resources and workshops to encourage parents in academic instruction and family dynamics. There were more than 200 families in the group and each month moms would straggle into the meetings looking haggard and discouraged. How different they looked by the end of the evening. They talked with others fighting the same battles, heard creative solutions to common problems, they laughed and cried together, and shared stories and ideas. Expectations were adjusted and they were reminded that they labored for a noble cause. They learned to view their stress differently. When they heard stories from other homeschooling families, they discovered their challenges and feelings were very normal and common. It was a great comfort to know that they were not alone in their struggles, and that parenting is hard work.

Multi-faceted remedy

I really appreciate that the Army field manual examines many different aspects of life in its attempts to reduce combat stress and prevent battle fatigue. There is not a simplistic, its-all-in-your-head approach. It's not just an emotional problem, or just a physical problem. It's not primarily a spiritual problem. It's more nuanced than that – it's complex – and the solution must be as well.

Let's look at a few of the key principles listed earlier in this chapter. It is incredibly practical how they apply to helping others in spiritual warfare and/or the battles of life:

a. Unit cohesion: People need to be drawn into a place to "belong." I thought it was interesting that the field manual talked about integrating new people into the unit quickly. Feeling like an outsider adds to the normal stress of battle. I love that it actually says to "assign buddies" to provide immediate support and to speed up the process of bringing that person into the fighting team. Trust and loyalty are vital to unit cohesion.

What is it we can do to be that kind of person? Can we spot the "outsider" and draw them in? What can we do to minimize division in our home, church, work, friendships?

b. Stabilize the home front: Ongoing home issues can cripple a person in the battles of life. This type of ministry can take many forms, too many to list out. Trench buddies help however they can in these areas with godly counsel, encouragement, practical assistance, etc.

c. Instill unit pride with examples of initiative, endurance and resilience, self-sacrifice and triumph. I have often been encouraged by hearing testimonies at church from those who have struggled deeply, yet found victory. Sadly, testimony time is very limited at many churches, yet it lifts up others engaged in similar battles and builds connection. Encouragement should not just promote the group looking inward to their own comfort and protection, but together they should be reaching out as well.

d. Assure physical fitness: In spiritual battles, this is often overlooked as a factor in battle fatigue. This can include regular exercise and healthy dietary habits. Getting active and outside brings a much-needed attitude adjustment when the battles are raging – even better with a friend.

e. Conduct tough, realistic training that is as much like the combat mission and environment as possible. This is probably the most neglected area in the arena of spiritual warfare, and was treated extensively in the three training chapters. Our lack of rigorous training and preparation for battle greatly increases our likelihood for battle fatigue.

f. Practice casualty care and evacuation routinely: We should practice caring for each other. What do we do when a brother or sister-in-the-Lord falls? What do we do when the leader falls? Do we train for the contingencies? Are we training junior leaders to fill the gaps to prevent costly breaks in the chain of command – or does everything come to a standstill when a leader is lost? If we face the contingencies – and prepare for them –the response is less catastrophic when the contingency happens.

g. Plan and practice sleep discipline: This concept is best illustrated by toddlers. Often their meltdown in the face of minor challenges is just an indication that they need a nap. A good night's sleep brings amazingly fresh energy and perspective to battle.

A good trench buddy will provide a comprehensive assessment to their buddy in battle – and be conscious of these elements in their own battles. If I find myself easily overwhelmed, what factor am I neglecting?

Pursue the hurting

A good trench buddy is aware, discerning, and picks up cues that battle fatigue is happening. I wish I had this information about five years ago when a former student of mine had all four factors causing battle fatigue, and I missed it. I knew she wasn't doing well, but I honestly did not know what my role was. I made a few feeble attempts to reach out to her and had limited contact because she was away at college and later living away from home. Eventually, she lost the capacity to fight her spiritual battles and succumbed to living against all she knew was true.

Happily, in the intervening years, she has been restored to faith and we have met several times since then. I asked if I could interview her to better understand the slide away from faith – what made her vulnerable, and what she wished (in hindsight) has been different. Her answer stunned me. I can't get it out of my mind. It is the fuel for this whole chapter. She said, "I wish someone had chased me."

The wrong influence and the lack of true trench buddies hastened a downward spiral of pain and confusion. This dear young woman needed a bold rescue. She needed someone who recognized her battle fatigue, and pursued her with love, truth, hope and healing.

There should be a better way

Brendan O'Byrne was one of the men from the Second Platoon, Battle Company that served at outpost Restrepo on the side of a ridge in Korengal Valley, Afghanistan. O'Byrne was part of a Q&A about PTSD after his duty in Afghanistan. He compared their experience processing stress to those that served in WWII, noting that past soldiers had the benefit of long ship voyages home to process their emotions with those who endured similar stressors. They were allowed to decompress, to validate their experiences and emotions, and prepare to re-enter civilian life.

According to O'Byrne, soldiers today are back home in 3-6 days attempting to resume civilian life without properly processing all they went through. He recommends an emphasis shift from treatment to prevention. "I can take apart an M-4 [rifle] in 30 seconds, but I have no idea how to handle my friend getting killed," he said. "I wish someone had said, 'You're going to see your friends die. How will you handle that?'" O'Byrne said.[7]

Avoiding our own breakdowns

How do we avoid our own battle fatigue in spiritual warfare? This list is hardly exhaustive, but can provide some warnings as we attempt to be trench buddies:

1. Be led by the Holy Spirit. Only the Holy Spirit can lead us into the battles that are truly ours. Stepping into battles you are not called to is a surefire way to burn out. When I am not called to a battle, I tend to battle in the flesh instead of in the power of the Holy Spirit. It is not pretty.

2. Minister in God's power, not yours. This is another subtle difference that can be hard to discern at first. We are not anyone's savior – God is. When we minister in our power and think we are the answer to their deepest needs, we will quickly stress to the point of being ineffective. We need to point them to God. Ministry can also be a subtle form of "hiding." There can be an imbalance where we are only ministering to others, but never letting others minister to us in our pain, or in areas where we need to be corrected.

3. Don't play God, show them God. Know your boundaries and keep them. When you show them God, you let God bring needed changes and don't stress out trying to create change yourself. As you walk through battles with another person, stay in constant communication with God in prayer to know when to act, how to act, and most importantly, when not to act. Don't ever steal God's glory.

4. Respect your priorities. God has given us all priorities to live by and when we violate them, we suffer. I have learned this the hard way. God, my husband, and my family are my first priorities. In my zeal for ministry, I have often struggled with conflicted priorities which increased my stress and my ineffectiveness. This also means that I need to keep myself healthy spiritually, or I can't help anyone.

5. Roll your burdens onto Jesus or you will be overwhelmed. This one catches me unaware at times. During periods of deep ministry, I notice that my joy has ebbed and heaviness has set in. In prayer, I realize that I have been carrying burdens I am not designed to carry. When I realize my mistake, I readily cast my burdens at the feet of Jesus, and walk away lighter.

6. Know when to walk away, or when you are over your head. Some trench buddy situations are seasonal. They are for a specified period of time. Don't be afraid to let go. They may need a different portion than yours to continue to grow. And, most importantly, know when the situation is extreme and needs ministry beyond your capacity. This may include people that are suicidal or causing hurt to themselves or others. These situations should be referred to professionals because the stakes are too high to dabble in inexperience.

7. Minister freely. Avoid ministry with "strings" attached. Does someone owe you because you poured yourself out in ministry to them? If so, it may be a good indicator that your ministry motivation is not healthy and is less than pure. We serve God and should expect nothing from the people we serve.

Respect the Sabbath

The military understands the importance of "R&R" (Rest and Recreation) to keep soldiers in the fight. There is a "Morale, Recreation and Welfare" (MWR) section at most every military installation – and their primary role is to provide opportunities to rest, play, and connect with other military members. As with so many other common sense and wise things – God prescribed R&R for His people in the Bible centuries ago. It's called the Sabbath.

God created a rhythm of life for His people that brought balance to their work, families, and battles. In the Old Testament, He created feast days throughout the harvest calendar to promote praise, fellowship, and rest. In fact, God is so serious about rest that those that did not rest on the Sabbath and appointed feast days were to be cut off from the people – or destroyed. (Leviticus 23)

Dr. John Barnett taught that Jesus invites us into His rest – to a cessation of our snowball lifestyles. He said the Sabbath thieves are: culture overload (primarily through media), legalism, busyness, hurry, and debt. "A personal Sabbath with God feeds our patience, strengthens obedience, focuses the spirit on God, and renews our strength," said Barnett.[8] So often, we do not feel God's presence in our battles because we have sped ahead of Him in our hurry – and find ourselves in battles of our own making. Respecting the Sabbath is one of the best deterrents against battle fatigue, but it must be intentional in our 24/7-always-on world.

Worth the fight – together

Spiritual warfare is a corporate battle. We do this together.

Staff Sergeant Sal Giunta provides a wonderful example of this mindset. He was awarded the Medal of Honor for his heroic actions in the Korengal Valley in 2007. It is a medal few soldiers merit, yet Giunta puts it in perfect perspective:

> "It's the nation's highest honor. It's given to me. Okay. But, just as much as me, every single person that I've been with deserves to wear it. They are just as much of me as I am," he said. "My name in lights doesn't look that good, but if I can bring everyone's name with me, then... cool. I think that looks pretty good with everyone else's name there."[9]

CHAPTER 23: BATTLE BREAKDOWNS

Most important "take-away" thought(s):

1. Do you belong to a unit? Are you involved in a local church, Bible study, or small group? Is it a cohesive unit? Do you feel someone in the unit "has your back?" Why, or why not?

2. What are the four main contributing factors that cause battle fatigue? Have you had seasons in life where you experienced most or all of them? How would you describe the "battle fatigue" you subsequently experienced>

3. What is your perception of the stressors in your life? Do you view them all as negative? Explain your viewpoint and how it fuels or fights battle fatigue.

4. Ministering to someone with battle fatigue is complex. Review the multi-faceted treatment list. Which ones do you tend to ignore while ministering to someone in crisis? What approaches does the church in general do well? Which ones does the church tend to ignore?

5. What are some of the ways we can minister poorly as a trench buddy? Have you experienced any of the pitfalls listed? Have you been on the receiving end of some of these errors? Explain.

THIS PAGE INTENTIONALLY LEFT BLANK

Section
6
Victory & Peace

VICTORY AND PEACE: A Personal Profile

It was a long, hard battle, but Jane found victory!

Now that she knows that life is a battle, she has a completely different mindset. Jane is resolute to fight for victory. She is realistic about her defeats and takes responsibility for her actions. She reminds herself that God has given her everything she needs for victory. She believes God, hears God and obeys God. God redeemed the ambush and brought sweet fruit into Jane's life.

She is no longer proud and independent, but strives to stay fully submitted to God in every area of her life. She realizes that if God is not her authority then the enemy will exert his authority instead – and the enemy has no legitimate right to her because of the cross. Jane never wants to go back to that bondage. Jane has made peace with God and enjoys the peace of God in her victory. She has learned to trust God for her life, and has come to see His blessings as overwhelmingly good. God is more real than ever before.

She and her husband did the hard work of counseling to pursue forgiveness and reconciliation. They both learned how their weaknesses were exploited to Satan's advantage. Both Jane and her husband developed regular habits of Bible study, prayer, and accountability with a strong community of believers. They know the battle is for life, but the battle is worth the outcome.

God gloriously restored their marriage. They now have a burden to help other couples in ambush mode – and to help even more couples avoid the ambush.

They share their testimony often. Glory to God for redemption!

Thine, O Lord, is the greatness, and the power, and the glory, and the victory, and the majesty: for all that is in the heaven and in the earth is thine; thine is the kingdom, O Lord, and thou art exalted as head above all."
I Chronicles 29:11

24
VICTORY

One minute after midnight on May 8, 1945, all hostilities ended. Germany surrendered. Hitler's dream of world conquest had come to an end.

Two million people celebrated for 24 hours in Times Square. A million more partied in the streets of Detroit, and thousands more in cities throughout the United States. Outside Buckingham Palace, throngs cheered for the victory they had feared would never come.

Winston Churchill announced the victory in Europe saying, "...we may allow ourselves a brief period of rejoicing..." because the war in the Pacific was not yet settled.[1] Three months, and two nuclear bombs later, Japan succumbed to the Allied forces and victory celebrations once again spilled out into the streets of our cities and communities.

V-E Day (Victory in Europe) and V-J Day (Victory in Japan) provide the quintessential snapshots of the joy and relief of victory – from a long and arduous war fought in Europe and Asia – the largest war in history.

It was a victory that came at a high price, because WWII was also the deadliest war in history, killing approximately 2.5 percent of the global population.[2] War tallies totaled more than 52 million military and civilian casualties from 25 countries. Other sources quote higher estimates of up to 80 million and include more countries. American casualties in the Pacific theater alone totaled 100,000.

Victory demands a high price.

The price of victory

President Harry S. Truman acknowledged the grim statistics of war in his address to the nation on V-E Day:

> "For this victory, we join in offering our thanks to the Providence which has guided and sustained us through the dark days of

adversity. Our rejoicing is sobered and subdued by a supreme consciousness of the terrible price we have paid to rid the world of Hitler and his evil band. Let us not forget, my fellow Americans, the sorrow and the heartache which today abide in the homes of so many of our neighbors--neighbors whose most priceless possession has been rendered as a sacrifice to redeem our liberty."[3]

Millions of people gave their lives for a war people said would end all wars. Sadly, WWII didn't end all wars.

Happily, there is a victory that ended a war of a different kind – originating from a different kingdom. It happened more than 2,000 years ago – a war for our souls – a war that saves us both from the fiery hell our enemy intends, and the unimaginable wrath our sin deserves. The cost of this "war-of-all-wars" was paid for on a gruesome cross by God Himself. Jesus Christ came to earth in the form of a man to bring victory to a war that we brought upon ourselves through rebellion – a rebellion that occurred from the beginning of creation.

Just before Jesus breathed His last breath from the cross, He proclaimed, "It is finished." The Godhead – the Father, Son and Holy Spirit – warred as the Supreme Allied Force to secure victory for our souls, and for our eternal destiny.

The apostle Paul reminded the Corinthians: "But thanks be to God, who gives us the victory through our Lord Jesus Christ." (I Corinthians 15:57) In another letter to Corinth, Paul writes: "But thanks be to God, who always leads us in triumph in Christ, and manifests through us the sweet aroma of the knowledge of Him in every place." (II Corinthians 2:14)

We could practice every principle in this book – and probably gain great advantage by applying them – but we will never have deep, transforming spiritual victories without Jesus Christ. An unbeliever could practice many of these strategies and win many of life's battles, but would never secure the most important victory of all – the victory over judgment and hell.

God is essential. While driving in the car just this morning, I listened to Bible teacher and San Diego pastor David Jeremiah teaching from the book of Hebrews. From just the first three verses of Hebrews, Jeremiah listed out some of the characteristics of this great God who has paid for our victory.

Christ is:
    ... the final word from God
    ... the future heir of all things
    ... the first cause of creation
    ... the fullness of the Godhead
    ... the facilitator of all things
    ... the forgiver of all sin
    ... the finisher of our faith[4]

Wow! What an awesome God to give us so great a victory! So, what difference should this victory make in our daily battles against the world, the flesh, and the devil?

Fighting from victory

I am intrigued by a thought: What if Allied soldiers had been certain of the outcome of WWII before it began? What if they had still faced uncertain battle outcomes, but were absolutely sure the war was already won? How would that knowledge have affected the Allied soldiers? Would it have provoked fear or fortitude? Carelessness or courage? Discouragement or delight? Think about it. What difference would it have actually made?

Why do I ask these questions? I ask because the Allied soldiers couldn't possibly have known the outcome of their war – but we do. They could only hope for victory; but our victory is assured.

What should that provoke in us? Are we fearful or brave? Careless or courageous? Discouraged or delighted? I am intrigued by these questions, but also convicted in my own life. Indeed, one of the main reasons for this book is that I see so few of us affected by the precious reality of victory. We don't seem to be encouraged by the overall victory we already have, and I have encountered too many believers who live in defeat in the battles along the way.

"Why?" is the question that begs to be asked.

In my own life, I ask, "Sandi, what would it look like if you really, really believed you have victory over the grave, death, sin, and strongholds?" One thing I know; it would look different than my present reality. God has paid for my victory. He has done His part. The problem then has to be my faith. My theology doesn't match my reality as it should. It's not enough to just know – I have to believe deeply. The apostle Paul often used the term "fully persuaded." That's the key. When we believe deeply, it flows naturally into our behavior.

The apostle John emphasized the link between faith and victory in his first short epistle written from his time of exile on the Isle of Patmos. He was the last apostle standing and had been through a lifetime of battles. This wizened veteran stated: "For whatever is born of God overcomes the world; and this is the victory that has overcome the world – our faith. Who is the one who overcomes the world, but he who believes that Jesus is the Son of God." (I John 5:4-5) John found victory in exile through faith and through believing all the implications that come with Jesus being the Son of God.

The next chapter is filled with victory testimonies, but I can't wait until then to share this one. About five years ago, Dorrie, a woman I served with in ministry for several years, found her 27-year-old son dead in his bedroom. He had suffered with intestinal issues and diabetes for years and died from a diabetes-related problem.

I've never seen anyone handle a painful death like Dorrie did. She was certainly saddened by her son's death as they were very close, but her faith was her comfort, her fortress, and her strength. When people expressed condolences at the "loss of her son," she would remark, "Oh, thank you, but he's not lost. We know right where he is." Her absolute confidence in the victory over death and promise of heaven brought her great relief. At the funeral ceremony, Dorrie brought comfort to many as they approached her standing by the casket in front of the altar. When she later spoke to the audience, she said, "People are worried that I'm in denial about John's death. I'm very sorry that he died, but do they think that I haven't been listening to the preaching here the past 20 years?" Dorrie gently portrayed the dynamic intersection between faith and life's battles.

When I asked her to contribute a victory testimony, she immediately thought of many, but one stood out in her mind. It was 10 days after John had died. "I remember it like it was yesterday," she said. "I was driving through the Wendy's drive-up and for one split second I thought, 'What if it's [faith beliefs] not true?'" Because of her strong foundation of faith (and incredible recall ability) she rattled off one truth after another to herself. She remembered the undeniable truths surrounding the resurrection, the historical reliability of Scripture, and the consistent evidence of God in her life. "There was absolutely no doubt in my mind," Dorrie said. "God instantly gave me complete victory over doubt."

Faith of victory

How comforting to know that Jesus Christ is the Author and Finisher of our faith!

Am I "more than a conqueror through Him who loves me" as it says in Romans 8:37? It really comes down to believing in Him, believing that He loves me, and just believing Him. Do I really believe? When I do, I can fend off the fiery darts of fear and doubt with the shield of FAITH. In fact, every part of the armor listed in Ephesians 6 is completely faith-related. So do we really believe we are saved – if so, what does that mean in the details of life? (the helmet) Do we really believe God's Word is truth? (the belt and the sword) Do we really believe that we are righteous IN Christ? (the breastplate) Do we really believe the gospel? (feet shod with gospel of peace) Even the prayer mentioned in Ephesians 6 is meaningless unless there is deep belief and confidence in the Object of our prayer.

I studied the armor of God so many times as a believer. I understood the concepts and knew they were important, but I've always struggled to live them strategically until I began to see warfare in the light of military parallels.

Standing in victory

Ephesians 6 also presents another extremely important aspect of victory. Verse 10-14a says:

> "Finally, be strong in the Lord and in the strength of His might. Put on the full armor of God, so that you will be able to *stand firm* against the schemes of the devil. For our struggle is not against flesh and blood, but against the rulers, against the powers, against the world forces of this darkness, against the spiritual forces of wickedness in the heavenly places. Therefore, take up the full armor of God, so that you will be able to resist in the evil day, and having done everything, to *stand firm*. *Stand firm* therefore...."

Because our strength comes from the Lord – the One who has already won the victory – we are to stand firm. We put on the collective armor of faith – and stand firm. Paul repeats the Ephesian message to the church in Galatia: "It was for freedom that Christ set us free; therefore keep *standing firm* and do not be subject again to a yoke of slavery." (Galatians 5:1)

Tony Evans pounds this point home in many of his messages of spiritual warfare. "Christians don't know they have the victory – so they keep fighting a fight that's been already won," he says often. "They need to learn to stand in the victory God has given them."[5]

"Stand firm" seems to be the answer to the previous question: "What if we knew the outcome?" The believer walks in a strange dichotomy – in a condition of certain war – but from a position of guaranteed victory. Sometimes it gets confusing because our Christian battles are full of dichotomies. We have to surrender to win. We have to die to live. We battle the unseen and not the seen. These realities are counterintuitive, but these are the truths we must stand firm in to experience the victories promised through faith.

The battles are real and relentless. We get bumped, bruised and bloody – and maybe even lose a limb or two. The desire to retreat and quit can be overwhelming. What keeps us in the battle? The perspective of victory instead of defeat. Standing in the final victory – but also embracing lively hope for victory in our present battle. There should be no more valiant soldier than the Christian.

Process of victory

So, we learned that we fight from a place and perspective of victory, and we fight for our faith in the daily drama of life. Chuck Swindoll offers some additional pointers in his message: "What's Necessary for Victory?"

As a pastor and former Marine, Swindoll brings a dual perspective to the quest for victory. He begins with describing the typical defeat – a slow life of compromise. Defeat is "when the zip, thrill, and excitement of fleshly investments begin to yield their carnal dividends… and you suffer as you've never suffered before."[6]

"Maybe you've ignored God's warnings and pushed your convictions aside; you've trafficked in unlived truth, but now you're at the end of your rope, and you are discouraged, maybe even depressed," he said.[7]

"Admit your defeat," Swindoll said. "Face your defeat, and then focus directly on the Lord, and not on the odds against you."[8]

"God did not create you to live this way," he said emphatically. "You've allowed someone else to call the shots. You are marching out of step with your Creator."[9]

Where are you right now? Living in victory or defeat? Assessing your current battle status is important – and the first step towards getting in step with the Commander Lord who brings consistent victory. Doing nothing is losing. According to Swindoll, passivity in our defeat is the greatest enemy of victory, and it is also the most subtle.

"Some of you have walked with the Lord Jesus for so long – you've forgotten there's a battle – because somewhere, back when you began to lose it, you just changed the rules," said Swindoll.[10] He assessed the soft state of the church:

> "We recoil at things that call for endurance and effort and sacrifice and self-control. We don't like those kinds of messages. We like comfortable messages. We like comforting talks. We like to be told our position in Christ, but not our responsibility as children of God. We love the benefits that come with our security in the Savior, but we are galled when someone pushes his finger on the nerve of responsibility."[11]

Ouch. There is that price for victory again. Jesus paid the ultimate price, but we will never gain personal victories without paying a price as well. Swindoll culled from I Corinthians 9:24-27 for principles that promote victory, and attack apathy:

1. ACTION: Paul borrows from an athletic example of a foot race. You can't win if you don't RUN. And you can't run very well if you don't train. An action is required from the participant if victory is ever a possibility.

2. AIM: The runner runs with an aim to win. A boxer doesn't beat the air, but makes contact with his opponent. According to Swindoll, a believer with the right aim doesn't stumble into temptation but knows full well how to get through it.

3. DISCIPLINE: A runner exercises control in all things. Paul makes his body a slave. Why? So he won't be disqualified. So he won't lose even before he gets to the finish line. Swindoll cited a quote he found in a Wheaton College bulletin: "The undisciplined is a headache to himself and a heartache to others, and is unprepared to face the stern realities of life."[12]

Swindoll thinks all God's people are championship material, but said many have adopted the flabby philosophy of our times – opting for comfort and mediocrity – yawning their way through life. He says:

"Nothing in this world will take the place of persistence. Talent will not. Nothing is more common that unsuccessful individuals with talent. Genius will not. Unrewarded genius is almost a proverb. Education will not. The world is full of educated derelicts. Persistence and determination alone are omnipotent. You are never too old."[13]

Our fight for victory must continue strong to the grave because of the every-present default of defeat – not in the "long war" – but defeat in our everyday battles.

What victory is not

With all this talk of victory, it is important to recognize real victory versus a false concept of victory. Once again, Swindoll provided valuable insights:

1. **Victory is not a once-for-all accomplishment.** Romans 8 ends with conquering through Jesus Christ who loves us, but the context is one of sheep being led to slaughter – of tribulation, distress, persecution, famine and sometimes death. There are no sounds of flashy battle, but a day-by-day steadfastness in the face of adversity.
2. **Victory is not an emotional high** – it is about volition – not how we feel that defines victory.
3. **Victory is not a dream, but a reality.** Victory is not reserved for "super saints" at only certain levels of spiritual maturity.
4. **Victory is not an independent achievement.** We overwhelmingly conquer _through_ Him who loves us. Victory is always linked to the Lord Jesus Christ.
5. **Victory is not something that happens to us as we passively wait on the sidelines.** Victory doesn't just occur.

That would be like a Olympic athlete not knowing how they earned a gold medal.[14]

Purpose of victory

What does victory look like for the believer in Jesus Christ? Victory should not cause us to swagger and strut, and look for accolades, but it should cause us to serve. In I Corinthians 9:1-12, the apostle Paul models victory. Paul chose to be a servant rather than a prima donna on a pedestal to be idolized. All of the apostles deflected attention when God gave them victory through miraculous signs. Our victories should bring God glory, not us. Paul used his victories to win others to Christ.

God always gives us victory for a purpose. In Beth Moore's teaching on the book of Deuteronomy she said, "God doesn't give us victory just for the sake of victory."[15] She quotes from Deuteronomy 6:23: "He brought us out from there in order to bring us in, to give us the land which He had sworn to our fathers." When God gave His people victory over the hard taskmasters of Egypt, it was to bring them out of Egypt and into the Promised Land. But, most of the Israelites that witnessed the amazing victory in Egypt never lived to see the full victory of the Promised Land because of their grumbling and lack of faith.

"He [God] brings us victory so we can walk in a promise – so we can fulfill our call," said Moore. "Yes, personal victory is sweet... but it is always for something bigger."[16] She gave the example of the man blind from birth. When he was healed, it was to his great personal benefit, but ultimately so God could receive glory. "Our victories should manifest the One who gives it to us," Moore said. "We should walk in it."[17]

Victory corpses

When our Bible study group studied the book of Numbers last year, I was deeply grieved by those that fell in the wilderness of disobedience and unbelief. God promised them victory but they squandered it:

> "The Lord spoke to Moses and Aaron, saying, 'How long shall I bear with this evil congregation who are grumbling against Me? I have heard the complaints of the sons of Israel, which they are making against Me. Say to them, 'As I live,' says the LORD, 'just as you have spoken in My hearing, so I will surely do to you; your *corpses will fall in this wilderness,* even all your numbered men, according to your complete number from twenty years old and upward, who have grumbled against Me. Surely you shall not come into the land in which I swore to settle you, except Caleb the son of Jephunneh and Joshua the son of Nun. Your children, however,

whom you said would become a prey – I will bring them in, and they will know the land which you have rejected. But as for you, *your corpses will fall in the wilderness.* Your sons shall be shepherds for forty years in the wilderness, and they will suffer for your unfaithfulness, until *your corpses lie in the wilderness.*'" Numbers 14:26-33

I have thought about this passage for months. It made me sad, and it scared me in the most healthy way. I wondered how many victories I have squandered in my life through unbelief. These people lost the fight of faith, and lost full victory as a result. Was I doing the same every time I grumbled, disobeyed God's Word, and simply did not believe what God promised?

"The reason for corpses in the wilderness is not because God is not able --- they had no faith in what God could do through them," taught Moore.[18]

The Israelites not only lacked the faith to fight for the fulfillment of their promise, but they actually fought God instead. They failed to surrender, so they failed to win. Miles McPhearson addresses those that battle against God in his message, "Why Surrender?" The pastor of Rock Church in San Diego said, "Some of you are fighting God – and you are getting your butts kicked…. Maybe it's time to give up and ask, 'God, what do you want me to do?' – and do it."[19]

The most ridiculous battle you will ever fight is against God. You will lose – every time. The Israelites did, and so will we.

Way of victory

Forty years after the Numbers account – after all the corpses fell – Moses spoke to another generation in Deuteronomy 8. They stood at the brink of the promise – the full victory from God. Moses' warning to them speaks to me also, if I want to walk in victory:

> "All the commandments that I am commanding you today you shall be careful to do, that you may live and multiply, and go in and possess the land which the Lord swore to give to your forefathers…. It shall come about if you ever forget the Lord your God and go after other gods and serve them and worship them, I testify against you today that you will surely perish. Like the nations that the Lord makes to perish before you, so you shall perish; because you would not listen to the voice of the Lord your God." Deuteronomy 8: 1, 19-20.

Three verses serve as a summary for walking in victory. Believe God, hear God, and obey God. Nothing else will do.

Caleb did that. Caleb and his faithful friend Joshua were the only two men (from the original group over 20-years-old) that enjoyed the victory of their promise in the "land of milk and honey."Caleb was one of the 12 spies that checked out the Promised Land right after God delivered the Israelites from Egypt. He and Joshua were the only ones that believed God for victory. They saw the giants and fortified cities of the enemy – just like the other 10 spies – but they believed God would keep His word and give them victory. Caleb received his full victory "because he followed the Lord his God fully" (see Joshua 14:8,9). This great man of faith is 85-years-old when he is about to get his allotted land of promise. He picks a hill country filled with giants and fortified cities! He still believes the Lord will be with him, and drive his enemies out – just like He promised. THAT is a victory mindset.

Victory enjoyed

I have a friend like Caleb. She believes God, hears God, and obeys God. She has been through more battles than most people I know, but I seldom speak with her when she doesn't have some great victory testimony. She is one of my trench buddies. Amazing things happen in her life – despite all that she has been through. She takes God's commands seriously. She worships God deeply and guards against idols in her life. She listens to God's voice, and acts obediently. She takes on big battles because she really believes God will show up. He does, consistently.

Caleb and my friend should be the norm for the Christian.

"God did not design for us a life of defeat," said Swindoll. "We are not supposed to have a 'whatever comes, I'll have to endure it' attitude. That is not in the Book."[20]

Submit, resist, and persist. In the end, V-E Day and V-J Day celebrations will pale in comparison to the final victory celebration in heaven on that great day!

CHAPTER 24: VICTORY

Most important "take-away" thought(s):

_____

1. Why is Jesus Christ the "linchpin" for all victory?

2. Are you currently living in mostly victory or mostly defeat? How does your level of belief factor into your assessment?

3. Why does God give us victory? What is the specific cost when we live in defeat?

4. Think. What is the biggest obstacle to victory in your life right now? Unbelief? Disobedience? Grumbling? Passivity? What steps can you take to move toward victory?

5. Read Deut 8:1,19-20 again. Evaluate your life against the prescription given by God. Are you careful? The command was also given to a nation. Where is our nation headed according to the passage? What three steps can change our course?

"And they overcame him because of the blood of the Lamb and because of the
word of their testimony, and they did not love their life
even when faced with death."
Revelation 12:11

25
THE WORD OF THEIR TESTIMONIES

This might be my favorite chapter – the fruit of the fight. In the midst of all the grueling training and pain, victory stories are massively encouraging. Testimonies reveal the reality of victory. It's possible. It happens all the time. It happens to others, and it can and should be happening to us.

I recently heard Gabe Wirth's victory testimony:

Gabe Wirth is a wiry, lean man. His body bears the symbols of his journey. His piercings are both physical and emotional – and tattoo sleeves ink his saga.

His story starts in California – walking the streets – going nowhere. Drugs and drinking had taken their toll in his early 20's. He attempted suicide and often thought of driving his car off a cliff. "My life was complete emptiness," he said, "despair, brokenness, and no goals."

Gabe married young, but with no training and guidance, his weakened marriage was dying. "I was completely helpless and hopeless. I didn't want my life to end this way," he said, on the verge of tears. "I thought there had to be more to this life than what I was experiencing right now."

As if staring back into time, Gabe spoke of a turning point in his life when he was invited to a church marriage retreat. "Listening to this pastor preach, I couldn't tell you one word he said, and I can't remember his face.... I can remember sitting in the middle of the crowd, and actually remember Jesus speaking right into my heart – just grabbing a hold of me. I just wept, and wept, and wept – and my life was forever changed after that weekend.

"It went on, and on, and on.... He [Jesus] was cleaning me up from the inside out. My heart was changing, my desires were changing, the drugs were not anything I was interested in anymore," he said. "God was tearing away fleshly desires and idols. I still battled alcohol and pornography." Gabe said it was an incredibly painful time of brokenness and marital separation – God was stripping away his former identity, but it took a while to understand his new identity in Christ.

Two years into the process, Gabe and his wife moved to Tennessee. In a tiny rural church, an old country preacher began to disciple Gabe. "He was my spiritual father," Gabe said. "He taught me to pray. He taught me how to really love Jesus."

Gabe said it took about four years before he actually awakened to what God was doing inside of him – through him – training him to be who he needed to be.

He remembers one night looking up at the stars, and asking, "God, what do you want for me for my life?" He clearly recalls the answer: "I want you to be a father. I want you to be a husband." Gabe tried to push this simple mission aside as not very meaningful. He expected something greater, but he had no idea how fitting God's answer was to his future calling.

Struggling to maintain his composure, Gabe explained: "Here I sit in Springfield, Mass. – all the way across the country...." Faltering, he finally continued: "I'm leading a wife and three children on mission at a house where we model family life to homeless women and their kids! The craziness and insanity of who God is, and how He works.... Now, I'm in this home and my life is completely changed. He has recreated me, and is continuing day-by-day to create me into somebody completely different. I am truly born again."

Yes! Applause! Another enemy victory stolen! Defeat redeemed! I am continually broken by the power of Almighty God to change lives. In my present battles, I often forget God's faithfulness in my past battles. Gabe's story makes me hungry for greater victories in my own life.

Surprise lessons

Victory can look very different on different people. It can be a full victory over an addiction – and a radically transformed life, like Gabe. It can also be a seemingly insignificant behavior or thought pattern – that one day you discern is completely gone – by God's grace and not behavior management!

It can be a relationship restored that seemed humanly impossible, or forgiveness you could not imagine – either receiving it, or giving it. It can be shattered marriages gloriously restored when, by sight, it looked impossible.

I was so excited about this chapter, but began to understand its importance even more as I began to solicit victory testimonies. Many people drew a blank. "I know I get them, but I can't think of one," was a frequent response. Fortunately, others said they had so many, it was hard to choose one or two. But, it was the first response that troubled me – and brought up other questions.

If people weren't getting victories, then why not? If they won victories, but couldn't recall them, how was that encouraging? It was an epiphany of sorts that it's really important to capture or catalog our victories – to celebrate each one, large or small. Why?

First of all, it causes me to intentionally give God the glory for what He has worked in my life. Secondly, it promotes thankfulness. Thirdly, it provokes courage for future battles.

David patterns these three points often in the Psalms. Discouraged in the battle, he whines to God. In Psalm 13, David writes: "How long, O Lord? Will you forget me forever? How long will you hide your face from me? How long shall I take counsel in my soul, having sorrow in my heart all the day? How long will my enemy be exalted over me?" (v. 1-2) By verse 5, David begins to turn. He is reminded of God's loving-kindness. Perhaps he recalled all the times God brought him victory in the past. In verse 6, David writes: "I will sing to the Lord, because He has dealt bountifully with me." Nothing had changed concerning David's present circumstances, at least what was recorded. What did change then? David's perspective did.

The fourth reason we should capture our victories is because it encourages others. I am encouraged by David and Caleb. I am provoked and inspired by the victories I see God giving my faith-filled friends. It makes me bolder in my own walk.

The last reason is that it promotes praise. When we proclaim our victories, we boast in the Lord – it is ultimately His victories.

It was startling to see all these victory testimony benefits. Conversely, I began to see how the enemy tries to keep us ignorant or silent regarding our victories. If our testimonies promote God's glory, thankfulness, courage, encouragement, and praise, then the enemy wins if we have none or never speak of our victories.

Karen captured this point:

> "I KNOW there have been victories in my life. It's probably my standards-driven self kicking back in, but when I think of the victories in my life I kind of shrug and say, 'Yeah, but they're no big deal.' ...or 'why should anyone care?' And there is the lie, isn't it? The enemy whispers that any victory I have is small and not worth sharing. But, more and more I see that if I can achieve these small

victories it gives confidence going forward. Maybe the next one will be bigger. Maybe I can build on what I have already accomplished through Christ and do something more. And, perhaps seeing that is a victory in its own right."

May these testimonies bless you, encourage you, and cause you to believe God for your own victories to share.

Victory over circumstances

"When I was first separated from my alcoholic abusive husband, I also lost my niece to breast cancer, my nephew to a heroin overdose, then another nephew to a heroin overdose. My finances were challenging and I was feeling like a failure in all areas of my life. A very wise Christian woman counseled me to "be in the Word" like it was my life line. I carried verses on cards with me, kept them tacked to my ceiling in my car, on my mirrors, in my bra (LOL), in my purse.... I slept with my Bible. This made me feel protected when I would wake in the night and feelings of failure would surface.

"I would have despaired unless I had believed that I would see the goodness of the LORD in the land of the living." (Psalm 27:13) This verse and many others got me though. They gave me victory!

For some reason, when I was driving in the car, my mind would go places it should not have gone. I would hear the whispers: 'I am a failure, I can't even keep a husband, blah, blah, blah....' I kept those verses written down and ready. I would read them over and over again. Satan loved to attack me with untruths, but I would recite Scripture over and over.

My victory is great. I am secure in who I am in Christ, but I still need to constantly be in the Word."

Donna Viens

Victory over health challenges

"I had it all under control. I was a successful teacher, healthy, and enjoying life with friends. I had everything I wanted, the old neighborhood, a great car, and I was dating the most beautiful teacher in the whole school. God was in the mix somewhere....

Things began to unravel. My perfect life hid an emptiness I couldn't explain. My relationship then failed – and so did my health. While on vacation in Florida, my kidneys stopped working. During my four months in the hospital in Florida, I found out I had won a teaching award, but I also lost my position due to my illness. I got worse and was eventually airlifted to Boston. I had a few brushes with death during my six-month hospitalization. I was eventually discharged, began dialysis, and moved in with my sister because I was no longer well enough to live alone. It seemed God had stripped me of all the things I loved.

Devoid of all that I had pursued for happiness, an unexpected joy began to form. Still very sick, I found new life in the Word of God, church, and ministry. I was happy to be alive, and God used my passions and talents in diverse ways in my new environment. I had come "home." God's promises, and the love of family and friends, helped me thrive. I began a weight loss program so I could qualify for a kidney transplant.

Nine years later, and I finally had a transplant date. A fellow church member had donated her kidney. Anticipating life without dialysis, I eagerly awaited the surgery. Long story, short: the transplanted kidney failed. Of course I was disappointed and wanted it all to work out, but I knew God was in control, and that He would use even this for His glory. He had taught me those lessons the last time I was in the hospital. He used my initial time of losing what I thought was everything to show me that even though the transplant had failed, I had Him, and that was enough.

God has rebuilt my life through trials and loss so I could withstand the storms of life. The whole Bible tells me that Jesus loved me before I loved Him back. Jesus did so much for me, and the Holy Spirit dwells in me. If we stay in the Word, and never lose sight of the Savior, how can we worry about the ins and outs of everyday? I'm not saying that you won't have a day where you think you can't handle it. You can't. Only God can handle it. Use what He has given you: His Word, His church, His people. It's not a battle you have to fight by yourself.

Remember, when things start to fall apart, are they the things you wanted, or the things God has for you?"

Luca Coppa

Finding victory for others

"My husband came home from work frustrated. He had been passed up for a promotion for the fourth time. He had the highest performance scores in his department. He was well-liked and always professional. He never took any time off and worked through his breaks. Because of corporate politics, my husband watched promotions given to unworthy and undeserving colleagues.

As his trench buddy, I watched him sit at the table angry and defeated. As my husband complained, I prayed, '*Lord open his heart and his mind. Help him to see that this is an attack.*' Finally I spoke. 'Have you prayed about this?' My husband honestly responded, 'I am too angry to pray.'

The next day my husband awoke upset again. As he drove to work he rehearsed how he was going to confront his supervisor. As he drove to work I prayed again. '*God have control over this situation. Lord your will be done.*' My husband's supervisor was in such a bad mood that morning that my husband decided to delay the conversation.

Hours later a coworker from another department approached him. There was a position opening up in her department – a perfect fit for him. My husband was shocked. Minutes later he got a phone call to setup an interview for the new position!

My husband came home and happily recounted what had unfolded throughout the day. Even though he had missed the attack, I was able to see it. I was able to battle for him. We both knew that God had protected him that day from his own foolishness. The Lord was control, and knew what He had in store for our family was better than what my husband had originally wanted."

– Camila Andre

Victory from secret sin

"When I was 13 years old, I was exposed to internet porn, and by the time I turned 15, I was moderately addicted to it. It wasn't just the porn that had me ensnared; it was the deception and hiding that was killing me. I grew up in a strong Christian home, filled with constant, positive spiritual investment; I really had no reason to search for, and get caught up in such a painful sin. But nevertheless, I was.

I found myself being sick all the time, ridden with guilt, and hiding lies to cover up other lies. I was fake. I'll never forget, in the midst of all that trash, I made an anniversary card for my parents filled with sweet words, and love notes. My mom hung it on the fridge, and every single time I walked by that card, it screamed at me, "This is not love. This is fake. What does real love look like?" It didn't look like the stuff I was doing in the darkness.

I'd like to say that one day I woke up, and decided to confess, but, that's not what happened. I wasn't strong enough for that. Instead, I got caught. And as much as that was very embarrassing, and shameful, it was God's perfect mercy and saving grace for me. From the moment I was caught, and everything was exposed, I never went back to that dark place. Ever.

Even though I got punished for my deception, my parents were also wise enough to usher in outside help for me to fully gain victory. I had mentors come to help me out of that pit, and follow me until I was far, far away from it. I wasn't just left alone after being exposed. I was carried to victory. And I was willing, and so ready to claim it. I pursued the Word with new purpose and vigor. I memorized Scripture and stayed accountable to godly women. My brush with hidden sin made me much more careful with lots of other areas in my life. It shattered my confidence in the flesh.

I am now 27 years old, and since that day I haven't even had a single desire to return to that pit. Of course I struggle with other temptations, as is the life of a sinful human, but the victory I experienced back then gave me such strength and wisdom for even greater victories now. The fight for faith is so worth it."

Anonymous

Victory at work

Our small dental practice was sold to a larger, corporate practice. They kept me on as a hygienist, but the work environment was completely different. The work pace doubled and I had to learn a new computer system. The office took on a corporate feel, and the new office manager was overwhelmingly negative, back-biting, and overbearing. One of the new dentists makes misery his lifestyle. I no longer had time to interact with my patients. I was stressed, tired and miserable.

As I prayed, I knew God was telling me to love and serve my new co-workers. I resolved to avoid the negativity and gossip. I creatively tried to bring a positive spin to conversations. I built up the staff. Despite the hectic schedule, I helped other hygienists whenever I could. I learned what their favorite snacks were and brought them to work. Every time I wanted to react (which was often) I simply kept quiet. I just concentrated on winning them over with love.

It was tiring to battle the situation with love and kindness, but it gradually began to change. They began to tease me about being a "church girl," but it was not mean-spirited. They began to soften, and began to ask me questions about my life. I was gradually able to share things that revealed the work of God in my life. The atmosphere is slowly changing.

Work is still challenging in some ways, but God brought about significant victory – a victory that came His way, by following His principles. God is so good! Cheryl

Victory over legalism

I have always held myself to unrealistic standards. Somewhere in my heart I knew they were unrealistic, but when I wasn't meeting them, I would label myself a failure – and then berate myself for being such a failure. I even mocked myself for failing to set realistic standards.

It was fine that others would not be able to meet those same standards. I never expected them to. I could be accepting, even gracious, with the shortcomings I saw in others but never with myself. If I actually attained one of my standards, then it must be because the bar was set too low. There was no room for grace with myself. Allowing grace was surely a license to keep falling short, wasn't it?

I was never really happy. I lived in bondage....until godly women helped me to see grace for what it really is: not a license to sin or an excuse for my failures, but a covering for both. God knows I fall short; He's always known I would, and that is why He gave me Jesus. The joy in my life today comes from allowing His perfect, everlasting standards to be mine and allowing His grace through Jesus to fill in the gaps where I fall short.

Some days I fall back into my standards-driven life, but even on these days there is grace. That grace is like a bolt-cutter snapping the chains of the heavy standards that have long weighed me down. Each time I allow God's grace to minister to me in my failures I find I want to live more and more in the freedom that it brings.

Karen Curran

Victory over anxiety

I can vividly remember the days when my daughter was growing up. They were filled with worry and anxiety over what would happen to her. When she was a teenager I would panic every time she was gone from our home. I would ask my husband time after time if he thought she was ok, and he always confidently answered, "Yes".

As I read my Bible for encouragement, I came across Philippians 4:6 "Do not be anxious about anything, but in every situation, by prayer and petition, with thanksgiving, present your requests to God." About this time, I was actively involved in the homeschool community and met with other homeschooling moms throughout the week. They encouraged me to pray and seek peace from the Lord. How freeing it was when the Lord freed me from my fear!

Now I rest in the knowledge that He is always in control & that He loves my daughter more than I ever could. I still need friends to remind & encourage me at times, but when I start to feel anxious I go back to the Word & find my reassurance there.

Deb Lapointe

Victory over fear

Patti was on her way back to Peru from Equador. Her husband Len was gravely ill and both their lives were in peril.

She and Len were on their last leg of a very successful mission trip. They had spent a week ministering in Lima before traveling to Kajamarca. Len's health began to tank at the higher elevation away from the coast. With diabetes and prior heart attacks, Len's heart struggled with the lower oxygen levels.

Patti and Len decided to risk the travel to Cuenca, Equador so Patti could present a women's conference there. The car ride to Cuenca was supposed to be 12 hours, but it stretched into 24 hours – a harrowing drive along narrow cliff roads with no guard rails.

The extended driving time took its toll on Len. He grew weaker, and began to experience more pain. Their location was remote, with no hospital nearby. Len tried to rest as Patti presented the conference – teaching mostly from Joshua 1. In fact, most of her teaching during the trip stressed the verse: "Be strong and very courageous for the Lord God is with you...."

To minimize the stress of the trip back to Lima, Patti and Len booked a return flight from a remote regional airport in Peru back to Lima. The bus ride to the regional airport was supposed to take 12 hours. It took 15 and while en route, they found out they missed their flight to Lima.

The outlook was grim. Len was suffering. The town they were heading to has a terrible reputation for crime and violence. Once the airport there shut down, they would be forced into the town, with no lodging. "I just started to cry," Patti said. "I was fainting in fear, imagining all the worst things happening – luggage stolen (including her recording equipment), kidnapping, or rape." Her husband was too sick to defend her, and his life was already in danger.

In the midst of her breakdown, Patti began to remember all the things she had taught over the past two weeks. She began to see the enemy behind her despair and panic. She sensed God's voice saying, "Do you really believe what you've been teaching? Do you believe I'm your Father, that I love you? Do you think I don't know what's going on? Do you believe I will take care of this?"

"God's truths washed over me, and I wiped my tears with my last scrap of toilet paper." Patti recalled. "I began to pray out loud on the bus: 'Lord, I believe you. I don't know how this will work out, but I believe You. You will be faithful. You will take care of everything.'"

"It's not that I didn't still feel fear. Fear just became subservient to the truth," Patti said. She began to take every fearful thought captive and compare it to truth. She said she felt her heavenly Father smile. She fully believed what she prayed, and anticipated what would happen in the next hour.

When they pulled up to the town next to the airport, they caught a ride on an open cart pulled by a bicycle. Patti draped her body over the luggage so no one could steal it as they drove through town. Patti recounted the victories from that point on:

Victory 1: They made it to the airport.

Victory 2: There was one last flight leaving the airport, and it was currently loading.

Victory 3: The woman at the airport counter spoke English.

Victory 4: God gave them favor. Tickets on this second flight cost $1600, but the woman contacted the airline headquarters and got approval to charge them only $248!

Victory 5: Their previously problematic charge card went through with no glitches.

Victory 6: More favor: A young man walked them personally through security, took their luggage, and signaled to them from the tarmac that their luggage was loaded.

Victory 7: They arrived safely in Lima, where Len's health rapidly improved at the sea-level location.

"When I sat on the bus sobbing, the problems were bigger than me," Patti said. "When I prayed, God became bigger than my problem." Now that she is safely back home, Patti said that the victories experienced on the mission field now bleed into the smaller challenges she faces in everyday life. "God is good."

Patti Spangler

Victory over bitterness

In my early twenties, I was going through a time of counseling trying to heal some hurts as a result of my parents' divorce. I previously had forgiven my father for many wrongful actions and words he had brought upon me and my family.

But, I was frustrated because real victory seemed to elude me. Over and over, new hurtful memories would surface, or new events occurred.

My wise, godly counselor pointed out that forgiveness is never a one-time action or heart attitude. In Matthew 18, Jesus said we are to forgive 70 x 7. Just as I need forgiveness from my heavenly Father over and over again, so I should extend forgiveness to others in my life.

God loves and forgives me when I don't deserve it, and it's the greatest gift I have ever received. I needed to share that gift with my earthly father.

I am now able to see him through Christ's eyes and forgive his faults – just as I am forgiven.

My father and I have enjoyed a good relationship for eight years now.

Margaret Patrick

Victory in marriage

In more than 60 years of marriage, I often wanted something so badly, I ignored what God had planned for me. I wanted my expectations for marriage met my way, and was not open to God's way.

Once I submitted to God's will, life turned around. God gave me what I wanted in life, it just came about differently than I expected. I learned to stop praying for what I wanted and pray instead for what God wanted. I learned to wait on God. I learned to be willing to let God be God.

My life became so much better. I enjoyed a peace that I never had before.

Grace

Believing God for victory

I love victory testimonies! I want more, but unbelief hinders me at times.

In Scripture, faith seems to play a huge role in God's actions. The Roman official believed and his son was healed that very hour. (John 4:49-53) Naaman believed God and dipped into the Jordan 10 times and was healed of his leprosy. (II Kings 5) The woman with the issue of blood was healed because of her faith. (Mark 5: 25-34) The Canaanite woman's daughter was delivered from demons because of her persistent faith. (Matthew 15: 22-28) In Mark 9, a father brings his demon-possessed son to Jesus. Jesus rebukes the crowd for their unbelief and says, "All things are possible to him who believes." (v. 23) The father repents of his unbelief and asks Jesus to help him with his unbelief, then Jesus heals the son.

By contrast, the Israelites lost access to the Promised Land because of unbelief. In Mark 13, Jesus returns to His hometown. Everyone was astonished by His teachings, but Jesus appears to be limited in some way by their unbelief. Mark 13:58 says: "And He did not do many miracles there because of their unbelief."

My prayer echoes that of the father in Mark 9: "Lord, I believe. Help me in my unbelief."

True, honest, authentic faith is the conduit through which all victories flow. The last-standing apostle, John, says it best: "This is the victory that has overcome the world, our faith." (I John 5:4)

DIGGING
DEEPER

CHAPTER 25: THE WORD OF THEIR TESTIMONIES

Most important "take-away" thought(s):

1. Could you relate to the people that said they couldn't think of any recent victories they experienced with God? Why or why not?

2. What five things do we miss out on when we don't take the time to capture the victories that God gives us in our walk of faith? Have you ever considered what is lost when we don't chronicle our victory testimonies?

3. If asked to give a personal victory testimony at church this Sunday, what would you share?

4. What is the most powerful victory testimony you have ever heard? Share it. What impact did it have on you?

5. What role does faith play in victory? How would you assess your own level of faith for victory? Bring your assessment to God in prayer.

*"These things I have spoken to you, so that in Me you may have peace.
In the world you have tribulation, but take courage,
I have overcome the world."*
John 16:33

26
PEACE THAT LASTS

The Egyptian-Hittite peace treaty is the oldest, known surviving peace treaty, created in 1259BC between the Egyptian Pharoah Ramesses II and Hittite King Hattusili III.[1] Peace was shattered by Assyria some 100 years later.

Hundreds of treaties were negotiated prior to 1259, and Wikipedia lists nearly 800 peace treaties from 1300 through 2000.[2]

The treaty that ended WWI illustrates a foundational principle about war and peace. President Harding signed the Treaty of Versailles on June 28, 1919, formally ending the war dubbed "the war to end all wars." The Paris Peace Conference in 1919 spawned the League of Nations as a further attempt to end future wars. Despite men's best efforts, the quest for lasting peace remains elusive.

Once a war is over, there is a "peace at last" mentality, but it rarely endures as a "peace that lasts." As of this writing (July 2014) warsintheworld.com lists 61 countries currently involved in wars involving 548 militias or separatists groups.[3] The current headlines highlight bombing between Hamas and Israel, and ongoing conflict in Eastern Europe as Russia takes over parts of the Ukraine. The war continues in Afghanistan, and Iraqi stability is crumbling as the Islamic State (ISIS) expands.

Grim news. "I thought this chapter was about peace," you might be thinking.

It is. Current events can be discouraging, but there is a peace that lasts. The best news is this peace that lasts does not demand the cessation of hostilities, but is found in the midst of hostilities. It is not dependent on what is going on outside of us, but on what is going on inside of us.

As with so many other principles presented in this book, the spiritual parallels of war and peace present paradox. They don't make sense to the natural mind.

Peace with God

We learned from the very first chapter that spiritual warfare involves two primary players: God and Satan. In this conflict, we are with one side or the other, or to put it more succinctly, we are under the authority of one side or the other. The Bible clearly delineates: God's people and "pagan" people, Jews and Gentiles, saved and lost, believing and unbelieving, redeemed and dead in sin, justified and condemned. The lines are drawn between the sides.

In John 8:44, Jesus is speaking to unbelieving Jews: "You are of your father the devil...." Romans 5:10 says that Christ died for us while we were still His enemies. James, the brother of Jesus writes: "You adulteresses, do you not know that friendship with the world is hostility toward God? Therefore whoever wishes to be a friend of the world makes himself an enemy of God." (James 4:4)

Throughout Scripture, it is clear that alienation from God makes us at war with God. Yet, the entire Bible reveals a loving God Who pursues rebellious, lost sinners – His enemies. Those that humbly come to Him find the path to peace.

In fact, one of God's names is "Jehovah Shalom," and the origin of the name is perfect for this chapter. The Israelites are living in rebellion and, subsequently, utter defeat. They are hiding out in the mountains and caves while the Midianites and Amalakites oppress them, stealing their crops and livestock, ravaging the land. Finally, in anguish, the Israelites cry out to God. God sends them a prophet to proclaim deliverance. An angel of the LORD (believed to be the pre-incarnate Christ) then commissions Gideon to lead the deliverance. Gideon prepares an offering, the Lord consumes the offering with fire, and God says to Gideon, "Peace to you, do not fear...." Gideon then builds an altar and proclaims God as "Jehovah Shalom" meaning "the Lord is our peace." (Judges 6:1-24)

God ultimately gave Gideon and his small band of soldiers an incredible victory but, it is significant that Gideon discovers the God of Peace while his circumstances are still very bad. It is from a place of peace, worship, and obedience that Gideon experiences profound internal victory. His peace was in the battle, not after the victory against the Midianites and Amalakites.

Provision of peace

The path to peace with God began in the Old Testament through a series of sacrifices or offerings. God's people were to observe these sacrifices at regular intervals prescribed throughout the year. One of these was a peace offering. Leviticus 3 outlines the requirements. The peace offering required the shed blood of an unblemished animal (bull, cow, lamb or goat) while the owner placed a hand on the animal as it was slain to identify with the sacrifice. The priest then sprinkled the blood around the altar, burned the animal, and then shared the meat with the owner and his friends. The subsequent meal was a thanksgiving celebration for unexpected blessings, answers to prayer, or general thankfulness.

To study the offerings in the Old Testament is fascinating, because they all point to the cumulative sacrifice of Jesus Christ in the New Testament. This perfect Lamb of God was slain and His blood applied for our sin so we could celebrate such an unexpected (and undeserved) blessing. Jesus Christ is the ultimate Peace Offering bringing us into right relationship for all that call on Him as Lord and Savior.

True peace is only possible from this starting point: peace with God. At the moment of salvation we become His sons and daughters instead of enemies. The cosmic war was won at the cross, and we gain the spoils of peace. Our eternal destiny is no longer in question. We belong to God. In John 6, Jesus says that He will not cast out the ones that come to him (v. 37), and four times in the same chapter it says that Jesus will raise us up on the last day (v. 39, 40, 44, 54). We are secure, and at peace regarding our eternal position.

This assurance should bring an abiding peace, that regardless of what happens along the way, we can rest in a future promise. "Who can mind the journey," asked the late, great Bible teacher James M. Gray, "when the road leads home?" Like Gideon, when we see God for Who He is, we can have peace in the midst of battle. We can say with the psalmist: "He will redeem my soul in peace from the battle which is against me, for they are many who strive with me." (Psalm 55:18)

Peace of God

Those that have peace with God can also have the peace of God – a peace which is often very different from our conceived notions of peace. In John 13-14, Jesus gives us a glimpse of His peace during a time of intense struggle. Jesus is about to be crucified and those that follow Him will experience great persecution by association. It's Jesus' last supper with His disciples, likely and ominously a pre-Passover feast for the soon-to-be crucified Lamb. Jesus washes their feet and offers His final teaching before His death. Their present looked bleak, but Jesus offered them a hope beyond the present. He offered them a parting gift of peace: "Peace I leave you; My peace I give to you; not as the world gives do I give to you. Do not let your heart be troubled, nor let it be fearful." (John 14: 27)

The peace of God is not like the world offers. The Jews had hoped for a mighty Messiah who would free them from Roman oppression – someone who would make their lives comfortable where they lived. But, God did not come to provide a temporal peace. God's peace is not a transient, dependent-on-circumstances peace. When Jesus offered His unique peace in John 14, He also brought practical encouragement. Jesus told them He was going to prepare a place for them, so they could be with Him in the end. He offered a future and final peace. He also promised the Holy Spirit to help them after He had departed.

God's peace is an abiding peace – a permeating peace for those that abide in Him. God, through His Son and the Word provides the answers to the fundamental questions of life: Where did I come from? Why am I here? What is the basis for morality? Where am I going when I die? It is no small thing to get solid answers to these important questions. When I am firmly set in who I am in Christ, why I am here, and where I will spend eternity, I can move forward with power and peace.

Process of peace

Often we have peace with God, and the peace of God, yet still do not experience peace. Why not? It appears, from Scripture, that God's peace is unconditional, but our experience of peace is conditional. Consider the verse in Isaiah 26:3: "The steadfast of mind You will keep in perfect peace, because he trusts in You." What are the implications? My mind must be steadfast and I must trust in God as the prerequisites to experiencing perfect peace. Psalm 119:165 offers another criterion: "Those who love Your law have great peace, and nothing causes them to stumble." Do I love God's Word? Does it show in my daily practices? If not, it may be a reason why I don't experience God's peace. Proverbs 3:7 says: "Her ways are pleasant ways and all her paths are peace." The context of this proverb is wisdom. Am I seeking wisdom in all my decisions and actions to experience greater peace?

Andy Stanley has some great advice when it comes to incorporating wisdom into our daily decisions. In his book, *The Best Question Ever*, he defines that question as, "Is this wise?"[4] In the most practical application, Stanley breaks the question down into three areas:

1. Is this wise based on my past?
2. Is this wise based on my present circumstances?
3. Is this wise based on my future plans?

In his book, Stanley elaborates on how to apply these questions and maintains that these questions could keep people from much turmoil in their lives. I found them helpful tools in making assessments.

Isaiah 32:17 says: "The word of righteousness will be peace, and the service of righteousness, quietness and confidence forever." Am I speaking righteously? Am I serving? I am righteous by the blood of Christ. Is my behavior consistent with my identity?

Probably the most important condition to experiencing God's peace is obedience. Full obedience. Have you ever felt that nagging unrest of conviction? Have you done something you shouldn't, or not done something you should? I know I have. Nothing ruins my peace like disobedience. No matter how hard I try to rationalize my behavior, I am still running from God, and forfeiting my peace in the process.

Am I right in my personal relationships? The Bible tells us: "If possible, so far as it depends on you, be at peace with all men."(Romans 12:18) Relational discord drains our experience of peace.

In fact, my lack of peace can be the best warning sign that something is not right in my life. It may be a decision, an action, a word spoken, or a deed undone. Once I repent openly and fully, peace flows freely. Once I obey, peace is no longer obstructed by my rebellion.

False peace

There is a manufactured peace we often try to create in our rebellion. The Bible is full of examples. Moses gives a chilling contrast in Deuteronomy 29. After decades of leading a stiff-necked people, Moses stood on the brink of the Promised Land and proclaimed his final warning in a covenant God commanded him to share. Moses warned them about following after the gods of other nations, saying they will be as "a root bearing poisonous fruit...." Moses said that some who hear this warning will boast, saying: "I have peace though I walk in the stubbornness of my heart...." (29:19) Not only will those people not experience God's peace, but in the next few verses Moses listed out the curses they will bring upon themselves. Scary stuff.

The Old Testament prophets constantly warned God's people of the consequences of their rebellion. God's tenderness always prompted Him to send messengers to draw His people back to Him, rather than watch them wallow in the squalor of their choosing, but they rarely listened. In their rebellious deception, God's people often thought they were fine – at peace, even though they were not. Isaiah emphatically states: "'There is no peace,' says my God, 'for the wicked.'" (Isaiah 57:21) The prophet Amos speaks to God's people as they are still bringing peace offerings, but God will not even look upon them because the people had departed from Him. God says, through Amos: "Even though you offer up to Me burnt offerings and your grain offerings, I will not accept them; and I will not even look at the peace offerings of your fatlings." (Amos 5:22) They were still going through "religious motions," but God was no longer involved. That might describe the reality of many churches today.

In Jeremiah 6, even the priests proclaimed false peace to the people. God says" their ears are closed.... The word of the Lord has become a reproach to them; they have no delight in it." (v.10) The prophet Jeremiah describes their situation vividly:

> "'For from the least of them even to the greatest of them,
> everyone is greedy for gain, and from the prophet even to the priest
> everyone deals falsely. They have healed the brokenness of My people

superficially, saying 'Peace, peace,' but there is no peace. Were they ashamed because of the abomination they have done? They were not even ashamed at all; they did not even know how to blush, therefore they shall fall among those who fall; at the time that I punish them, they shall be cast down,' says the Lord." (v. 13-15)

Sound familiar? Sound like today?

Fast forward about 650 years from Jeremiah's times and the apostles pick up the same theme. The whole book of II Peter is an exhortation against false belief and false peace. Consider chapter 2:

"But false prophets also arose among the people, just as there will also be false teachers among you, who will secretly introduce destructive heresies, even denying the Master who bought them, bringing swift destruction upon themselves. Many will follow their sensuality, and because of them, the way of the truth will be maligned; and in their greed they will exploit you with false words; their judgment from long ago is not idle, and their destruction is not asleep." (v. 1-3)

Sound familiar? Sound like today?

Over and over, God's people grope to find their own peace outside of God's loving commands. The lure is ever-present for us as well. The things of the world draw us. They seem attractive. They are right now, and we hate waiting. Sometimes I read the Bible and wonder how God's people could be so stubborn and rebellious, but, unfortunately, it often reveals the very same things in me. The author of Hebrews tells us that the Word of God is "able to judge the thoughts and intents of the heart." (4:12) That's uncomfortable. It makes me squirm. But, it also makes me much more likely to enjoy God's peace when I respond in humility and obedience to the teaching of His Word.

Practical peace

Sometimes our experience of peace is hindered by something simple, something practical. It may be as basic as rest, or as foundational as belief.

We are a hurry-scurry society. Like gerbils on a wheel, our pace of life doesn't necessarily get us to a good destination – and it often takes us further from the destination of peace. Our culture prizes productivity, a tangible outcome for our labors. But, peace is cultivated in the intangible soil of rest. It is in the quiet that we realize the deepest truths of peace – peace with God and the peace of God. The treasure we find in the place of quiet, we bring into our battles. Ravi Zacharias often says: "The biggest battle you will face in life is your daily appointment with God. Keep it, or every other battle will become bigger."

James MacDonald presented some other practical points of peace when he spoke at Moody Bible College's Founders Week. He first defined God's peace as: "a calm assurance that what God is doing is best."[5]

McDonald then offered five useful habits that promote peace:

1. Resolve conflict: Take care of relational conflicts to promote peace of mind and a clear conscience.
2. Rejoice: Purpose to pursue a supernatural delight in the person, purposes and people of God.
3. Reject reasonableness: Life doesn't always work out the way we want, or reason it should. Let go of petty differences, and forego your rights for the sake of peace. "Christ is coming, let it go," he said.[6]
4. Do not be anxious: Nothing steals peace like divided care. "PRAY – alone, on your knees, out loud, fervent, with a list," said MacDonald.[7]
5. Think on:
    a. Whatever is true... true peace is lost in deception and dissonance
    b. Whatever is honorable... peace is lost on the low road
    c. Whatever is pure... peace is lost in a dirty mind
    d. Whatever is beautiful... train yourself to see the beauty in everything
    e. Whatever is excellent... what is in agreement with wisdom?
    f. Whatever is praiseworthy.... Peace is found in God alone.

Good advice.

God is the originator of both victory and peace, but we are responsible to live according to Scripture to partner in the process. God provides peace, but we can quench the result by our choices.

Peace through strength

Few countries disband their armies once a peace treaty is signed. They understand the need for continued vigilance to maintain peace – peace through strength. Most peace treaties also contain terms of agreement – conditions both sides must comply with to maintain the peace. Often, they include some type of inspection to ensure compliance. Similarly, God has given us the peace treaty of His Word – a new covenant. His part is perfect. There is nothing more God needs to do, but His Word outlines our responsibility to maintain a strong walk, and gives criteria to inspect our compliance

God's Treaty gives us the right to bear arms – spiritual armor and spiritual ammo. The classic passages of Ephesians 6 give us our marching orders from a place of peace. The first three chapters of Ephesians speak of our position in Christ, and the second three reveal how we should live based on that position. Ephesians 6 explains how we bring it all into battle – through strength:

"Finally, be strong in the Lord and in the strength of His might. Put on the full armor of God, so that you will be able to stand firm against the schemes of the devil." (6:10-11)

Full strength is accomplished through prayer: "With all prayer and petition pray at all times in the Spirit, and with this in view, be on the alert with all perseverance and petition for all the saints." (v. 18) There is that Trench Buddy mandate again – "be on the alert with all perseverance and petition for all the saints." We are in this battle together, and we seek to enjoy peace in the battles – together. In fact, Paul ends the epistle by praying "peace to the brethren, and love from faith, from God the Father and the Lord Jesus Christ."(v.23) Peace with God, peace of God, and peace with each other in the battles of life.

Peace and strength through suffering

Strength is found in God. Strength is found in obedience. Strength is also found through battles. We usually try to avoid battles, but they can play a significant role in our strength for peace. Combat Journalist Sebastian Junger found this out after struggling with PTSD from his time in Afghanistan and other war zones. Mostly everyone knows about perils of PTSD, but a therapist told Junger about "PT-growth." She said it is the positive aspect of trauma. "Trauma deepens you emotionally, and that's a good thing," the therapist told Junger.[8]

"Frankly, it made me a much more emotional person.... I came out of the Korengal after a year and I had no problems being emotional anymore," said Junger. "It was traumatic, but actually really good."[9]

Tim Keller concurs that our suffering is never wasted. He cites psychologist Jonathan Haidt, who acknowledges the harmful effects of trauma but also maintains that there is empirical support for the view that "people need adversity, setbacks, and perhaps even trauma to reach the highest levels of strength, fulfillment, and personal development."[10] Haidt observes three benefits of suffering:

"First, many people who survive suffering become more resilient. Once they have learned to cope, they know they can do it again and live life with less anxiety.... Second, it strengthens relationships, usually bonding the sufferer permanently into a set of deeper friendships or family times that serve to nurture and strengthen for years.... And, thirdly, suffering changes priorities and philosophies."[11]

Keller also cites psychologist Robert Emmons who highlights the priorities mentioned by Haidt: "People who invest much or most of their energy into the goals of personal achievement and happiness are the most vulnerable to the adverse circumstances of life."[12]

Suffering can wring the life out of us, but it can also bring great strength. The apostle Paul faced a string of battles few of us will ever experience. He models an amazing attitude for our example: "Therefore, I am well content with weaknesses, with insults, with distresses, with persecution, with difficulties, for Christ's sake; for when I am weak, then I am strong." (II Corinthians 12:10) Seems like an odd way to strength. Another paradox of faith.

Peace through strength is a continual process. It takes effort, discipline and discernment. It is a process that only ends with the grave.

Perfect peace

There is coming a day when we will experience perfect peace. The battles will be over – forever.

Until then, our battles are real – and everything about our fight should be to the glory of God.

In his book, *Hope for the Hurting*, Chuck Swindoll offers perspective for life: "God has given us a purpose for our existence, a reason to go on, even though that existence includes tough times. By our living through suffering, we become sanctified – in other words, set apart for the glory of God. We gain perspective. We grow deeper. We grow up!"[13]

Compared to the future prospect of heaven, Swindoll writes that nothing that occurs to us on this earth falls into the "final chapter," and that chapter will not be completed until we arrive in heaven and step into the presence of the living God.

Until that great day – either by death or His return – may we battle as shoulder-to-shoulder spiritual soldiers. In our battles, God is not only the God of Peace, but He is Jehovah Jireh (the Lord will provide), He is Jehovah Nissi (the Lord is my banner – to lead His people to victory). He is Jehovah Sabbaoth (the Lord of hosts) our Commander leading the armies of heaven, and He is Adonai (Almighty God) signifying His majesty.

To God be the glory forever and ever. Amen!

DIGGING
DEEPER

CHAPTER 26: PEACE THAT LASTS

Most important "take-away" thought(s):

_____

1. How did the peace with God shift from the Old Testament to the New Testament? Why does it matter to your Christian experience today?

2. On a scale of 1-10, how would you rate your typical experience of peace? Explain your rating.

3. What are some of the reasons we don't experience God's peace? Which ones apply to you personally?

4. Explain how people can experience a false peace. What is false peace so dangerous – both in war and in our own lives.

5. What is the role of suffering in peace? Is peace dependent on circumstances? Defend your answer.

You did it! You finished the book!

Whether you read the book individually or with a study group, I hope you found the training practical and relevant to your life. I pray that it's not "just another book," but that practicing the principles will bring you greater spiritual victories – and train you to be a better trench buddy. Please re-visit the content often and share it with others.

If you would like to host a **TRENCH Buddies** conference, contact me at: sandi@trenchbuddies.com, or give me a call at 413-237-0168. Feel free to visit the website: www.trenchbuddies.com for more information.

I would love your feedback! Let me know what impacted you the most. Send me your victory testimonies, or share how a trench buddy has made a difference in your life. Send them to the e-mail above. With your permission, I may feature you as a guest blogger on the **TRENCH Buddies** blog.

ENDNOTES

CHAPTER 1: WAR 101

1. http://dictionary.reference.com/browse/war?s=t
2. http://www.brainyquote.com/quotes/authors/e/edmund_burke.html
3. http://www.chesteron.org/quotations-of-g-k-chesteron/
4. http://www.quotationspage.com/quote/27169.html
5. http://thinkexist.com/quotations/there_is_nothing_so_likely_to_produce_peace_as_to/262864.html
6. John MacArthur, *The Truth War: Fighting for Certainty in an Age of Deception* (Nashville: Thomas Nelson, Inc., 2007), 29.
7. *Ibid.* 31.
8. *Ibid.* xvii

CHAPTER 2: THE REALITY OF AN ENEMY

1. http://acc6.its.brooklyn.cuny.edu/~phalsall/texts/artofwar.html
2. http://www.brainyquote.com/quotes/quotes/a/abrahamlin138223.html
3. http://www.brainyquote.com/quotes/quotes/w/waltkelly114887.html
4. http://thinkexist.com/quotation/beware_of_no_man_more_than_of_yourself-we_carry/260515.html
5. MacArthur, xx.
6. https://www.gordonstate.edu/PT_Faculty/jmallory/index_files/page0508.htm
7. MacArthur, xxvii.

CHAPTER 3: THE ALERTNESS OF WAR

1. http://www.insightforliving.com/pdf/messagemates/12.09.2009-mm.pdf

CHAPTER 4: IMPORTANCE OF STRATEGY

1. http://www.artofwarquotes.com/
2. http://thinkexist.com/quotation/you_may_not_be_interested_in_strategy-but/340121.html
3. http://womenofchristianity.com/quotes/elisabeth-elliot-quotes/
4. http://www.goodreads.com/quotes/69071-when-the-time-comes-to-die-make-sure-that-all
5. Oswald Chambers, *My Utmost for His Highest, Classic Edition* (Uhrichsville, OH: Barbour Publishing, 1963).
6. http://www.reformed.org/documents/WSC.html

CHAPTER 5: LEADERSHIP AND AUTHORITY

1. Merriam Webster Collegiate Dictionary, Tenth Edition (Springfield, MA: Merriam Webster, Inc., 1973), 78.
2. Charles Kraft, *I Give You Authority* (Grand Rapids, MI: Chosen Books, 1997), 138.
3. John Bevere, *Enemy Access Denied* (Lake Mary, FL: Charisma House, 2006), 106.
4. *Ibid.*

CHAPTER 6: SIGNING UP FOR PAIN

1. Lt. Carey Cash, *A Table in His Presence* (Nashville: W Publishing Group, 2004), 173.
2. *Ibid.* 174.

CHAPTER 7: PARALLELS THAT WORK

1. Francis Chan, *Multiply* (Colorado Springs: David C. Cook, 2012), 16-17.
2. *Ibid.* 32-33.
3. Ron Luce, *Battle Cry for a Generation: The Fight to Save America's Youth* (Colorado Springs: Cook Communications Ministries, 2005), 57.
4. *Ibid.*
5. http://www.brainyquote.com/quotes/quotes/e/earthakitt106382.html
6. Jeff Wise, "The Brave Among Us," *Reader's Digest*, January 2014.
7. *Ibid.*
8. http://www.4kidsofsfl.org/page.aspx?pid=327
9. *Ibid.*
10. Dr. Spiros Zodhiates, editor, *Hebrew Greek Key Word Study Bible* (Chattanooga: AMG Publishers, 1996), 1607.
11. *Ibid.*

CHAPTER 8: THE SOUL OF THE SOLDIER

1. Cash, *A Table in His Presence*, 11.
2. *Ibid.*
3. *Ibid.* 16-17.
4. *Ibid.* 21.
5. http://www.airforce.com/learn-about/our-mission/
6. http://www.navy.mil/navydata/nav_legacy.asp?id=193
7. http://www.army.mil/values/
8. Andy Stanley, *Enemies of the Heart: Breaking Free from the Four Emotions that Control You* (Colorado Springs: Multnomah Press, 2011), 161..
9. Kris Lundgaard, *The Enemy Within: Straight Talk About the Power and Defeat of Sin* (Phillipsburg, NJ: P&R Publishing Company, 1998), 79.
10. http://www.goodreads.com/quotes/105350-integrity-without-knowledge-is-weak-and-useless-and-knowledge-without
11. http://www.merriam-webster.com/dictionary/integrity
12. Chuck Swindoll, "Plea for Integrity," aired on oneplace.com, July 12, 2013.
13. *Ibid.*
14. *Ibid.*
15. http://www.breakpoint.org/search-library/search?view=searchdetail&id=1338
16. https://www.goodreads.com/quotes/156299-in-a-sort-of-ghastly-simplicity-we-remove-the-organ
17. https://tombguard.org/column/2012/06/the-sentinels-creed-line-6/
18. http://dictionary.reference.com/browse/hero?s=t
19. http://thinkexist.com/quotation/courage_is_contagious-when_a_brave_man_takes_a/200524.html
20. http://afbmt.com/before-bmt/things-to-memorize-before-bmt/

21. Timothy Keller, *Reason for God: Belief in an Age of Skepticism* (New York: Riverhead Books, 2008), 168.
22. *Ibid.*

CHAPTER 9: CAN YOU HEAR ME NOW?

1. Charles W. Sasser, *God in the Foxhole: Inspiring True Stories of Miracles on the Battlefield* (New York: Threshold Editions, 2008), 44.
2. Cash, *A Table in His Presence*, 120.
3. *Ibid.* 121.
4. Chip Ingram, *The Invisible War Series*, "How to Gain Deliverance from Demonic Influence," Part 1, www.oneplace.com/ministries/living-on-the-edge/how-to-gain-deliverance-from-demonic-influence-part-1
5. E. M. Bounds, "The Weapon of Prayer: Putting God to Work," www.cbn.com/spirituallife/prayerandcounseling/intercession/weapon_prayer_0303b.aspx
6. *Ibid.*
7. Ingram.
8. Cash, 162.
9. Ingram.
10. http://www.armystudyguide.com/content/publications/field_manuals/fm-2433.shtml
11. *Ibid.*
12. Dr. Archibald Hart and Sylvia Hart Freid, *Digital Invasion: How Technology is Shaping You and Your Relationships* (Grand Rapids: Baker Books, 2013), 29.
13. Richard P. Hallion, "Airpower From the Ground Up," in *Air Force Magazine*, Vol. 83, No. 11, November 2000.
14. Wikipedia, http://en.wikipedia.org/wiki/Fog_of_war

CHAPTER 10: TAKEN CAPTIVE

1. Ray Pritchard, *Stealth Attack* (Chicago: Moody Publishers, 2007), 147-149.

CHAPTER 11: THE WEAPONS OF OUR WARFARE

1. *Merriam Webster's Collegiate Dictionary, Tenth Edition* (Springfield, MA: Merriam-Webster, Inc., 1993), 423.
2. Jentezen Franklin, *Fasting: Opening the Door to a Deeper, More Intimate, More Powerful Relationship with God* (Lake Mary, FL: Charisma House, 2008), 9.
3. *Ibid.* 35-36.
4. Timothy Keller, "Spiritual Warfare" podcast; available at https://itunes.apple.com/us/podcast/timothy-keller-podcast/id352660924?mt=2
5.*Ibid.*

CHAPTER 12: SHOOTING AT THE RIGHT TARGETS

1. http://www.nationalgeographic.com/pearlharbor/history/pearlharbor_timeline.html
2. *Merriam Webster's Collegiate Dictionary, Tenth Edition*, 1167.
3. Dr. Spiros Zodhiates, editor, *Hebrew Greek Key Word Study Bible*, 2089.

4. *Ibid.*
5. David Noebel, *Understanding the Times: The Collision of Today's Competing Worldviews* (Manitou Springs, CO: Summit Press, 2006).
6. http://dictionary.reference.com/browse/lust?s=t
7. Ravi Zacharias, "What is Worthwhile Under the Sun" podcast, www.RZIM.org
8. *Ibid.*
9. *Ibid.*
10. *Ibid.*
11. Warren Wiersbe, *What to Wear to War* (Lincoln, NB: Back to the Bible, 1986), 12.
12. *Ibid.* 18.
13. Timothy Keller, *Encounters with Jesus: Unexpected Answers to Life's Biggest Questions* (New York, NY: Penguin Group, 2013), 122.
14. *Ibid.* 123.
15. *Ibid.* 124.
16. *Ibid.* 126.
17. http://www.gracegems.org/Ryle/holiness5.htm
18. http://en.wikipedia.org/wiki/Isoroku_Yamamoto%27s_sleeping_giant_quote

CHAPTER 13: WEAPONS TRAINING

1. Tony Evans, "The Weapons of Authority," http://www.oneplace.com/ministries/the-alternative/listen/the-weapons-of-authority-393398.html
2. *Ibid.*
3. http://users.wfu.edu/price/Biblefunny.htm
4. MacArthur, *The Truth War*, 49.
5. Chuck Swindoll, *A Look at the Book: Traveling the Original Route 66* (Anaheim, CA: Insight for Living, 1994), 25.
6. http://dictionary.reference.com/browse/hermeneutics?s=t
7. http://www.nationalmuseum.af.mil/factsheets/factsheet.asp?id=15559
8. Evans, "The Weapons of Authority."
9. *AFPAM 10-100*, 102, http://static.e-publishing.af.mil/production/1/af_a3_5/publication/afpam10-100/afpam10-100.pdf
10. Ron Powers, "Rules of War," http://usmilitary.about.com/cs/wars/a/loac.htm
11. *Ibid.*
12. Evan, "The Weapons of Authority."

CHAPTER 14: GOING BOOM

1. Gregg Zoroya, "How the IED Changed the US Military," in *USA Today*, December 19, 2013, http://www.usatoday.com/story/news/nation/2013/12/18/ied-10-years-blast-wounds/amputations/3803017
2. *Ibid.*
3. *Ibid.*
4. Greg Foley, *Journal of a Christian Soldier in Iraq: A young Army officer's personal testimony* (Maitland, FL: Zulon Press, 2012), 172.

5. *Ibid.*

6. Liz Klimas, "The Amazing Story of Soldier Hit by Nine IEDs Who Has Now Been Awarded the Bronze Star," June 20, 2013, http://www.theblaze.com/stories/2013/06/20/the-amazing-story-of-soldier-hit-by-nine-ieds-who-has-now-been-awarded-the-bronze-star/

7. Charles F. Stanley, *Landmines in the Path of the Believer* (Nashville: Thomas Nelson, Inc., 2007), ix.

8. *Ibid.* x.

9. *Ibid.* xi.

CHAPTER 15: ORDINANCE OR ORDNANCE?

1. http://publicintelligence.net/u-s-army-improvised-explosive-device-ied-awareness-guide-iraq-and-afghanistan/2010

2. *AFPAM 1-100*, March 1, 2009, *www.e-publishing.af.mil*, 126.

3. Karl Menninger, M.D., *Whatever Became of Sin?* (Portland, OR:Hawthorne Books, 1973), 16.

4. *Ibid.* 22.

5. Oswald Chambes, *The Philosophy of Sin* (Ft. Washington, PA: Christian Literature Crusade, 1960), 56.

6. *Ibid.* 10.

7. *Ibid.* 11.

8. *Ibid.* 53.

9. *Ibid.* 11.

10. Gerry Bridges, *Respectable Sins* (Colorado Springs: Navpress, 2007), 51.

CHAPTER 17: DIRTY BOMBS

1. Sharon Jacobs, "Chemical Warfare, from Rome to Syria: A Timeline," *National Geographic News*, August 22, 2013, http://news.nationalgeographic.com/news/2013/08/130822-syria-chemical-biological-weapons-sarin-war-history-science/

2. *Ibid.*

3. *Ibid.*

4. *Ibid.*

5. *Ibid.*

6. Organisation for the Prohibition of Chemical Weapons, "History of Chemical Weapon Use," *https://www.opcw.org/about-chemical-weapons/history-of-cw-use/*

7. Tim Keller, *Walking with God through Pain and Suffering* (New York, NY: Dutton/Penguin Group, 2013), 3.

CHAPTER 18: SECURITY: CAN I SEE AN ID?

1. Kris Lundgaard, *The Enemy Within*, 38.

2. www.oneplace.com/ministries/insight-for-living/player/strengthening-your-grip-on-purity-part-3-402239.html

3. Lundgaard, 92-93.

4. *Ibid.*
5. Dr. Caroline Leaf, "13 Steps to Detox Your Thought Life," from *Your Body, His Temple: God's Plan for Achieving Emotional Wholeness*, Audio CD (Life Outreach International, 2007).
6. *Ibid.*
7. *Ibid.*

CHAPTER 19: THREAT LEVELS
1. Kris Lundgaard, *The Enemy Within*, 88.

CHAPTER 20: OUTSIDE THE WIRE
1. www.oneplace.com/ministries/insight-for-living/player/strengthening-your-grip-on-purity-part-3-402239.html
2. *Ibid.*
3. Kris Lungaard, *The Enemy Within*, 76.

CHAPTER 21: SABC: SELF-AID-AND-BUDDY-CARE
1. http://www.wpafb.af.mil/library/factsheets/factsheet.asp?id=9135
2. *Ibid.*
3. *Ibid.*
4. Tim Dilena, "I Can't Do This Without You," *www.brooklyntabernacle.org/medi/sermons/May182014*
5. *Ibid.*
6. *Ibid.*
7. *Ibid.*
8. Jeff Wise, "The Brave Among Us", in *Reader's Digest*, January 2013, 72.
9. Kelly McGonigal, "How to Make Stress Your Friend," TEDGlobal 2013, June 2013, *https://www.ted.com/talks/kelly_mcgonigal_how_to_make_stress_your_friend*
10. *Ibid.*
11. *Ibid.*
12. *Ibid.*

CHAPTER 22: TRENCH BUDDIES
1. http://www.va.gov/opa/speceven/memday/history.asp?utm_source=3birds&utm_medium=Web&utm_campaign=GANLEYHONDA_Fun+Facts+About+Memorial+Day
2. Tim Keller, *Walking with God through Pain and Suffering*, 163.
3. Ray Ortlund, "'One Anothers' I Can't Find in the New Testament," *http://thegospelcoalition.org/blogs/rayortlund/2014/05/24/one-anothers-i-cant-find-in-the-new-testament-2/*
4. *Ibid.*
5. *Ibid.*
6. Beth Moore, *Wising Up Whenever Life Happens*, "A Wise Friend" (Living Proof Ministries, 2007).

7. *Ibid.*
8. *Ibid.*
9. Sebastian Junger, "Why Veterans Miss War," January 2014, *https://www.ted.com/talks/sebastian_junger_why_veterans_miss_war/transc ript*
10. *Ibid.*
11. *Ibid.*
12. *Ibid.*

CHAPTER 23: BATTLE BREAKDOWNS

1. *Army Field Manual 22-51*, Chapter 5, armypubs.army.mil/doctrine/DR_pubs/dr_a/pdf/fm6_22x5.pdf
2. http://www.medterms.com/script/main/art.asp?articlekey=2443
3. *Battle Fatigue – Military Veterans PTSD Reference Manual,* www.ptsdmanual.com/fm22-51/ch5.pdf
4. *Army Field Manual 22-51*, Appendix E, http://www.patriotoutreach.org/fm_22-51_appendix-e.html
5. Helen Walters, "The Upside of Stress: Kelly McGonigal at TEDGlobal 2013," TEDBlog, June 11, 2013, *http://blog.ted.com/2013/06/11/the-upside-of-stress-kelly-mcgonigal-at-tedglobal-2013/*
6. *Army Field Manual 22-51*, Appendix E.
7. "*Restrepo* Q&A – Coming Home from War and Battling PTSD," *restrepothemovie.com/video.*
8. Dr. John Barnett, "How to End Hurry in My Life," from *Psalm 119: The Power of a Word-Filled Life* audio CD series (Discover the Book Ministries, November 2004).
9. *Restrepo: One Platoon, One Valley, One Year*, a film by Sebastian Junger and Tim Hetherington (Outpost Films, 2009).

CHAPTER 24: VICTORY

1. "VE Day," http://www.youtube.com/watch?v=psgYiOU-3iU
2. www.historyplace.com/worldwar2/timeline/statistics.htm
3. http://www.presidency.ucsb.edu/ws/?pid=12248
4. David Jeremiah, "The Awesomeness of Jesus," www.oneplace.com/ministries/turning-point/player/the-awasomeness-of-jesus-part-2-413535.html
5. Evans, "The Weapons of Authority."

6. Chuck Swindoll, "What's Necessary for Victory?" www.oneplace.com/ministries/insight-for-living/listen/what's-necessary-for-victory-part-1-378846.html
7. *Ibid.*
8. *Ibid.*
9. *Ibid.*
10. *Ibid.*
11. *Ibid.*

12. *Ibid.*
13. *Ibid.*
14. *Ibid.*
15. Beth Moore, *Law of Love: Lessons from the Pages of Deuteronomy* (Nashville, TN: Lifeway Christian Resources, 2012).
16. *Ibid.*
17. *Ibid.*
18. *Ibid.*
19. Miles McPhearson, "Why Surrender?", *http://www.sdrock.com/messages/2014-06-15*
20. Swindoll, "What's Necessary for Victory?"

CHAPTER 26: PEACE THAT LASTS

1. Stephanie Fitzgerald, *Ramses II: Egyptian Pharaoh, Warrior, and Builder* (North Mankato, MN: Compass Point Books, 2008), 64.
2. Wikipedia, *http://en.wikipedia.org/wiki/List_of_treaties*
3. http://www.warsintheworld.com/?page=static1258254223
4. Andy Stanley, *The Best Question Ever* (Colorado Springs, CO: Multnomah Books, 2004).
5. James MacDonald at Moody Bible College's Founders Week, *http://www.youtube.com/watch?v=ewhqcQowSs8*
6. *Ibid.*
7. *Ibid.*
8. Sebastian Junger, "Why Soldiers Miss War."
9. *Ibid.*
10. Keller, *Walking with God through Pain and Suffering*, 164.
11. *Ibid.* 164-165.
12. *Ibid.* 165-166.
13. Chuck Swindoll, *Hope for the Hurting* (Plano, TX: IFL Publishing House, 2010), 4-5.

38546674R00181

Made in the USA
Lexington, KY
16 January 2015